PRAISE FOR

THE CEREBRAL SYMPHONY

"Calvin takes the reader for a walk along the foreshore of brain science, and he is a wonderful companion. He wades into the sea and returns with a writhing new theory of the human mind . . . Darwin would have loved it."
—Nicholas Humphrey,
author of *Consciousness Regained*

"An especially inventive new book . . . an intriguing theory. This is the best popular volume on the mind in a long time . . . a highly instructive look deep into the very nature of what we are and why we behave as we do." —*The Sacramento Bee*

"[Calvin's] format of chatty, ordinary events, interwoven with his great insights . . . has become a landmark." —Hugh Downs

"With a deft use of astute observations of everyday life around a marine biological research laboratory on Cape Cod, William H. Calvin brings into unexpected focus the quintessence of the human mind—the phenomenon of consciousness. His relaxed and often lyrical prose makes *The Cerebral Symphony* a joy to read and stimulating to contemplate." —Roger Lewin,
author of *Bones of Contention*

"Aiming and throwing led our species literally to project; Calvin's new psychology is deeply imbedded in knowledge of the origin and evolution of the nervous system."
—Lynn Margulis,
co-author of *Microcosmos: Four Billion Years of Microbial Evolution*

"Thinking along with Calvin is sheer delight. This book has the most vivid and lucid explanations of brain function I have seen."
—Daniel C. Dennett, co-author of *The Mind's I*

THE CEREBRAL SYMPHONY

SEASHORE REFLECTIONS
———ON THE———
STRUCTURE OF CONSCIOUSNESS

WILLIAM H. CALVIN

BANTAM BOOKS
NEW YORK · TORONTO · LONDON · SYDNEY · AUCKLAND

THE CEREBRAL SYMPHONY
A Bantam Book
Bantam hardcover edition / January 1990
Bantam trade paperback edition / December 1990

ACKNOWLEDGMENTS
Portions of this book have been adapted from articles by the author that were previously published in *Nature, Science, Reality Club #1* and *#3*, and in the *Whole Earth Review #60*.

Bantam New Age and the accompanying figure design as well as the statement "the search for meaning, growth and change" are trademarks of Bantam Books, a division of Bantam Doubleday Dell Publishing Group, Inc.

ISBN 0-553-34994-5

Published simultaneously in the United States and Canada

Bantam Books are published by Bantam Books, a division of Bantam Doubleday Dell Publishing Group, Inc. Its trademark, consisting of the words "Bantam Books" and the portrayal of a rooster, is Registered in U.S. Patent and Trademark Office and in other countries. Marca Registrada. Bantam Books, 666 Fifth Avenue, New York, New York 10103.

PRINTED IN THE UNITED STATES OF AMERICA

0 9 8 7 6 5 4 3 2 1

For
Blanche Kazon Graubard
and
Seymour Graubard

CONTENTS

1.
MAKING UP THE MIND:
Morning on Eel Pond   7

Woods Hole, on the southern tip of Cape Cod. Cormorant, skunk, and robot behavior: How do they decide what to do next? Thinking about thought: Movement programs and "brainstorming" creativity. Why pianists and ferryboat captains can't rely on feedback: When the perfect plan is needed. Our sense of self, of voluntary decision.

2.
THE RANDOM ROAD TO REASON:
Off-line Trial and Error   27

Trial, error, and selectivity. Purpose and chance in philosopher's eyes. *E. coli*'s random walk. Selling short darwinism again. Experience as the elimination of bad guesses, but we humans can think through an action without acting. Owner's test for boaters (and prospective parents) and why planning ahead isn't common.

Venturing out Cape Cod. Stupidity in freeway (and cormorant) design. Elaine's head injury, amnesia, and the stages of recovery of function. The fantastic juxtapositions of nocturnal dreams. Injury to motor strip, premotor, and prefrontal cortex. Planning sequences and a violinist's performance at the MBL Centennial. Sense of volition and how dreams violate it, promote the notion of a soul that wanders abroad. Monitoring narratives, telling the truth. The frontal lobe's role in worry, compulsions, and schizophrenia.

Coast Guard Beach, the Outermost House. Horseshoe crabs and dangers of overdoing defensive armor. Consciousness as overused word: Sleep/wakefulness, awareness, perception/cognition, even worldview. The *Narrator* seems the most important aspect of consciousness—but that brings up the homunculus problem, and the need to know the parts from which an explanation can be constructed.

Churchyard; graves of Otto Loewi and Stephen Kuffler. *Fin de siècle* arguments. Loewi's discovery of puff of perfume used to bridge gap between two nerve cells. Atropine and a heart-stopping story. Kuffler's inhibitory neuron and how it turns up its sensitivity when deprived. Basic research as the major industry of Woods Hole.

schemas. Marshaling yard metaphor. Sequential aspects of consciousness can come from a Darwin Machine too. Hazards of remembering everything. Lateral inhibition circuits for declaring "the best": Does this provide our "unity of consciousness"? Is the subconscious all of the tracks but the best one, which is what one is "conscious of"? Chunking due to seven-unit buffer length.

Multiple planning tracks create a Darwin Machine analogous to biology's variation plus selection: If operate tracks independently, get a Darwin Machine for planning all sorts of future scenarios. The problem of value: How does machinery judge "better" and "best"? The economists' *Subjective Estimated Utility* function as the scorecard. Ready, get set, and go: Random Thoughts Mode of the Darwin Machine. Variations-on-a-theme Mode when we focus our attention. Choral Mode of near-clones from "get set." Constructing sentences with sensory and movement schemas ("nouns" and "verbs") in a Darwin Machine. The emerging consensus among sequencers. Music may be another secondary use of the same neural machinery in the off-hours when not needed for throwing or talking. The Woods Hole Cantata concert at the Church of the Messiah in Woods Hole, scientists *en famille*.

Niche specialization: Can the cormorants and the Great Blue Heron manage to share the resources of Eel Pond? Getting around niche-fixity with a nice jump to a new function and the virtues of discovering an "empty niche". Labor Day in Woods Hole and the hazards of amateur truck drivers. Sunset from Nobska Lighthouse and the green spots escaping sunset. Stringing things together and free will. Subconscious problem-solving and premature closure; fundamentalist haz-

FIGURE LIST

—— PROLOGUE ——

FINDING MIND AMID THE NERVE CELLS

We shall, sooner or later, arrive at a mechanical equivalent of consciousness.

THOMAS HENRY HUXLEY (1825–1895)

To most people, Huxley's prophesy is still improbably distant. I hope to persuade the reader that, on the contrary, there is already one mechanistic analogy for consciousness. It isn't yet implemented in computer hardware, and it may well prove to be insufficient, but it shows that human consciousness has proved capable of thinking about its own roots in the brain, about how it differs from the sensibility of other animals, and about how it came to be that way.

And I don't mean consciousness in any superficial sense; important as it is, I'm not simply talking about the brain-stem region that controls sleep and wakefulness, nor am I only talking about cognition, how we become aware of something. I really do mean *consciousness* in the sense of the metaphorical "little person inside the head," the conductor of our cerebral symphony, who contemplates the past and forecasts the future, makes decisions about relative worth, plans what to do tomorrow, feels dismay when seeing a tragedy unfold, and narrates our life story.

And I mean *machine* too—not specific machines such as are currently on the drawing boards, but a class of computing device that I call a Darwin Machine, so named because one of this new type works like a greatly speeded-up version of biological evolution (or of our immune system) rather than like the familiar programmed computer. The Darwin Machine can evolve an idea, using variation-then-selection, in much the same way that biology evolves a new species using Darwin's natural selection to edit random genetic variations and so shape new body styles. Our conscious and subconscious thought processes constitute a Darwin Machine. It shapes up new thoughts in milliseconds rather than new species in millennia, using innocuous remembered environments rather than the noxious real-life ones. This suggests that consciousness is due to the same darwinian principle as evolved life on earth, but simply on an accelerated time scale.

It is impossible to conceptualize the power of a symphony just from knowing the technical specifications of each instrument of the orchestra, just as it is impossible to imagine a ballet from knowing how nerves and muscles work. Many people use such an analogy when contemplating the anatomy and physiology of the human cerebral cortex—that many of the uses made of this machinery are far removed from the nuts and bolts of neurons. But I think we can do much better than merely wave our hands about the machinery, as is the common practice among psychologists and humanists. I believe that we now understand how our brain creates the narrator of our conscious experience, the conductor of that cerebral symphony—not in all its complexity, but at least in principle—and that knowledge of the narrator machinery is going to revolutionize our concept of consciousness, make it much easier to appreciate the richness of our cerebral symphonies.

Consciousness is fundamentally a *process*, not a place or product: *How* is the fundamental question, not the *where* or *what* of the classical "seat of the soul" searches. I address the mechanisms of animal consciousness, discuss how human consciousness elaborates that, and propose how humans could create machines that would have much of what we call consciousness. This book covers both the neurological mechanism and its machine mimic: We are conscious machines (among other things), and we can probably create mechanical consciousness as well. Creating "mind" in a machine comes closer to "playing God" than any amount of genetic tinkering—and to exercise suitable caution, we must understand our own mental processes and how they occasionally fail us.

As in several of my previous books, I have again used a narrative style to permit the nonscientist reader to temporarily skip over any difficult sections and resume the travelogue. And I have again taken a few (hopefully inconsequential) liberties with time and place in order to keep this narrative from becoming as cluttered as real life and a real diary. The Marine Biological Laboratory celebrated its centennial in 1988; I hope that, in passing, I manage to communicate some of the special flavor of Woods Hole, an intellectual atmosphere built up by thousands of thoughtful people over the century.

W.H.C.

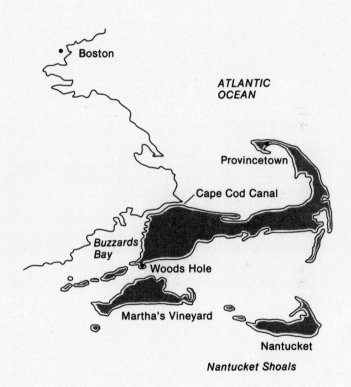

Boston

ATLANTIC
OCEAN

Provincetown

Cape Cod Canal

Buzzards
Bay

Woods Hole

Martha's Vineyard

Nantucket

Nantucket Shoals

Map of Massachusetts Shoreline

1

MAKING UP THE MIND: MORNING ON EEL POND

*Animals are molded by natural forces they do not compre-
hend. To their minds there is no past and no future. There is
only the everlasting present of a single generation—its trails
in the forest, its hidden pathways in the air and in the sea.*

the anthropologist LOREN EISELEY (1907–1977)

Looking out over Eel Pond, I see the same cormorant every morning. Breakfast time is his time for sitting atop that spherical white buoy amid the sailboats in the little harbor, his wings held in the shape of an *M*. They look as if pinned up to a clothesline to dry.

Then he begins flapping his wings furiously, as if revving up his motor before takeoff. But he doesn't take off. Flap, flap, flap. After a few moments of this standing-in-place exercise, he collects himself, tucks in his wings, somehow smoothes his surface. Soon he looks like a dark bronze statue of a sleek diving bird, perched atop a white pedestal.

Not only is he there every morning, but my wife insists that he was there several years ago as well. He seems to be one of the permanent residents, unlike the dozens of scientists who sit in the cafeteria of the Marine Biological Laboratory watching him over their first cup of coffee or tea. Some discuss him in German, others in Japanese or Hebrew or Chinese. It is morning in Woods Hole.

Again the cormorant revs up his wings, and one of the children exclaims that he is about to take off. But no, just more morning exercise in wing-flapping. Time enough to go fishing, to plunge deep below the surface and snatch a meal. Soon the cormorant is very sleek again, truly unruffled.

How does he decide when it's time to fish, or time to flap? Or time to flee? Cormorants probably don't worry very much about predators. I haven't seen any cats around here that would be hungry enough to consider swimming out to the buoy. The local cats make a very good living on the fishermen's leavings.

As do the skunks. I was walking around Eel Pond the other day, trying to get some thoughts in order, when I was intercepted by a curious skunk. And thoroughly inspected. Not while in some secluded spot in the woods but on the main street of Woods Hole,

Cape Cod, Massachusetts, U.S.A. I saw this skunk heading my way from across the street. I stopped, wondering what a skunk had been doing in the bookstore. The skunk waddled past the cars and hopped up the curb, then came right toward me. It thoroughly sniffed my feet from the front. And then from the rear, as I peered down over my shoulder to observe it.

Disdaining my shoes, it took off down the sidewalk. But it immediately stopped again, finding a stick from an ice cream bar. It turned the stick over with a deft swipe of a forepaw, then licked off the remaining ice cream. It reconsidered me for a moment, as if trying to make up its mind about something—our eyes met as I stood there turned halfway around, and we contemplated one another. Inspection over, the skunk set off down the sidewalk once more. I watched it turn the corner as I stood, twisted around in wonder, rooted to the spot where I'd first seen it leave the bookstore.

At first I thought that surely it was someone's pet skunk, perhaps the bookstore owner's? But it was merely a thoroughly urban skunk, not afraid of anything. I do wish they were more afraid of cars. Evolution prepared them well for dealing with cats and other carnivores, but not hit-and-run vehicles speeding along winding roads. Skunks often travel in groups of two or three, and so one fatality often leads to another as a sociable skunk comes back to nudge its suddenly lifeless companion, and yet another car rounds the blind curve going too fast to stop. Evolution prepared humans well for making a good living on the Ice Age frontiers. And we too often seem oblivious to the hazards of our new environs, despite our occasional abilities to look ahead in a manner unlike any other animal. It's a paradox—humans have amazing abilities to look ahead, but only occasionally use them.

THIS IS A BOOK about consciousness, even that of cormorants and skunks. Or at least those aspects of consciousness that are closely related to the question "What shall I do next?" Posing that question surely isn't uniquely human. Making choices between fairly standard behaviors is something that all animals do. But humans are always devising novel sequences of action and comparing them to the conventional. We contemplate them, estimating their probable consequences, then perhaps implement one with some new combination of words or movements that we've never used before. Our cousins the monkeys and apes also innovate, but novelty is a small part of their daily lives—and looking ahead seldom extends to tomorrow.

And so this book is about behavioral choice in animals, about how humans greatly elaborate such capabilities (especially in the frontal lobes of our enlarged brains), and about some of the principles involved—one of which is so similar to darwinian evolution that we might almost call the thought process a Darwin Machine. This leads to a discussion of how to build thinking robots that would have much of our own consciousness, creativity, and—potentially—ethical behavior.

Except in passing, this is not a book about the many other things that have been called consciousness; plants may be sensitive to the environment, but they do not—so far as anyone knows—spin alternative scenarios about the future, then pick and choose after winnowing down a lot of random possibilities on the basis of memories about what worked well in the past. I am a biophysically oriented neurophysiologist by training, one who has wandered a bit into anthropology and evolutionary biology in search of answers to why hominid brains enlarged fourfold so quickly, but who otherwise tends to think in bottom-up terms involving creatively nonlinear nerve cells and the powerful circuits they form. I have enough trouble trying to explain how we plan ahead and construct sentences to speak without getting into the wondrous awareness enthusiasms—and while my thinking-about-thought efforts may have, fortuitously, illuminated such diverse things as our musical abilities and pitching performances, that isn't everything that brains do.

And "everything that brains do" is about the only definition of consciousness that encompasses the many entries in the dictionary. The other connotations of consciousness are interesting, but other neurobiologists, psychologists, and philosophers will have to undertake their explanation. Or engineer their disappearance—one must remember that many important-appearing questions simply turn out to be poorly posed, as in the natural philosophers' debates a few centuries ago about "appearance" and "substance," a distinction that vanished as empirical science advanced. Our dualistic distinction between mind and brain may similarly disappear as our science matures.

Science progresses not only at the laboratory bench, at the patient's bedside, and when studying animals in the field, but also in the incessant contemplation of how things fit together— particularly the interlocking findings from different research specialties such as animal behavior, brain research, developmental biology, evolutionary theory, and anthropology-linguistics. Often such contemplation is best done when taking long walks, especially along shorelines—one might almost call this book *Seashore Speculations on Darwinian Designs*.

THE CORMORANT seems to cruise around Eel Pond on a schedule, covering about the same distance with each dive. He swims along the surface about the same four seconds each time, then pops back under, searching the bottom of Eel Pond with the efficiency of a search-and-rescue airplane quartering a sector. The skunks make their rounds of the docks at night, but in an entirely different style.

Skunks seem to stop and investigate with far more curiosity than any night watchman I've ever seen. I can imagine programming a robot to make watchman's rounds, looking for intruders and sniffing for smoke, but it will be awhile before robots become as sophisticated as those skunks that prowl around under the cars, into the trash cans, and gregariously interact with one another, as if gossiping about what humans throw out and who is the most profligate. Since they often hold their ground when nonskunks approach, one of the hazards of taking a nighttime stroll in Woods Hole is tripping over a skunk—at which they do take offense.

The skunks' food-finding tours could be considered variations on a theme, just as in music where the familiar melody shifts into a new key, blends in another melody, plays one familiar tune off against the other as in the *Goldberg Variations*, and then returns to the original melody—of which the skunks' seems to be "Grand Tour of the Waterfront." Their motions are more complicated than the narrowly rule-bound foraging habits of a bee. I could program a robot to duplicate the bee's patrol pattern (and maybe even that of the cormorant), but to mimic a cat or skunk seems to require a consideration of "will"—even of whim, a decision-making process with unpredictable elements.

NO ONE, I TRUST, will think that only humans have "will"—though the term has become somewhat unpopular; the *Encyclopaedia Britannica* has, magisterially, eliminated its entry. But both will and whim were invented long before humans were.

Our cat has been having a war of wills with the neighbor's Siamese for months now. And with us for years. She likes to sleep on our bed, and usually in an inconvenient location. And so we wedge a foot under her, from beneath the covers, and try to shove her over to one corner of the bed. She pretends not to notice, even though obviously wide-awake. You can wedge her until practically propped upright—and still she will pretend that your foot isn't there. It's a little matter of territory, asserting one's rights.

My wife has learned to take advantage of this. The cat makes an excellent foot-warmer. It would have been quite impossible to train the cat to perform a foot-warming task, even with a chopped liver reward system; cats are terribly suspicious of training schemes. And lacking the territorial dispute, the cat would never put up with a foot beneath her for very long. But provided that the foot pushes on her every few minutes and stokes the cat's resolve, the "hot pad" game will continue for a long time. Sometimes my wife even gets both feet warmed up, thanks to the cat's willpower.

DECIDING WHAT TO DO NEXT need not involve such obvious considerations of willpower. Take that cormorant drying its wings, for example. Its patrol pattern seems to involve a routine (that underwater tour of Eel Pond's circumference), as does its wing-drying atop the buoy. Each can be viewed as a movement program (even holding a statuesque pose is a program), and the daily routine can be seen as a changing repertoire of programs.

But how does the cormorant decide when it is time to stop fishing and time instead to sun itself with wings outstretched? When to stop wing-flapping and just sit there looking around? When to move on to another pond? Different cormorants do things different ways; they're not ruled by the sun in quite the fashion that bees seem to be. How does an animal's brain make these big decisions, starting up one movement program rather than another? Is it the same way we decide to get up from a chair and take a stretch? And perhaps raid the refrigerator? Surely we humans have some fancier kinds of decision-making, but are they variations on a primitive theme, or of an entirely novel kind?

One of the children in the cafeteria is pestering her parents with "What are we going to do next?" And that prompts one of the computer programmers to observe that the Three Primal Questions, as told to him by his sister, are:

1. Where are we going?
2. When do we get there?
3. Why do I have to sit in the middle?

And they really do have a lot to recommend them to the philosophers. Deciding what to do next is, after all, the primary job of the "little person inside the head," that metaphorical midget who seems at the center of everything. Is cormorant consciousness all that different from ours?

Consciousness can mean, depending on whom you're talking to, vastly different things. For some idealist philosophers and Zen enthusiasts, even plants have consciousness—but to some philosophical scientists, consciousness is instead defined so narrowly as to be the ineffable nonmechanical essence. If you can explain how the brain carries out something, then that something isn't part of consciousness, they claim.

It all reminds me of the argument that I heard once again last night, on whether computers could possibly produce art. A local artist claimed that if a computer could do it, then it wasn't art! In the case of both consciousness and art, one suspects that progress, a better understanding of what they're all about, isn't desired by such people—that they're offended by the notion that something so personal is somehow explainable.

> *When was I born?*
> *Where did I come from?*
> *Where am I going?*
> *What am I?*
>
> THE HOPI QUESTIONS

THREE HOURS AFTER BREAKFAST, that cormorant is still there. I haven't seen it move except when a rowboat passed by, and then it promptly returned. It inspects its feathers, spreads them once or twice. But mostly it just sits there, looking around.

Oops! It isn't the only cormorant after all. Another cormorant just surfaced near shore, a fish held in its beak. The cormorant shakes the fish violently, probably crushing its spinal cord. A practiced flip of the cormorant's head, and the flaccid fish disappears into its open mouth. That slim neck is easily expanded. The cormorant promptly dives under the water surface again, checking if there are any more foolish fish about. I think that cormorants know all about the tendency of fish to school.

When the cormorant is on the surface, it is usually swimming steadily, only its S-shaped neck and head extending above the water, rather like a submarine cruising along with only its conning tower above the surface. Except that patrolling cormorants hold their heads with their beaks pointed up in the air at an angle, a sleek social snob cruising among the fat ducks that sit atop the pond's surface like feathered rowboats.

The busy cormorant has worked its way clear across the harbor in only a few minutes, swimming underwater most of the way, emerging about three times. I've gotten so that I can predict about where this cormorant will surface next, as it seems not easily distracted from its regular rounds of Eel Pond. Straight-line paths certainly are different from random walks, the crazy paths taken by the proverbial drunkards as they wander aimlessly around a street lamp, deciding on new directions every now and then, and so tracing a path that is very different from the cormorant's purposeful culinary cruise.

Randomness seems so very different from purpose—but that doesn't mean purposeful paths weren't generated by randomness. That's the great intellectual message of Charles Darwin, which we're so slow to appreciate. Variations, then selections—but not always expressed in behavior, as they can be done inside the head too, off-line. We often do the right thing the very first time—but that's because we do the random trial-and-error inside our heads.

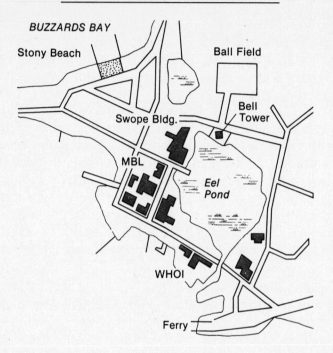

THE CORMORANT IS BACK AGAIN on its mooring buoy. He didn't fly in, but hopped out of the water with a brief flap of wings—it looked so effortless, compared to a human trying to haul himself up out of the water into a boat. Now, the cormorant is standing there with his wings hung out to dry. I haven't seen one of these cormorants really fly yet. They just cruise around Eel Pond, head held high for about three seconds, then disappear with a little dip of the S-shaped neck into the water, which the rest of their body seems to automatically follow, as if pulled in by some underwater assistant. You have to look carefully to spot the ripples from the dive; a small pebble thrown into Eel Pond would leave more lingering traces. Ducks are graceless in comparison.

Both diving and the patrol pattern seem like rolls for a player piano, "canned" movement programs (a "motor tape," as neurobiologists are wont to say). It's like my cat's washing routine. Sometimes while she is running across the room at home, she will suddenly stop to wash, as if some irresistible urge had struck her and started up the washing program. After which, it's just one thing after another.

Following Motion X usually comes Motion Y—though sometimes Motion Z instead. Motion X probably "brings to mind" both possibilities Y and Z—certainly it does for the cat. "Cat" (as readers of *The Throwing Madonna* may remember, though I've taken to calling her "Noise" in recent years as she has a Siamese-like vocal repertoire) likes to play with my shoelaces when I'm getting dressed in the morning. I suppose that the shoelace is reminiscent of a mouse's tail; she certainly treats it that way, cupping it with a paw and bringing it toward her open mouth. And then a funny thing often happens—she starts washing the paw and moves on to washing her face, ignoring the shoelace long enough for me to finish tying my shoe (if I hurry). In short, she switches in midstream from a food-acquisition movement program to a grooming movement program.

And the paw-cupping movement subprogram is the *initial* part of each of those two major movement programs. In one case, it is followed by biting—in the other case, by licking and then wiping the paw over the head, and so on into one of the best-practiced and most graceful of feline movement programs. If the paw-cupping doesn't bring with it something solid on which to bite, I suppose that the switch from food acquisition to grooming has a nice logic to it: Both setups involve cupped paw and open mouth. Some of our own mistaken actions are in the same class, as when I finish slicing the ends off of some carrots with a paring knife, open the dishwasher—and put a carrot into the silverware compartment.

We would like, of course, to take apart movement programs into primitive elements, the "atoms" from which they might be composed. But even animal grooming is harder to characterize than you might initially think. In hopes of being able to break up animal grooming into its components, some of the animal behavior people have sought the aid of choreographers, since they have developed a notation scheme for movements that can be used to annotate the musical scores. The robotics people are eagerly awaiting the results, since melding together the separate jerky movements of robots into the smooth, dexterous motions of an assembly-line worker has proved exasperating.

Well-practiced movement programs are likely to be seamless, just one movement flowing into another without a definable end to one and beginning of another. That is, of course, what any tennis coach or golf pro attempts to achieve: to blend the beginner's jerky separate movements into one integrated whole, without any components remaining visible.

I'm sitting outside in the shade of the only tree in the patio of the Swope Center, and listening to someone practice the piano up in the Meigs Room, where the Sunday evening concerts are held. The pianist is trying to get an arpeggio right, but it still doesn't flow as gracefully as that diving cormorant. Now there's a "motor tape" for you: That arpeggio is so fast that feedback cannot help the pianist. She simply has to send out exactly the right commands, at exactly the right times, and not wait around for progress reports before continuing. She needs a perfect plan, in advance.

The "conscious mind" relates to dealings with the outside world, which require elaborate analysis in the light of the past, and preparation of future courses of action. We think things over and make plans; there would be no sense in doing this consciously every time that we speed up the heart when we go upstairs, or dilate the blood vessels of the leg muscles to do the work. These things are arranged to happen automatically every time that one has set in motion the action of climbing. Conscious control of the details of these activities would overload the cerebral computer.

the neurobiologist J. Z. YOUNG, 1987

THINKING ABOUT THOUGHT isn't as circular as it sounds, but it demands a fairly fancy mental construct that the cormorant probably lacks. And certainly I suspect that plants lack that ability, whatever the Zen enthusiasts say. Trains of thought seem a lot like trains of muscle commands, as if they were movement programs being planned out before being started up. But not all movement programs need be conscious; indeed, the well-practiced ones, like those for my bicycle riding and the cat's grooming, seem to require little conscious effort. *Consciousness* is a term we seem to apply to choosing between alternative scenarios for what we might do next.

So is the cormorant's decision to take another dive "conscious"? Maybe, but that also might make my cat's reflex scratching of her collar "conscious" too. And therefore my reflex rubbing of my nose, which I've always considered largely unaided by conscious decision.

Still, every situation is unique, and responses often are modified with the conditions. How about choosing between nonautomatic, more novel scenarios? But that might leave out the cormorant almost altogether, since novelty is such a small part of its life. Still, unless we define consciousness so narrowly as to make it a sudden step from none in apes to full-blown in humans, we expect a gradation. And the increasing utilization of novel movement scenarios (such as speaking a novel sentence, or dancing to a new rhythm) does capture something of the likely differences between cormorant and human consciousness. And it leaves room for the insightful behaviors which apes display more than monkeys.

There's another sense in which consciousness is only the uncommon. As you become highly practiced at a skill, so that it no longer qualifies as novel, maybe it does move from conscious control to less-than-conscious—as in Zen archery, where the object is to become so practiced that no conscious will is required to release the arrow at the right moment. You can simply watch the arrow being released, as if someone else were doing it. In Zen archery, according to Eugen Herrigel, "The shot will only go smoothly when it takes the archer himself by surprise. It must be as if the bowstring suddenly cut through the thumb that held it."

THE DERELICT BOAT called *Ovalipes* is even lower in the water today, the thunderstorm in the middle of the night having soaked everything. That boat looks as if it tried to sneak into Eel Pond after hours and sheared off its superstructure on the drawbridge. There is also a curious de-masted sailboat in the middle of the harbor, on which someone lives. They suggest that someone didn't think ahead very far.

Except for small rowboats and motorboats without windshields, getting in and out of Eel Pond is a matter of remembering the schedule of the drawbridge operator. If you return later than midevening, you wait until morning (one is reminded of the days of *in loco parentis* when college dorms were locked up at midnight). People memorize the drawbridge schedule (including the operator's coffee-break hours) in the way that other people memorize the ferry schedule to Martha's Vineyard and Nantucket, the large offshore islands connected by ferries to Woods Hole.

Both schedules occasion much beeping, the squeaky boat horns used to signal the drawbridge operator sounding quite different from the solid tenor notes of departing ferries as they try to blast small boats out of their way. Atop these sounds, the robotic foghorn at the Nobska lighthouse can sometimes be heard as a bass rumble.

Heard in the middle of the night, the foghorn sounds like a metallic cow, mooing insistently. But sometimes the sound is broken up, deflected by a shifting breeze somewhere between Nobska and Eel Pond. Then it resembles broken speech rather than a moo. Sometimes I think that it's saying, "Feed me. . . . Feed me. . . ."—like some Cape Cod minotaur monster.

EEL POND is changing again. Some fishermen returned, and several sailboats went out for a late afternoon on the ocean. Eel Pond is a tidal basin opening off the salty straits between Vineyard Sound and Buzzards Bay. Over the last century, the possessive apostrophe has been eliminated from Wood's and Buzzard's, but not yet from Martha's—but then everyone around here just calls it *"the* Vineyard" instead.

The town of Woods Hole grew up around Eel Pond. Walking around town is always an experience, even if you're not one of the regulars, as Susan Allport noted in her book *Explorers of the Black Box*:

> Woods Hole could never be mistaken for one of the many other summer resorts that dot Cape Cod. . . . It's the scientists themselves who give Woods Hole its unmistakable air. Whether waiting for the drawbridge that bisects the town to be lowered or for a bowl of chowder in a local restaurant, they are in constant conversation. Their scientific jargon— "ATP," "calcium spikes," "symbiotic bacteria"—always fills the air, mingling at the beach with the lapping of the waves or in a restaurant with the smells of coffee and fried clams.

And it's not just their conversations but also their behavior that distinguishes them from nonscientists. In this town full of observers of nature, everyone makes eye contact with everyone else. It doesn't matter whether you are passing on foot—in the hall, on the beach, or on one of the small roads that wind through Woods Hole's warren of cottages and beach houses—or even in cars. It's a bit disconcerting at first, but before long you begin to feel that you're part of some greater intelligence, that this is a place where knowledge is being accumulated and communicated.

Taking the loop clockwise, I pass the Bell Tower, stop to talk to some physiologist friends who have been out fishing, and then continue on past the schoolhouse. On reaching the main street near where the skunk intercepted me earlier, I start seeing ships rather than the pond's sailboats. Just outside the drawbridge spanning the neck of Eel Pond, the big boats dock: funny-looking ferryboats, destroyer-sized oceanographic research vessels, an old-fashioned sailing ship of the era before engines, and the occasional graceful white yacht with a uniformed crew treading softly on a teak staircase between decks.

Here are some of the buildings and piers of the Woods Hole Oceanographic Institution, WHOI being known hereabouts as "who-ee," and of the National Marine Fisheries Service. And sticking out into the Great Harbor is the pier and pumphouse for the Marine Biological Lab's sea water supply, what keeps the animals in MBL's aquariums alive.

In 1975 a Vineyard ferryboat, the *M.V. Islander*, while maneuvering to avoid a small boat, collided with this pumphouse pier and nearly destroyed it. The ferry's captain, seeing that he was about to back into the pier, must have set the engines on full speed ahead—but big ships respond slowly because of their considerable inertia. And so, after the MBL pier was extensively damaged, the ferryboat charged full speed ahead and thereby plowed into WHOI's pier across the way, narrowly missing one of their brand-new oceangoing ships tied up there.

Such evenhanded treatment of Woods Hole's two leading institutions was the talk of the town for months. The captain of a big ship has to plan far ahead because the ship responds so slowly;

feedback is pretty inadequate when it takes so long from initiating an action to getting some reaction. It's similar to the pianist's problem with feedback, but on a much longer time scale: The pianist's loop time from action to correction is at least a tenth of a second, but the captain's is many seconds. So how do they do it (when successful)?

Which reminds me: I'm still watching for the classy sailboat named *Fantasy* that is said to inhabit this place. *Fantasy* is notable for its small dinghy that trails along behind on a leash. The dinghy too has a name painted on its rear: Its name, though you have to squint to read it, turns out to be *Reality*. Overblown fantasy first, trailed by scaled-down reality. Remember that technique for stimulating creativity called "brainstorming," where you're not allowed to criticize anyone's suggestions until several dozen are on the table, the wilder the better? I suspect that each individual works much the same way subconsciously, that our brains generate a lot of random possibilities and then pick the best—but that we're only conscious of the best one, and not of all the inferior discards. And that this procedure is responsible for not only for the success of pianists and ferry captains, but for how we think great thoughts.

HUMAN CHOICES include versions of the cormorant's fishing, fleeing, and basking in the sun—all are popular here in Woods Hole. But our range of choice is much greater, especially as we plan for tomorrow.

Setting aside great thoughts for the moment, instead consider an undergraduate trying to choose between elective courses. I remember having only one opening each term outside my load of math-physics-chemistry, and a wide range of candidates. Should I take a course in public speaking, since that seemed appropriate for anyone interested in teaching? Or a philosophy course in logic, which might help me understand mathematics better? Or the composition elective, important to a writing career? Or Richard Ellman's course on the novel as a literary form, also important for the writing option? Or a history course on the early Greek scientist-philosophers that seemed to fit with no particular career option, but was intriguing? Or the Melville Herskovits course on theories of culture, important if I wanted to pursue my tentative interest in anthropology? Or Steve Glickman's physiological psychology seminar, important to my budding interest in brains?

Each choice had to be viewed in terms of a whole scenario involving past, present, and future. Some choices had prerequisites, a typical scenario constraint. But part of scenario-spinning is discovering shortcuts: After a year's experience, I learned that some prerequisites were essential (you really can't take differential equations without a year of calculus) and that others weren't. The rules said that I had to take introductory anthropology before the theories of culture seminar, introductory psychology before the physiological psychology seminar, and a literature survey course before the special course on the novel—but I was willing to gamble on having to do some extra background reading, and so discovered that the aforementioned professors were willing to gamble too, that they would waive the rules when asked. Nearly all of my most memorable undergraduate courses involved such gambles.

But beyond prerequisites, there was a whole career scenario: What did one actually *do* as a physicist, as an anthropologist, as a writer? Did they bring one into contact with interesting people and important problems, involve travel to exotic places, provide stable employment—or chancy roads to riches, fame, and glory? What reactions might a given choice evoke from my physics advisor, from my girlfriend, from my parents?

It is this sort of scenario spinning, involving both past and future, that makes human consciousness so different from the behavioral choices of the cormorant, the skunk, and even the chimpanzee. It isn't that animals lack fancy concepts like mathematics and physiology and novels—it's that they so seldom chain together the concepts that they do have, to generate a novel course of action.

CHIMPANZEES COME THE CLOSEST to human-level novel planning when they engage in little deceptions (a behavior rarely observed in monkeys). A chimpanzee who comes upon a bountiful food resource—say, a tree full of ripe fruit—usually utters a joyful "food cry" that quickly attracts the other chimpanzees of the band, who similarly exclaim in delight upon seeing the bounty. But if the first chimp sees that there are only a few fruit to be had, it may keep quiet, attempting to silently eat all the fruit before any other chimp wanders along.

Foresight-prompted deception occurs when the lone chimp, hearing the approach of other chimps and worried that it will be deprived of the rest of its feast, leaves the limited bounty, casually strolls over in a different direction, and issues a food cry in the midst of dense foliage—where there is no food! This decoys the other chimps away from the limited supply of fruit. While the others are excitedly looking around the false site, the first chimp circuitously returns to the true site and finishes off the feast.

So it seems as if the chimpanzee can foresee the scenario of losing its remaining feast to competitors, and that it can spin a decoy scenario that involves "telling a lie." One might argue that these deceptions are only occasionally novel: Losing food to a higher-ranking animal is an everyday occurrence, and most decoy deceptions are probably just repeats of an earlier success. But still, there is some element of novelty in the animal's "first lie" that begins to look like the scenario-spinning deceptions common in humans. Do chimpanzees spin alternative scenarios, pick and choose between them, spin more when dissatisfied with the early choices? If so, it would begin to look like the human scenario-spinning abilities that we associate with contemplative consciousness.

Now there's a Philosopher's Primal Question for you: How do we "consciously" choose between alternatives? Indeed, how do we imagine the alternatives from which to choose? Neurophysiology ought to be able to provide some answers about neural mechanisms, such as whether the sequencing machinery for throwing can also be used for arpeggios, language, and scenario-spinning—though surely sociobiology will have to answer questions about the evolution of social expertise and intellect. And neurophysiologists, together with philosophers, ought to be able to provide some insights about our sense of self and voluntary choice—perhaps even why we often conceive of a "soul" that commands the body during the day and wanders abroad at night.

It has been the persuasion of an immense majority of human beings that sensibility and thought [as opposed to matter] are, in their own nature, less susceptible of division and decay, and when the body is resolved into its elements, the principle which animated it will remain perpetual and unchanged. However, it is probable that what we call thought is not an actual being, but no more than the relation between certain parts of that infinitely varied mass, of which the rest of the universe is composed, and which ceases to exist as soon as those parts change their position with respect to each other.

PERCY BYSSHE SHELLEY (1792–1822)

I am sincerely of the opinion that the views . . . propounded by Mr. Darwin may be understood hereafter as constituting an epoch in the intellectual history of the human race. They will modify the whole system of our thought and opinion, our most intimate convictions.

THOMAS HENRY HUXLEY (1825–1895)

2

THE RANDOM ROAD TO REASON: OFF-LINE TRIAL AND ERROR

Human problem solving, from the most blundering to the most insightful, involves nothing more than varying mixtures of trial and error and selectivity.

the computer scientist HERBERT SIMON, 1969

It takes two to invent anything. The one makes up combinations; the other one chooses, recognizes what he wishes and what is important to him in the mass of the things which the former has imparted to him. What we call genius is much less the work of the first one than the readiness of the second one to grasp the value of what has been laid before him and to choose it.

the poet and philosopher PAUL VALÉRY (1871–1945)

Three centuries ago, Leibnitz propounded what might now be called the *physiologist's premise:* "Everything that happens in man's body is as mechanical as what happens in a watch."

Does that apply to the mind too? Most people initially thought it unlikely. But perhaps Spinoza suspected as much when he said, "The order and connection of ideas is the same as the order and connection of things." Earlier in the seventeenth century, Descartes was bold enough to conceive of a completely self-sufficing nervous mechanism able to perform complicated and apparently intelligent acts. Unfortunately, he still had a conceptual problem regarding followers and leaders, and so mired us even deeper in the dualistic body-and-soul metaphors of an earlier age.

But by the late nineteenth century, Thomas Henry Huxley had explicitly prophesied that we would find a mechanical equivalent of consciousness—and this is manifestly the premise of most of my fellow neurophysiologists. Huxley reflected not only the biologists' mood in the wake of Darwin's revolution; the physicist Ernst Mach summarized in 1895 what many psychologists and philosophers had also begun to say, about how mental mechanisms could use the potent variation-and-selection combination:

> [From] the teeming, swelling host of fancies which a free and high-flown imagination calls forth, suddenly that particular form arises to the light which harmonizes perfectly with the ruling idea, mood, or design. Then it is that, which has resulted slowly as the result of a gradual selection, [which then] appears as if it were the outcome of a deliberate act of creation. Thus are to be explained the statements of Newton, Mozart, Richard Wagner, and others, when they say that thoughts, melodies, and harmonies had poured in upon them, and that they had simply retained the right ones.

PURPOSE SEEMS SO DIFFERENT FROM CHANCE, but darwinism suggests that you might be able to have your cake and eat it too: Chance plus selection, repeated for many rounds, can achieve much. Can darwinism achieve purposeful behavior, especially our planning-for-the-future behavior that has been such a powerful drive toward both civilization and ethics? Is it, indeed, the foundation of consciousness?

That is, alas, not how traditional philosophers usually phrase the question. Friedrich Nietzsche said that the creative person works by instinct and checks himself by reason; Socrates had said that it was just the reverse order and so influenced Western thinking for a long time. Likely neither was right. Philosophers (and many scientists too) have a problem with randomness in any form. It is probably because so many think in oversimplified cause-and-effect terms and so, following Laplace, infer that things must be "determined" if there are physical laws. And thus random outcomes (horrors!) would result from random causes. People often yearn for certainty: T. E. Lawrence wrote, "Perhaps in determinism complete lies the perfect peace I have so longed for. Free-will, I've tried, and rejected it."

We keep expecting human reasoning processes to be orderly— at least as orderly as those patrol cruises of an Eel Pond cormorant. To say that the height of human achievement usually contains a large dose of randomness is heresy, though people will readily admit to a role of randomness in preventing animals from "getting stuck." Remember Burdian's Ass, who was equally hungry and thirsty? And who was poised halfway between food and water, and so starved? Or Hamlet's inertia? But randomness has a far more important role than merely to act as a dice-tossing tiebreaker. A lowly bacterium would never get stuck like the apocryphal ass; indeed, bacteria find their way to food simply through selectively modifying randomness.

The philosophers can perhaps be forgiven for being overly impressed with thought as the highest of the higher cerebral functions, what's left over if one stops looking for the seat of the soul. But it might be better to start with how animals make behavioral choices, like that sunbathing cormorant or the bookish skunk, and work our way up to logic. When looking at an *E. coli* bacterium swimming around, it is easier to see how randomness can buy food:

> Organisms are problem-solvers seeking better conditions— even the lowest organism performs trial and error measurements with a distinct aim. This image brought to mind Howard Berg's striking film of chemotaxic bacteria. He showed how a bacterium's flagellar motor makes it run and tumble randomly until the bacterium senses a gradient of nutrient. The bacterium then reduces the frequency of tumbling and lengthens the runs towards a greater concentration of nutrient.
>
> the molecular biologist MAX PERUTZ, 1986

The random element is the tumbling: The new direction of swimming bears little relationship to the previous path before the tumble. And so the cell's path is a random walk unless something else happens. And the something else is simply suppressing the tumbling: When finding more and more food, the bacterium swims longer on its current straight path. This enables it to "home in" on the food source, perhaps a decaying morsel whose organic molecules are diffusing away into the water near the bottom of the pond (remember what a sugar cube looks like when dissolving in the bottom of a cup, how the sugar gradually spreads out).

I can make a little working model of the bacterium in my computer, not unlike the way a child can build a model crane with an Erector Set. First I create some "food," particles scattered around about like a sugar cube dissolving in the bottom of a glass. Somewhere in the bottom of the glass, I place the bacterium, swimming in some random direction. I make the simulated cell tumble (reset its path to a new randomly chosen direction) about once a second, but suppress the tumble if the nutrient concentration is higher than a few seconds before. This shows the path taken with this suppression of randomness:

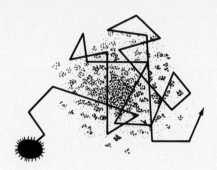

And so the simulated cell homes in on the richest concentration of nutrient and usually comes back if it strays away. If I make it tumble every half second instead (or if I slow down its swimming rate by half, or make the food source richer), then it stays even closer to the center. When the food is gone, tumbling again causes the cell to seek a new source.

Now most philosophers looking through a magnifying glass at that food-finding path would have ascribed intelligence to that purposeful performance of the little bacterium. At such a marginal magnification, it would seem to "home in" on the morsel. But the bacterium has no brain: It's just a single cell with some inherited simple abilities such as swimming, tumbling, and sensing increasing yield. The properties of the environment are all-important too: That diffusion of decaying molecules from the morsel gives rise to a fall-off in nutrient concentration, the same way that the smell of baking bread gets weaker as one gets farther away from the oven.

There are some people who hope to mine gold (and more useful metals) from the ocean floor—and they're thinking of locating the rich spots by turning loose a lot of underwater robots that seek out the highest concentrations by exactly such a regulated random walk. But unlike a metal-hungry bacterium, they'll shout, "Eureka!" in some secret code that will be heard and deciphered by their owners, who will come and stake a claim on the ocean floor.

One of the problems with prospecting robots is that they get fooled by weak lodes of gold while missing the rich one next door. But the randomness of the bacterium helps prevent sticking with false maxima: After all, the random walk will sometimes carry it far enough away from the weak source to sense the stronger source. Consider the simulated bacterium feeding on the weaker of a pair of morsels:

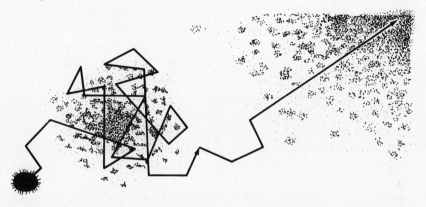

If the run lengths are always short before taking another sniff, the bacterium can get fooled into sticking close to the minor source. But if we make it sniff every 2 seconds instead of every second, its uninterrupted swim will sometimes carry it far enough away to be captured by the major source. It may take a while before it escapes, but randomness does have its virtues: Now the simulated bacterium would seem, to those philosophers peering through the magnifying glass, to have purposefully approached the two morsels and decided which was bigger! And it wouldn't have been easy to persuade the philosophers that randomness did the trick, because they were accustomed to thinking of random-ness as the exact opposite of purpose.

Now the owner of those prospecting robots has goals that are different from those of the randomly walking bacterium. For the *E. coli* cell, one has the "a bird in the hand is worth two in the bush" phenomenon: It may prefer to refuel rather than search out the all-time champion of rich foods. The robot master may wish reassurance that a region has been reliably covered for sources richer than a minimal concentration, so that he can call home all the robots and move the whole operation to Hawaii. Random walks will sometimes miss substantial patches that are surrounded by distracting small morsels. Of course, when one can install a microcomputer inside a robot, one is tempted to design search strategies that are more sophisticated than the bacterium's "cheap and good enough" scheme.

It might be easier to train some cormorants so that they think gold is food; after all, dolphins have been persuaded to find lost torpedoes in exchange for frozen fish, and people have been persuaded to dig ditches in exchange for money that can be exchanged elsewhere for frozen fish. But maybe cormorants are too smart to fall for that scheme.

NO ONE NEEDS A WEATHER VANE around here to tell which direction the wind is blowing: All of the sunning cormorants in Eel Pond turn to face into the wind. The other morning was dead calm, the pond like a mirror, reflecting every detail of the sailboat rigging. And so the cormorants and boats got a little disorganized, without any wind to orient them. But let a breeze come up and they will fall into formation; let the breeze switch around and, like a gaggle of geese, they'll follow it *en masse*.

Today, you can see the breeze: The ivy facade of the colonial-style oceanography building down on Water Street is being rippled by gusts. There are waves flowing from one end of the building to the other. Sometimes two or three ripples can be seen at the same time, all propagating along the ivy blanket. And I used to think of wind waves as being whitecapped horizontal waves: These waves stand up and move sideways.

PEOPLE ARE FANCIER THAN BACTERIA, the philosophers might justly reply when confronted with the purposeful appearance of food-finding that is based on suppressed randomness. Common sense says that human behaviors couldn't be based on something so "irrational"—except, perhaps, for a drunkard's random walk?

A wave of *déjà vu* sweeps over me each time I hear randomness sold short again. The same arguments were used against evolutionary thinking a century ago in the wake of Darwin: Few people's imaginations could see how random walks could yield the optics of the eye or the circuitry of the brain. A century later, newcomers still make the same mistake—until they study the anatomy long enough to see all those hallmarks of variation and selection. And I suspect we're repeating this history by selling short the power of randomness for producing the interesting things that minds do.

Of course, randomness by itself cannot produce such elaborate results, for all the usual reasons having to do with a roomful of monkeys typing a page of Shakespeare—it would take more time than the universe has existed (15 billion years) to arrive at that particular combination of words. We're always talking about randomness *plus* selective retention of some sort, and repeated cycles of this back-and-forth two-step dance serving to gradually shape up the unlikely. Richard Dawkins nicely illustrates this in *The Blind Watchmaker* by a little computer program that shapes up a random set of words into a near-mimic of a line from Shakespeare.

It's the combination of randomness and selection that is so powerful, not just selection, not just randomness. They are inseparable sides of the same coin (well, you *can* separate them—as when selection acts on a highly inbred gene pool with little combinatorial variability remaining—but they don't go anywhere). The foraging bacterium selectively retains those paths that seem successful, simply by postponing the next bout of random tumbling. Evolution, however, always involves a great number of individuals and many generations, making natural selection's cumulative editing of randomness harder to demonstrate within the observer's own lifetime. But it's much the same story.

Biological evolution usually involves variations on some theme (short or tall, fat or thin, naked or hairy, slowly or rapidly maturing). The environment "selects" the most successful and, provided that some tendency toward the theme is inheritable, their enhanced reproduction means that the average body style shifts toward the most suitable, simply because fewer of the less favorable body styles grow up to become parents themselves.

Of course, there are many cultural innovations which don't *appear* to be such variations on a theme: logical reasoning and *Eureka!* discoveries, for example. But as with "brainstorming" generating lots of variants (but preventing premature closure, selecting too soon), maybe each person's brain uses the same technique, but subconsciously, so we're not aware of randomly generating a lot of nonsensical possibilities before we then select a reasonable one.

> *If man was to think beyond what the senses had directly given him, he must first throw some wild guess-work into the air, and then, by comparing it bit by bit with nature, improve and shape it into a truth.*
>
> the geologist WILLIAM SMITH, 1817

> *A blind-variation-and-selective-retention process is fundamental to all inductive achievements, to all genuine increases in knowledge, to all increases in fit of system to environment.*
>
> the psychologist DONALD T. CAMPBELL, 1974

EXPERIENCE CAN BE CONSIDERED the elimination of bad guesses, but a guess can be much more elaborate than merely the bacterium's tumbling, the random choice of a new direction. It doesn't take a brain to choose a random direction—indeed, the *E. coli* isn't even a specialized cell like a nerve cell, much less a brain. But with a little more machinery, a cell can engage in more specialized locomotion, such as the way that a paramecium backs up when it bumps into an inedible obstacle, then turns to zoom off in a new random direction. And with a collection of nerve cells called a nerve net or a ganglion, behavior gets even fancier. With the head ganglion arrangement that we call a brain, the random elements can often be carried out inside the neural machinery itself—and *in advance*, so that the expressed behavior no longer looks random but rather purposeful, even insightful or logical.

Thanks to memory, the brain can carry around a rough representation of the environment: whether hot/cold is good/bad, whether bright lights are a good thing to approach or avoid, whether that particular item of the diet made one sick the last time it was eaten, etc. Of the many possible plans for one's next movement, some will evoke bad memories of what happened the last time something similar was attempted. Others will evoke fond memories of a feast or a snug nesting place. Depending on other factors such as hunger or reproductive drives, some plans will rate higher than others. Fancier organisms can solve fancier problems and thus utilize new resources—which is probably how they evolved to be fancier in the first place.

In particular, some animals have gotten to be so fancy that they seem to simulate extensively a course of action before taking even a tentative first step. While the chess master who looks a half dozen moves ahead and the army general who attempts bluff and counterbluff are extreme examples of how to make and compare alternative plans, even our pet cat seems to contemplate choices. One occasionally sees an animal seemingly plan several steps ahead, even engage in deception:

> One evening I was sitting in a chair at my home, the *only* chair my dog is allowed to sleep in. The dog was lying in front of me, whimpering. She was getting nowhere in her trying to "convince" me to give up the chair to her. . . . She stood up, and went to the front door where I could still easily see her. She scratched the door, giving me the impression that she had given up trying to get the chair and had decided to go out. However, as soon as I reached the door to let her out, she ran back across the room and climbed into her chair, the chair she had "forced" me to leave.

> PETER ASHLEY, 1981

While "aren't they clever" animal stories abound, most of them have potentially simpler explanations (e.g., the dog didn't plan but merely saw the empty chair while at the door—and its desire to sleep then exceeded its desire to explore outdoors). Still, I suspect that humans merely have substantially greater (what scientists like to call "order-of-magnitude greater," meaning about tenfold) abilities to mentally compute future alternatives, not that humans are unique in having foresight.

Indeed, looking ahead is so powerful a technique that the big problem is why don't we see more extensive examples of it in the animal kingdom. Jacob Bronowski put it very well in his 1967 Silliman Lecture at Yale:

> [None of the termite-fishing chimps] spends the evening going round and tearing off a nice tidy supply of a dozen probes for

tomorrow. Foresight is so obviously of great evolutionary advantage that one would say, "Why haven't all animals used it and come up with it?" But the fact is that obviously it is a very strange accident. And I guess as human beings we must all pray that it will not strike any other species.

The combination of biological and cultural evolution has happily provided us with foresight, an ability to look ahead and assess the probable consequences of our actions and so choose the better course without actually traveling the others and then comparing. Planning ahead, taking account of the nonroutine, is a key element of what is called consciousness, as Bronowski observed:

> [Humans' unique abilities] to imagine, to make plans . . . are generally included in the catchall phrase "free will." What we really mean by free will, of course, is the visualizing of alternatives and making a choice between them. In my view, which not everyone shares, the central problem of human consciousness depends on this ability to imagine....

And that in turn raises the question of why humans don't plan ahead more than we do, given our extensive abilities and how handsomely they pay off.

I'VE ALWAYS WANTED A SAILBOAT like the one now sailing out of Eel Pond beneath the raised drawbridge, but I flunked the ownership test. There is a special test for prospective boat owners, designed to weed out those who aren't temperamentally suited to the rigors of boat ownership.

First you figure out an annual budget; divide the cost of your desired boat by about six, and that is your capital cost per year. Add moorage, then an equivalent amount for insurance and repairs. Add the cost of the annual renovations to the interior. Add new sails, one each year, on the assumption that they are constructed of spun gold. Sum up and add 20 percent for good measure; this gives your annual budget.

Then estimate about how many times each year you'll take the boat out, and for how many hours, to give you the hours of pleasure you'll maximally achieve; deduct the hours you'll spend arranging repairs and writing checks. If the sum is greater than zero, correct for over-optimism, especially if your schedule or the local weather is more fickle than average.

To complete this first stage of the boater's qualification test, you must not be standing up. Sit down in a comfortable chair and divide these hours into the annual cost. This gives you the actual cost per running hour.

If you pass this stage of the test, you are allowed to go out and buy the most comfortable life jacket you can find, along with rain gear and a small camp stool. You must also stop at the bank and get a nice stack of $20 bills, amounting to the cost of a weekend's running time. Be sure *not* to ask for new, crisp bills.

The next morning, you arise before dawn and make yourself a day's supply of sandwiches and a Thermos of coffee. Then you place them and your camp stool in your shower stall, don your life jacket and rain gear, pocket a packet of $20 bills representing the day's running cost, sit down on the stool, and turn on the shower. You adjust it to the temperature of the local rain less 20°, to compensate for the wind chill factor (unless your shower stall is located in a wind tunnel).

You sit there all day, slowly tearing up $20 bills and stuffing the soggy scraps down the drain.

Those who pass this second stage of the test are allowed another day in the shower stall with the water turned off and a suntanning lamp substituted. The $20 bills are somewhat harder to stuff down the drain when not soggy, so you are allowed some bilge water to soften them up. Your lunch will get soggy whether it is raining or not, so the water underfoot will aid in realistically simulating conditions at sea. Upon successful completion of stage three, you are finally allowed to buy a boat, if still interested.

This test is quite safe, involving none of the usual hazards of falling overboard, or getting hit by the boom when the wind shifts unexpectedly, or becoming stranded on a sandbar, or being snagged by a fishhook. The mental hazards of this test are considerable, and I hereby disclaim all responsibility for what might happen to you, but they are surely no worse than actual boat ownership.

Only prospective boat owners who pass this test are truly suited to the rigorous life of the sailor. The number of boats around Vineyard Sound presumably attest to the number of people who find the shower-stall test invigorating—the alternative being that boat owners don't think ahead. At least, not any more than prospective parents volunteer to spend a weekend caring for the neighbor's squalling infant, giving the parents a respite and "test driving" before they acquire one themselves.

PLANNING AHEAD is thought to have something to do with our oversized frontal lobes, as injuries there sometimes disrupt abilities to change strategies. While frontal-lobe damage may occur from tumors and strokes, perhaps the most common cause (and certainly the most easily preventable) is a head injury due to a car accident. Even if the skull isn't fractured by the impact, the soft brain rattles around inside its bony case and gets bruised.

Seat belt usage shows an interesting "a little knowledge is a dangerous thing" aspect of looking ahead: Your conclusion depends on how far ahead you look. If you only look ahead to the grocery store, then of course the chance of anything happening is very small. Having succeeded many times in making such trips without incident, everyone except beginners tends to be very aware of the low probability of immediate injury—and some use it to rationalize ignoring "do this, it's good for you" parental-sounding advice about wearing seat belts.

But most people are not capable of looking years ahead and drawing valid inferences from the accident records. Those who are so skilled, however, have discovered that you have a one-in-three chance of being in a serious-injury car accident sometime during your life. That arithmetic works out to "someone in your family is likely to be in a bad accident."

The trouble is: You don't know when it's going to happen. It's as likely to happen on a short trip as on a highway trip. And so, the only solution that I know, until we reform drivers and redesign cars, is routine precautions: refusing to ride in the front seat of taxicabs with protruding fare meters, pencils, and other things you wouldn't want your head to collide with. Foremost, however, is making a habit of always buckling the seat belt and pulling it tight, just as you make a habit out of brushing your teeth every night. That way, you'll be wearing the seat belt some year when something does unexpectedly happen to you. *A seat belt reduces death and injury by about half,* so it seems an exceedingly rational choice. And quite the opposite conclusion to the one you form looking ahead only a little. It thus becomes a particularly dramatic "use it or lose it" principle: Failure to use one's frontal lobes can result in the loss of them, given the way in which they are the "leading edge" of one's forward trajectory in a collision.

TO POSTULATE MENTAL MACHINERY for simulating the future is one thing, but to demonstrate its properties is another. In particular, we want to know on what occasions we use it and when we don't. We want to know how it develops, both in children (they start enjoying fantasy and planning "tea parties" by the age of three) and in evolutionary terms (certainly by the apes, but what about monkeys?). And we want to know how *planning ahead* evolved via good old darwinian advantages.

But as the seat belt rationalizations demonstrate, evolving foresight may not be a straightforward problem: A little foresight can even be a disadvantage. Furthermore, the relative lack of other foresightful animals suggests that this is a rare route we're seeking to uncover, not a commonplace one. So the evolution of foresight via the usual more-is-better route starts looking pretty slow and uncertain.

Yet something has got to explain our consciousness, and if halfway versions of foresight seem unlikely to bootstrap it up to its present level, perhaps there is some missing scaffolding. Arches cannot stand until complete; during their construction, something else has to hold them up temporarily. Is there some missing scaffolding where foresight is concerned? Perhaps planning evolved via good old darwinian *side steps:* As Charles Darwin noted, sometimes new functions emerge from old machinery, a conversion of function.

Scaffolding and new uses for old anatomy: Can either help explain why we're so good at planning ahead, or seeing ourselves as the narrator of our life's story?

I have in my possession photostatic copies of several pages of Beethoven's sketches for the last movement of his "Hammer-klavier Sonata"; the sketches show him carefully modeling, then testing in systematic and apparently cold-blooded fashion, the theme of the fugue. Where, one might ask, is the inspiration here? Yet if the word has any meaning at all, it is certainly appropriate to this movement, with its irresistible and titanic energy of expression, already present in the theme. The inspiration takes the form, however, not of a sudden flash of music, but of a clearly-envisaged impulse toward a certain goal for which the composer was obligated to strive. When this perfection was attained, however, there could have been no hesitation—rather a flash of recognition that this was exactly what he wanted.

the composer and conductor ROGER SESSIONS, 1941

3

ORCHESTRATING THE STREAM OF CONSCIOUSNESS: PREFRONTAL-CORTEX PERFORMANCES

To classify consciousness as the action of organic machinery is in no way to underestimate its power. In Sir Charles Sherrington's splendid metaphor, the brain is an "enchanted loom where millions of flashing shuttles weave a dissolving pattern." Since the mind recreates reality from the abstractions of sense impressions, it can equally well simulate reality by recall and fantasy. The brain invents stories and runs imagined and remembered events back and forth through time.

the sociobiologist EDWARD O. WILSON, 1978

We drove further out the Cape today, and with considerable caution, too, particularly after we came upon an accident in a blind curve, a smashed-up car nosed into a tree and blocking the opposite lane; a truck was stopped just past it. The accident had evidently just happened, and I looked quickly for injured persons needing help. But there was no one in the damaged car, and the truck driver was walking along the shoulder, looking like business-as-usual.

After my second incredulous look at the truck, I figured out what had happened: The flatbed truck held three damaged (and partly flattened) junk cars, two in front (one perched atop the other)—but there was only one car at the rear. The car on the road had evidently fallen off its precarious perch atop the other junk car when rounding the curve. And dropped down into the opposite lane of traffic—fortunately unoccupied at that particular moment— and rolled over, finally coming to rest against the tree. If the driver was worried about being jailed for recklessly endangering other drivers via his improperly secured load, he sure didn't look it. "No problem, no problem!" his expression seemed to say. Evidently, this sort of thing is not taken very seriously around here.

We may not hold animals responsible for failures to look ahead; we realize that their brains are not capable of the foresight that ours are. We do expect operators of dangerous equipment to uphold a high standard in that department. I have no idea what the general standards are among Massachusetts truck drivers, but anyone driving around Cape Cod for a day can see for himself the standards among the public officials responsible for the roads. The roads are well paved but poorly designed—and not just because blind curves haven't been straightened out since the horse-and-buggy days.

Like a haunted-house movie, some situations contain so many traps for the unwary as to seem quite unnatural. The Mid-Cape

Highway, Cape Cod's only modern limited-access highway, is a good idea—but with fatal flaws that have never been corrected. At one point in the eastbound lanes just before the Hyannis exit, there is a hill that crests so sharply that the driver cannot see more than a few car-lengths ahead, suggesting that one should slow down to half the speed limit in order to be able to stop for anything on the road (few drivers do).

That's bad enough. But it is also at the end of a blind curve. *And* it is where the highway designers chose to locate a rest area of the block-long, extra-wide-shoulders variety, so that cars enter the high-speed lanes from a variety of places (there are two more rest areas in the next few miles, so this wasn't the only possible location). Having eliminated blind intersections with the limited-access design, they seem to have recreated a few for old times' sake.

Even more incredibly, they put such rest areas on *both* sides of the eastbound lanes, facing each other across this blind stretch of two-lane hilltop highway, tempting people out stretching their legs on the right shoulder to walk across the highway in search of a rest room (indeed, there is a flight of stairs and a paved path leading off into the median, seemingly promising facilities somewhere near the westbound lanes). In the middle of the road, the pedestrians are likely to see a speeding car rising up out of invisibility, coming out of the blind curve.

Such compounded asking for trouble isn't a failure of the Pilgrims to look ahead to motorcars: It is the stupidity of recent generations. Not just the designers either, but the politicians who fail to fix it and the voters whose priorities run to "well paved" rather than "well designed." At least such are the dark thoughts that one tends to think while cautiously navigating their highways and contemplating foresight as a defining characteristic of post-ape brain evolution.

Evolution, you may say, surely does better just by trial and error. Just think of those sleek cormorants, swallowing a fish with a deft flip of the head. But, alas, evolutionary design is full of stupidities too, such as our nearsightedness and sore backs. Biological evolution at least has the excuse of lacking foresight; one expects better of human cultural evolution.

DWELLING UPON STUPIDITIES, much as I dislike doing it, is a valuable exercise when thinking about human evolution, as we have a tendency to portray the grand process as perfecting things, with humans as the pinnacle of progress. Those who no longer believe that humans were designed according to some grand plan still have a tendency to substitute the evolutionary process as some guarantee that humans were, nonetheless, well designed. Or at least pretested.

But there is no reason to assume that humans are any better prepared for our present world than is the skunk, with its striking vulnerability to speeding cars. Nature is full of examples of "good enough engineering" where a sufficient solution to a problem (say, the cormorant wing-flapping to fluff up waterlogged feathers) tends to remove the problem from exposure to further selection pressures that might evolve a better design (such as the duck's waterproofing oil glands). Much evolutionary progress is far too slow and iffy to do us much good: Despite the undoubted importance of good vision for survival, human evolution has somehow let nearsightedness continue in a considerable proportion of the population. This optical myopia has, over the generations, been even more stupid than the metaphoric myopia of the Massachusetts road builders. And cultural evolution has given us eyeglasses only in the last dozen generations, of the 100,000 since the brain started enlarging and making lots of tools.

One might think that the skunk-cormorant style of behavioral choice would have been a "good enough" solution to the problems of deciding what to do next. And that little improvements in foresight might have landed their possessor in as much trouble as they avoided. Which all makes the evolution of foresight—at least via standard darwinian always-getting-better improvements—a bit problematic, not at all the straightforward course of evolution that it initially seems. So what scaffolding, or conversion of function, might have aided foresight? Or what new niche might we have invented that made natural selection so weak that the usual niche-confining rules were suspended for long enough that some rule-breaking exceptions evolved?

A major clue to such inquiries is the human brain itself, looking at what functions are located next to others. And a tradi-

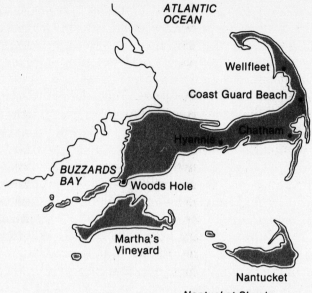

tional way of investigating brain organization is seeing what goes wrong, when it does—as it recently did to a friend of ours.

OUR FRIEND ELAINE lives out near Wellfleet's literary colony, along a protected stretch of waterway. Escaping from the car, we joined Elaine and all walked along the waterfront. "Big Blue" flies by every so often, Elaine's name for the Great Blue Heron that inhabits the place, along with numerous cormorants. The first time that you see Big Blue gliding along, you think that you've seen a hang glider—until he begins flapping his wings in that graceful beat.

Along the "river," one sees horseshoe crabs scurrying along the sandy bottom. Prehistoric tanks? Imagine a parade float, its wide skirts completely covering the truck that is underneath. Battle tanks were once made this way, to shield their vulnerable treads, but all that extra iron made them too slow and cumbersome. Yet that's the strategy evolution tried to protect the underside of *Limulus polyphemus*, and it seems to have worked for a very long time: *Limulus* is a "living fossil," very similar species being seen in the fossil record for the last 350 million years, even back before mammals invented themselves. Settled into the sandy bottom, the crablike legs of the horseshoe crab are completely concealed by the broad skirt of the shell; it almost looks like a bony version of a ray, hiding there in the sand. When it gets up and moves on, it leaves behind a horseshoe-shaped imprint in the sandy bottom. It's no crab, but rather a close relative of the modern spiders; they live from Maine to the Yucatán, and there are three other species in the Orient.

We haven't seen Elaine since she was severely injured in a car accident several years ago. An oncoming car swerved across the center line and crashed into her car head-on; the other driver was killed. It was fortunate that, through long habit, Elaine was wearing her seat belt, or there might have been two fatalities. Still, she was unconscious for a week with a severe head injury from the sudden stop, not to mention a shattered hip and rup-tured spleen. And it was another month before she knew where she was ("oriented to time and place," as the neurologists say). Except for getting used to the reconstructed hip, Elaine is back to normal now, but it was a long two years of hospitals and rehabili-tation therapy ("Try to imagine spending two years in a prisoner-of-war camp," she says, "unable to do anything that you really want to do").

Her friends have told her some of the stories of how she talked during her amnesiac period, while in traction.

"Did you have any visitors today?"

"Oh, yes—lots of visitors," Elaine would reply.

"What were their names?"

"Well, there were Adam and Eve. And the Magi too," Elaine said.

"You're kidding me."

"Oh, no. The Magi really were here," and Elaine went on to give their names.

At one point, Elaine asked one of the hospital staff if she personally knew anyone who had been in the California Gold Rush of 1848. Elaine insisted that she herself knew some veterans of it.

As she got better at recognizing people, she was always introducing arriving visitors to the ones already there, as if she were a cocktail-party hostess. She would often get the name right but sometimes describe the person inaccurately; an antique dealer became the head of the water department, and she described her surgeon at one point as a merchant from Boston.

The stories she told in her amnesiac period in the hospital sound much like my nighttime dreams, always changing direction in midstream to explore a new avenue. One recollection of Elaine's shows the dreamlike string of concepts particularly clearly:

> A friend brought me a present—a small painting of sand dunes to hang at the foot of my bed. I was in traction for several months and always looking at that one spot, being unable to move. When people would visit, I would describe the painting—which features a tall sand dune towering above a sandy beach—like an art dealer would, saying who painted it and when.
>
> But then I would tell them that it showed an island off of Hyannis, that the name of the island was Calypso. I told them that an island gets its name from a ship that has gone aground there, and that a ship named *Calypso* had run aground on this island. I'd draw their attention to the top of the sand dune and say that there was a hole in it, and that if they put their ear down to the hole, they'd hear the ocean surf.
>
> So I'd attributed a whole lot to the painting that wasn't there at all. The *Calypso* comes from another nineteenth-century painting of mine that hung at home—it's a portrait of a ship named *Calypso*. I'd somehow visualized that very ship, from the painting at home, going aground in the new painting which hung at the foot of my hospital bed. Obviously, I'd gotten the sound of the sea coming out of the hole atop the hill from the hole-in-the-seashell tale that all children get told sometime or another, where you hear your own heartbeat and mistake it for the sighing sound of the surf.

THE PROBLEM with investigating how the brain makes up sequences of mental constructs, such as our plans for what we'll do for our next act, is that we are ordinarily quite good at making logical plans. But when the brain isn't working well, we can sometimes see flawed sequences being rearranged and improved.

And they involve phenomena much the same as we can recall from dreams when we awake in the morning: In spite of a dream's resemblance to a scenario or narrative, there are all those strange juxtapositions. Compare Elaine's story with a description of the typical nocturnal dream that we all experience:

Persons, places, and time change suddenly, without notice. There may be abrupt jumps, cuts, and interpolations. There may be fusions: impossible combinations of people, places, times, and activity abound. Other natural laws are disobeyed, and sometimes pleasantly so: gravity can be overcome in the sensational flying dream.

J. ALLAN HOBSON, *The Dreaming Brain*, 1988

Indeed, the typical content of a dream, were we instead awake and without brain injury, would qualify us as mad (they constitute the symptoms of delirium, dementia, and psychosis). The fact that our brains engage in such fantasy for several hours every night suggests that maybe fantasy is its normal mode of operation, that we avoid the slipshod scenarios (when both awake and sane) only by a sustained process of editing out the nonsense, shaping up the imagined scenarios into a thing of quality by a process analogous to the way that bacterium converges on the morsel of food.

Inserting something wrong into a sequence can be readily seen in the amnesia that follows a head injury (indeed, the presence of memory problems is your basic definition of a "concussion"). Sometimes the patient will simply say that he can't recall, but often he'll just recall the wrong thing. The textbook examples are the patients who confabulate, the neurologist's word for "making up stories" when you can't remember what really happened. A patient with a head injury, when asked what he had for breakfast that morning, may tell a plausible story of fixing bacon and eggs for himself as he usually does at home—but, in fact, he ate in a hotel that morning. And he's forgotten about the hotel too. Patients often recover their memories in clusters, and gaps will remain between two accurately recalled events. Into such a gap, the patient may insert another plausible story that didn't really happen. We're always making up stories, I suspect, and relating only the best candidate—which is, if things are going well, the true story.

The patients who confabulate aren't lying, in the usual sense of the word. They probably relate the best story that they were able to construct from the data available to them and think it true; all their lives, the best candidate scenario has been pretty reliable. They're not as bad off as the normal person during a nocturnal dream, making all sorts of inappropriate juxtapositions of people and places; indeed, mild cases of confabulation are near the opposite end of the spectrum, almost perfect except for that one little unknowing substitution.

It shows you that our memories are not like tape recordings which keep the events in an immutable sequence; we remember the elements by recognition, and recall the sequence by ties between those elements. But each recognized element has usually been seen before, and combinations have likely occurred in various orders, and so our memories of individual episodes are often jumbled and unreliable—unless we've made a special effort to keep things in the right order, as may happen if we are trained observers such as football referees. But, as the instant television replay sometimes shows, even trained observers get things wrong. Our brains just weren't designed to be tape recorders—despite their obvious penchant for chaining things together.

THE FOREMOST SIGN OF FRONTAL LOBE INJURY is surely distractibility: You set out to say something or do something, and you can get easily distracted into saying or doing something else. The ability to maintain a mental agenda disappears. That certainly fits Elaine's condition during that first month after she came out of coma—as in that dreamlike sequence where she shifted from subject to subject in talking about the little painting. And her confabulation, such as filling in Adam and Eve when she couldn't recall her earlier visitors, is characteristic of injuries to the inner surface of the frontal lobes, where the left and right halves face each other behind the forehead.

Neurologists are the great natural historians of our day, not only helping the patient but collecting illuminating case histories in the way that Charles Darwin collected bugs in his youth. And then they think about the patterns that emerge from the array of symptoms and injury locations. None has hit the jackpot in quite the manner that Darwin did when he figured out how new species evolve from old ones, but in the century since the beginning of neurology a picture of the frontal lobe has gradually emerged. Most scientists lack the temperament for such a demanding task, instead focusing on quick-payoff investigations that take things apart into their component parts—and then take apart those parts too. But frontal lobe is all about putting things together, and the sum is often something quite different from the collection of parts.

Still, there is no point in waving one's hands and ignoring the known subdivisions of the frontal lobe. It's very useful to know that confabulations occur only with injuries to the frontal lobe's inside surfaces—and not to injuries to the side or top of the frontal lobe. Which, of course, brings up the question: Well, what does the rest of the frontal lobe do? For that, one must look for patients who have a small tumor or suffered a blockage of a small blood vessel; people with head injuries, like Elaine, are always injured in multiple places, usually making it difficult to sort out what symptom comes from which place. A. R. Luria, the great

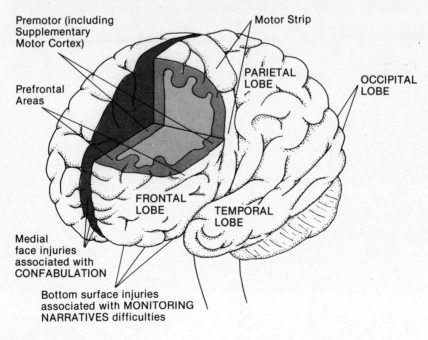

Premotor (including Supplementary Motor Cortex)

Motor Strip

Prefrontal Areas

PARIETAL LOBE

OCCIPITAL LOBE

FRONTAL LOBE

TEMPORAL LOBE

Medial face injuries associated with CONFABULATION

Bottom surface injuries associated with MONITORING NARRATIVES difficulties

Soviet neuropsychologist (1902–1977), pieced together the stories and lesions of a great many patients. Clearly, there are three major functional subdivisions of the frontal lobe: the motor strip itself, the premotor areas, and the *terra incognita* in front of them, including the prefrontal cortex.

MOTOR STRIP is at the back boundary of frontal lobe, a bit in front of your ear. Injuries there result in muscle weakness or, when damage is extensive enough, paralysis. There is a map of the body surface, though upside down in some sense: Starting nearest your ear is the machinery for throat and tongue and face, then fingers and hand and arm, with the trunk arching up over the fold down over onto the midline surface of the hemisphere, with legs and feet thereafter. But it doesn't follow that someone paralyzed on his entire right body has a big injury to the motor strip; someone with a weak right arm and right leg likely was injured where a bundle of the "wires" (we call them axons) emerging from motor strip pass through a bottleneck in the lower reaches of the brain—and so even the blockage of a small blood vessel there can affect both an arm and a leg. Someone with no leg problems, but a sagging right face and weak right hand— that's likely a person with an injury to the left hemisphere's motor strip, usually from a blockage of part of the middle cerebral artery supplying the motor strip with oxygen.

But nowhere else in frontal lobe will an injury cause paralysis: Damage to premotor and prefrontal regions is much more subtle, more like Elaine's confabulation and distractibility. And the farther forward we go, the closer we seem to get to the machinery we use to change from one behavior to another: our versions of the skunk's problem of deciding whether to sniff my foot again or waddle off down the street, or the cormorant's decision whether to go foraging underwater again or dry its wings a little longer.

PREMOTOR CORTEX is just in front of the motor strip, though the portion on the middle side of the hemisphere (in front of the leg's muscle controller) often gets called the supplementary motor cortex instead. It too has a "map" of the body—indeed, three of them, arm in front of leg in each case. And unlike the motor strip where the left hemisphere controls the right body and the right hemisphere the left body, the left premotor cortex has the reputation of controlling both sides of the body to a much greater extent than right premotor does. The lateral portion just in front of the motor strip's area for mouth and face is called "Broca's area."

Premotor isn't "pre" in the sense of its output funneling into motor strip and then down to spinal cord motorneurons; premotor has as many direct connections to spinal cord as motor strip does, as well as feeding into motor strip. It has extensive connections to parietal lobe (and thus information about body image and other spatial matters) and to ventral thalamus (and thus basal ganglia, another major component of the movement-control system) that motor strip doesn't. If you imagine making finger movements (but don't actually move), premotor works a lot harder than the rest of the brain; if you then actually move, motor strip also becomes active. Patients with strokes injuring supplementary motor cortex usually have trouble with such willed movements as speech and gestures. But attempts to fit premotor cortex into a hierarchy have failed; movement decisions don't start there and move on to motor strip. The best rationale that I know for naming it "pre" is because it lies in front of motor strip.

It specializes in setting up sequences of actions, as when you insert a key into the lock, turn it, turn the doorknob, and finally push open the door. Patients with damage only to left premotor cortex will be able to perform each action separately—there is no inability to move, as in motor strip injuries—but will have trouble chaining the actions together into a fluent motion, what Luria called a "kinetic melody." When we practice playing the piano, or practice our tennis serve or golf drive, we are tuning up the premotor cortex, particularly the left one (in right-handers and most left-handers).

Indeed, to tap your fingers rapidly is a typical request made by a neurologist who wants to check out premotor performance. Sometimes patients with premotor problems cannot easily change from one rhythm to another; asked to draw a sawtooth line and then change in the midst of the task to making square corners or smooth arches, the patient may be able to do each pattern separately but not switch back and forth between patterns. Premotor cortex is all about setting up sequences, chaining movements together. Musicians couldn't do without it.

THE STAGE OF LILLIE AUDITORIUM is not unaccustomed to white dinner jackets; at some of the Friday night lectures, the person introducing the evening's scientific speaker will come so attired. And it is usually a sign that some mischief is planned (baby pictures of the speaker may be shown at some point during the introduction, or the prediction read from his high school yearbook); the introductions are often as memorable as the speech that follows.

But tonight there are multiple dinner jackets on stage. And it has multiple music stands rather than a single podium. The fancy blackboard has also been removed, to permit eight performers at a time on the stage for the final work, J. S. Bach's Brandenburg Concerto No. 4. And the six players needed for the world premiere of Ezra Laderman's MBL Suite, commissioned to commemorate MBL's first hundred years. All of the four works on the program tonight feature at least one flute, if not two.

The featured flutist (and probably the reason that the $50 benefit tickets sold out in only 90 minutes when they went on sale five weeks ago) is Jean-Pierre Rampal. And the second flutist is Jelle Atema, once a student of Rampal's in Nice but for the last two decades a biologist at MBL studying the world of odors utilized by lobsters, fish, moths, dogs, bees, and other animals that live in a rich world of characteristic smells. When not in the lab, Atema may be conducting the Falmouth Chamber Orchestra.

But there is no conductor tonight, and I miss seeing those body movements synchronized with the music, fond as I am of conducting the Hallelujah Chorus from Handel's *Messiah*—from recordings. So I thought that the evening was stolen by Julie Rosenfeld, the first violinist with the Colorado Quartet (which formed the nucleus of tonight's group of performers), particularly her performance of the Brandenburg. A violinist playing such an energetic piece is always interesting to watch, as the instrument almost becomes part of her body, as glued as her head is to the violin's sounding board.

If you know your neurology of sequential movements, you realize that the music is flowing from the left frontal lobe, just above that chin on the sounding board of the violin, out the right arm holding the bow, and then back to the performer's left side, where left hand, violin, chin, and left brain all resonate in synchrony. That dramatic bowing movement of right arm, and the quick fingering by the left hand, is all focused on that left-sided resonance, as are the performer's eyes staring down at the string and the fingering. The violinist's bow is often said to "behave like an extension of her right arm"—but the real simile is that arms and violin behave like an extension of her brain, the part of her left brain that is just above the chin rest.

And where in evolution did we get such capabilities? Surely our musical abilities are unlikely to have been shaped up by usefulness. But if the left-brain sequencing abilities were shaped up by something else more closely related to making a living, perhaps music can use those sequencers in the spare time.

THE LIBRARY of the Marine Biological Lab is on the floor above the auditorium; it is now amalgamated with that of WHOI and is one of the world's better libraries for basic biological science. Many books have been written in its carrels and little offices (there's something about the smell of books that puts one in the right mood for such labors). It is certainly one of the nicest of libraries, being open day and night; the only other library where I can reliably check out a book at three in the morning is also at a marine lab, the one at Friday Harbor, Washington.

The MBL library is, however, not the place to read up on frontal lobe injuries and many other matters medical, once you want more than the standard textbook physiology. But since the library of Harvard Medical School was where I was first introduced to such neurological matters, I ventured up to Boston in search of some of Elaine's symptoms. And wound up reading Donald Stuss and Frank Benson's little book, *The Frontal Lobes*.

Prefrontal cortex is the front of the frontal lobe, most everything in front of the better-known portions of frontal lobe, premotor and motor strip. Some animals, such as the dolphins, have relatively little prefrontal cortex. Perhaps the best-known function of prefrontal cortex is strategy: deciding which movement sequences to activate, and evaluating the results. "Getting stuck" with a strategy that no longer works can be a symptom of prefrontal problems. The standard way in which the neuropsychologists test this is with a special deck of cards, though a standard deck of playing cards will suffice: The patient is handed a shuffled deck of cards and asked to sort them into two piles. But on what basis, which cards go in the left pile, which in the right? Ah, that's what the patient has to figure out, based on trying a scheme and the doctor saying "yes" or "no" after each card is laid down. Pretty soon the patient gets the idea that the doctor wants all the red cards in the left pile, all the black cards in the right one, and so zips along getting one "yes" after another.

But all of a sudden, the patient starts hearing "no" and then another "no"—the doctor has, without warning, changed the name of the game in midstream. Most patients get the idea that there is a new strategy to discover, and most will figure out within a half dozen cards that what the doctor now wants is for all the face cards to be put in the left pile, the numbered cards in the right one. But patients with prefrontal injuries often will not change strategies—they'll figure out the first strategy, but they won't change strategies when the first one no longer works. They get stuck, obstinately persevering, despite a long string of "no" responses. Monitoring the success of a strategy is something that prefrontal cortex seems to do for us.

Another prefrontal function is helping get sequences in the right order for the premotor cortex to execute. For example, a patient is in bed with his arms under the covers. He is asked to raise his arm. He doesn't seem able to do so. But if you ask him to remove his arm from under the covers, he can do that. If you then ask him to raise it up and down in the air, he does it all correctly and smoothly. Again no motor-strip-like paralysis, and no premotor-like difficulty with executing a fluent sequence—just a difficulty in planning the sequence, getting stuck on the condition of working around the obstacle of the confining bedcovers. Prefrontal problems give patients such difficulties in unfolding a proper sequence of actions. This isn't a conceptual problem, since the patient could probably look at another similar patient and analyze his difficulty, yet not be able to unfold the proper sequence himself.

Storytelling that meanders (more than usual!) can be another sign of prefrontal trouble, especially with damage to the bottom surface of the frontal lobe. Elaine's meandering story was not unlike a dream's wandering quality, making one wonder if sleep shuts down the orbital frontal cortex. But more than just story-telling, prefrontal cortex seems to monitor narratives, help keep things on track in spite of distractions.

And, of course, we tell stories to ourselves: The narrator of our conscious experience is the "self" we so prize, following its development in the third year of life. "Our need for chronological and causal connection defines and limits us—helps to make us what we are," in the words of one literary school. Stories about the past help us to understand patterns of causation; we "analyze" what happened, and so we can experience regret for doing the "wrong thing." Stories about the future help us to plan an agenda for the day's activities, as well as a career; we can anticipate in much more detail than other animals, largely because of the chains of possible events that we string together in our heads.

Things can go wrong with this storytelling—not merely erro-neous stories, but excessive attention paid to this narration. Worry is the most common problem, the unproductive repetition of an imagined scenario. "Getting stuck" on a regular basis is indeed associated with excessive metabolic activity in frontal lobes and basal ganglia as we "spin our wheels."

Patients with obsessive-compulsive disorder have a tendency to be overabstract and overintellectual, to worry and plan excessively for the future, and to repeat serial-sequential behaviors (that is, compulsions) as if locked into a "do-loop" that they are unable to escape.

the psychiatrist NANCY C. ANDREASEN, 1988

Nancy Andreasen is always kidding her psychoanalytically in-clined colleagues that they ought to stop talking about patients with overdeveloped egos and start talking instead of patients with overdeveloped (or at least hyperactive) frontal lobes. Patients with obsessions (such as a paralyzing fear that keeps them from being able to leave their room) or compulsions (such as those patients who have to wash their hands every few minutes) indeed illustrate in extreme degree those very things that frontal lobes are supposed to do for us: think ahead and organize serial movements. Such people often seem "stuck in a loop" and unable to move on to other behaviors.

The imaging methods that allow us to see how hard various regions of the brain are working now show that such obsessive-compulsives have midline frontal lobe regions that are indeed working overtime, compared to the rest of their brains and to normal brains. Normal people increase their frontal lobe activity when challenged with such serial tasks as the Tower of London game, where one has to imagine how to rearrange rings on a series of posts in order to get them all on one post with as few manipulations as possible. Schizophrenics, on the contrary, do not increase their frontal lobe activity—though some, such as those in catatonia, may have high resting levels of metabolic activity, spinning their wheels again.

Some schizophrenics have the so-called positive symptoms: They hallucinate, seeing things that aren't there. They may have delusions, thinking that God is out to punish them. Some have bizarre behaviors or thought disorders. Such patients are often helped by the antischizophrenic drugs and may spontaneously improve as well. These probably aren't primarily frontal lobe disorders; disorders of subcortical structures (such as basal ganglia and amygdala) come to mind, as does temporal lobe.

The schizophrenics with negative symptoms are the ones likely to suffer from a frontal lobe disorder. These people are drastically slowed down in their thought and speech, have blunted emotions (they don't even smile back at you when you greet them) and seem unable to enjoy anything in life. They seem unable to express empathy with others, and their attention spans may be shortened. There are many other sources of such symptoms (garden-variety depressions, for example); the combination of symptoms that the psychiatrists associate with schizophrenia by a process of elimination, however, have a poorer prognosis—and they often have structural brain abnormalities, such as enlarged reservoirs (known as the lateral ventricles) for cerebrospinal fluid.

Variations in brain structure are not necessarily a problem. For example, normal dizygotic "fraternal" twins have ventricular sizes that are about 50 percent larger than the general population (crowding *in utero* makes twins more vulnerable to many things). But a monozygotic "identical" twin who happens to have schizophrenia is likely to have ventricles twice as large as the average healthy population—while his or her healthy twin doesn't. These fluid spaces don't affect behavior directly, of course, but they indicate that there were abnormalities during the brain's development.

So prefrontal functions seem to include abstract and creative thinking, fluency of thought and language, affective responses and the capacity for emotional attachments, social judgment, volition and drive, and selective attention. If obsessive-compulsive behavior is an exaggeration of frontal function, then the negative symptoms of schizophrenia might be considered a result of a low level of functioning up front.

BUT NONE OF THESE "localizations of function" is at all comparable to the relatively predictable location of the hand in the middle of the motor strip. Especially when talking about higher functions such as strategy, which require the integrated action of many parts of the brain, one must be careful of speaking as if strategy were "located" in the prefrontal cortex, or that narratives came from its bottom surface.

If some function (say, planning a four-course meal) is particularly disruptable from a particular piece of cortex, that doesn't mean the function resides there. It may only mean that the function cannot survive loss of that particular piece of the larger circuit. Other parts of the brain may be equally involved in strategy, but their injury may not disrupt the function because another region can readily substitute for them. Injury (whether from bruising, strokes, and tumors or from gunshot and stab wounds) or temporary problems (such as epileptic seizures and migraine attacks) are only crude indicators of an area's function. This need to equivocate about localization of function is a source of enduring frustration to the neurophysiologist and neurologist.

Another reason for caution about localizing functions to particular places is that individuals are so variable. The anatomy is much more variable than textbooks tend to mention: For example, the primary visual cortex (that first big cortical-level map of the visual world in the back of the brain) varies threefold in size between seemingly normal adult humans. The motor strip isn't always in the same order, and patches of sensory cortex are sometimes found in front of motor strip, completely contrary to the motor-in-front, sensory-behind notions of the textbooks. If subdivisions as seemingly stereotyped as the "primary maps" can vary so much, we should be especially careful when generalizing about the brain's *terra incognita* up front.

But such variability is also cause for suspecting that the frontal lobe may, in a given person, be much more specialized here and there than this general picture has indicated: The general picture pieced together by those natural-historianlike neurologists has emerged from hundreds of patients, each with a different lesion—but each with perhaps a different organization. This jitter will blur the overall *average* organization; if we could map one individual and know all of his frontal-lobe areas in some detail, we might get the impression of considerable specialization, each little patch of cortex doing a somewhat different job. Neurosurgeons mapping the language cortex of individual patients have found much local specialization, though the overall map varies enormously from one patient to another. As neurosurgeons begin to operate on frontal-lobe tumor patients under local anesthesia in the same way as they routinely operate on temporal-lobe epileptics, and as functional brain-imaging techniques improve, it is possible that a more detailed pattern of localization in frontal lobe will emerge as well.

HARVARD MED and its library were all very nice, but I also knew an expert on monkey frontal lobe and its anatomical connections to the rest of the brain. My friend Terry Deacon can be found over in Harvard's anthropology department. Terry has been tracing the connections of primate frontal lobe, seeing whom it talks to, and who talks to it. And it's odd, Terry says, but frontal lobe's mappings to and from other regions have a marked similarity with how the deep tectum (what animals without cerebral cortex tend to use instead for higher functions) is organized: That midbrain structure, sitting atop the reticular formation, is what most animals (even those with an extensive cerebral cortex) seem to use to orient to new things in the environment. If my cat hears the can opener, you see her ears twist around to point that way, her eyes turn in that direction, and then her head turns too. That's exactly how midbrain is organized, serving to orient the sense organs via simple motor programs. It isn't a map of the body surface or of the visual field or of the muscles per se—it's a "map" of orienting movements. That's what frontal lobe may be duplicating in a big way—and then, of course, elaborating for even fancier versions of "What do I do next?"

If you are searching for the center of everything, the seat of executive power in a brain, that's the kind of wiring that is needed for selective attention, focusing both sensation and movement. For people who believe in dualism of a sort, it suggests getting close to the seat of the soul, the place where the interface occurs between the immaterial and the material. I stick to the "physiologists' premise" myself (it seems to be one of the occupational hazards of physiology), but one can understand why even a thoroughgoing atheist might wonder if some external agency wasn't occasionally at work. Consider this analysis of the sense of volition, by a leading sleep researcher:

Dreams are so strange—and so involuntary—as to challenge and deny the twin notions of rationality and responsibility. To be responsible, I must be rational; but in dreaming I appear irrational. And I lose my sense of volition. How, then, can I be responsible for my dreams? Surely they occur whether I will them or not. If I do not will them, then how can I cause them? And if not I, then who does will or cause them? While clearly involving me, dreams seem to happen regardless of my will; and they run their course—with few exceptions—no matter what I say, think, or feel.

Human intelligence has balked at two aspects of this experience. First, common sense says that there can be no effects without causes. Next, the individual sense of personal responsibility—and the freedom that is the basis of one's sense of will, choice, and morality—refuses to be held accountable for unwilled phenomena. One obvious conclusion: dreams are caused by some *external* agency over which we have no control; on the contrary, it is this external agency that during dreams controls the dreamer. Such assumptions have led naturally to religious theories and religious practices, in the effort to placate and appease the forces (or gods) that seem to drive our destiny.

People are, and have been, unhappy with the idea of gods

as insane, and must believe that their nocturnal visitations
have a point, however obscure. . . . Complementing the notion
of an external agency is the out-of-body experience that may
occur in nocturnal dreams or in the transitional states between
waking and sleep. In these states, it seems that a part of the
self (the soul or the ego) leaves the body and becomes an
external agency. It may even seem that the soul wanders
abroad, exerting its action in places remote from the body.
In this way, magical interventions can be achieved, and the
notion of gods as external agents is complemented by the
sense of being visited by disembodied spirits, with agency
power. [Hobson goes on to develop his thesis that dreams
are largely meaningless, except as evidence that there are
free-wheeling mechanisms in the brain juxtaposing things].

the neurophysiologist J. ALLAN HOBSON, 1988

AND SO THE INEVITABLE PRIMAL QUESTION: Where do
I live, where do *I* control it all from? And its corollary: Does
something control me, or am I truly autonomous?

If all this neural machinery is like a manufacturing plant
presided over by executives, where does the president sit? If this
is like a computer, where is the programmer? Deep in the frontal
lobe? Surely to make a conscious machine, we're going to have to
understand this center of it all in order to construct a mimic.

Yet it isn't like a corporation, and it isn't like a computer; our
consciousness is mechanically implemented by a process more
analogous to an economy or a political party, a distributed system
without much central authority. There is no central place from which
we consciously look out as a voyeur, from which a puppeteer pulls
our strings. Yet starting sometime in the third year of life, there is
a *narrator* for much of our conscious experience. One must understand what our narrator is, and in its own terms and phenomena
(such as what happens in delirium and dreams), before one can
appreciate how the lower-level machinery is voluntarily commanded
when we finally "make up our minds" about a shopping trip or a
career. Or, indeed, to glimpse a route to building a conscious robot.

But it is hard to see the narrator because of a thicket of
man-made obstructions: all of those multiple meanings of a much-
overused word, *consciousness*.

There is no term [consciousness] at once so popular and so devoid of standard meaning. How can a term mean anything when it is employed to connote anything and everything, including its own negation? One hears of the object of consciousness and the subject of consciousness, and the union of the two in self-consciousness; of the private consciousness, the social consciousness, and the transcendental consciousness; the inner and the outer, the higher and the lower, the temporal and the eternal consciousness; the activity and the state of consciousness. Then there is consciousness-stuff, and unconscious consciousness . . . , and unconscious physical states or subconsciousness. . . . The list is not complete, but sufficiently amazing. Consciousness comprises everything that is, and indefinitely much more. It is small wonder that the definition of it is little attempted.

the psychologist RALPH BARTON PERRY, 1904

4

VARIETIES OF CONSCIOUSNESS: FROM COMA TO REVERIE

[C]reation is still going on, . . . the creative forces are as great and as active to-day as they have ever been, and . . . to-morrow's morning will be as heroic as any of the world. Creation is here and now. *So near is man to the creative pageant, so much a part is he of the endless and incredible experiment, that any glimpse he may have will be but the revelation of a moment, a solitary note heard in a symphony thundering through debatable existences of time. Poetry is as necessary to comprehension as science. It is as impossible to live without reverence as it is without joy.*

the natural historian HENRY BESTON, 1928

I stand in awe of my body, this matter to which I am bound has become so strange to me. . . . Talk of mysteries!—Think of our life in nature—daily to be shown matter, to come in contact with it,—rocks, trees, wind on our cheeks! the solid earth! *the* actual *world! the* common sense! Contact! Contact! Who *are we?* where *are we?*

the essayist HENRY DAVID THOREAU, 1864

Eastham is as far east as you can go around here. The Outermost House is somewhere outside Eastham on the Cape's elbow, the isolated cabin from which Henry Beston chronicled a year in the life cycle of the Cape in his 1928 book, *The Outermost House*. Parts of the Cape north of the elbow have since been made into a national park of sorts, a patchwork of crazy compromises officially known as the Cape Cod National Seashore. Earlier, Beston's beach cabin was designated a National Historic Site.

Asking directions from the park ranger reveals that the Outermost House no longer exists. It lasted a half century, the great winter storm of 1978 having swept it away while rearranging the sand dunes. That is, as Beston pointed out, part of the life cycle of beaches (and, he might have added, offshore barrier islands such as Palm Beach and Miami Beach): to be rearranged every century or so. Anyone who builds within walking distance of a beach has to accept the consequences as part of the price of admission. Not that they always do: Like the people who build in the flood plain of a river, some expect the lawmakers (i.e., the other taxpayers) to protect them from erosion, as if it were some sort of manufacturing defect for which there ought to be warranty recourse.

Beaches are swept clean daily by the tides, and the sand dunes are cleaned out by the storms on a less regular schedule (even National Historic Sites); it is part of the charm of the place, what makes it so different from Woods Hole. There, alas, it is hard to find any original beach or headlands. The stony beaches have been covered here and there with imported sand. The Woods Hole headlands have been plastered with rows of giant boulders, to protect the houses that someone lacking foresight built too close to the water; though more neatly arranged than most riprap jobs, it's all very ersatz, something like those German forests where the trees grow only in orderly rows and not a scrap of undergrowth is to be seen.

This Atlantic Coast is very different. I was attracted here by Beston's 1928 description of Coast Guard Beach:

At the foot of this cliff a great ocean beach runs north and south unbroken, mile lengthening into mile. Solitary and elemental, unsullied and remote, visited and possessed by the outer sea, these sands might be the end or the beginning of a world. Age by age, the sea here gives battle to the land; age by age, the earth struggles for her own, calling to her defence her energies and her creations, bidding her plants steal down upon the beach, and holding the frontier sands in a net of grass and roots which the storms wash free. The great rhythms of nature, to-day so dully disregarded, wounded even, have here their spacious and primeval liberty; cloud and shadow of cloud, wind and tide, tremor of night and day. Journeying birds alight here and fly away again all unseen, schools of fish move beneath the waves, the surf flings its spray against the sun.

I'm not sure Beston would recognize the place today. I just saw someone riding a little motorized dune buggy, put-putting up the beach like a lawn mower, chewing away at the sand with its tractor tires (if that happened on a national park beach on the West Coast, a crowd of indignant hikers and bathers would probably rise up and throw the offending vehicle into the surf). But there was no point in my complaining to the nearest park ranger: The person riding the thing was a park ranger on patrol. That's an inauspicious sign.

I set off walking down Coast Guard Beach in the other direction, toward where the Outermost House was last seen, if only to get away from the road end. The cluster of well-oiled bodies and mindless radios on the beach, while repelling me, has attracted a buzzing pest circling around them. And a rather large one at that. The labored-sounding airplane is towing an advertising banner around an endless circle in the sky, promoting one of the fast foods whose throwaway containers contribute both to litter and to the depletion of the ozone layer (via the "refrigerator"-type gas used in the construction of the foamlike boxes). And the depletion of ozone will let more ultraviolet light through, making beaches like this uninhabitable and driving cities underground.

Grumble, grumble. Advertising promoting the destruction of the environment, and this supposedly a park. What will the National Park Service allow next? Park rangers on trail bikes zooming past hikers at Mount Rainier, all in the name of "efficiency"?

A QUARTER-HOUR WALK south of the road end, and suddenly there are no more people for a long while (fortunately, many of the people who come to the beach for a suntan tend to cluster together). There are, however, plenty of the natural inhabitants. I sit and watch a sea gull watching me. It sits there in the sand, moving only its head. Every ten seconds or so, it rotates its head suddenly to a new position. Within a minute or two, it covers the whole horizon, left around to right, just like a well-trained lookout on the bridge of a ship at sea. Occasionally, it breaks the regularity of the advance, coming back to look at something. Unless I move, it seems to ignore me, apportioning its attention equally to all points of the compass.

Washed up on the shore nearby is the shell of a horseshoe crab, a *Limulus* no more. It is upside down, its vulnerable underside exposed to the sun, and it might have died that way, as an inverted *Limulus* can have some trouble righting itself, what with that flaring skirt of armor. The wider the skirt, the more resistant to flipping—but the more serious the consequences if he does flip.

Sounds familiar, like knights in ever-heavier armor when knocked off their horses—and more recent nuclear-tipped "defensive armaments" with their ever-more-suicidal scenarios if a computer makes a mistake. It's too bad that there aren't any *Limulus* on the West Coast where all of those aerospace companies are located, to serve as a "Star Wars" warning (come to think of it, West Coast museums are also poor places to see displays of medieval suits of armor, escalating from chain mail up through behemoth walking coffins).

[Because aircraft carriers are so vulnerable, defenses are] the first order of business—the loss of a carrier would be an unthinkable catastrophe, an unbearable humiliation—and

protective systems are layered and lavished upon the carrier group with unstinting prodigality. In such fashion, the modern carrier group is slowly evolving toward a splendid solipsism, plying the seas in isolated grandeur, ever more invulnerable and ever more harmless, its own final cause and final end, the realization in the modern world of the Hegelian nous, *the ultimate self-regarding system.*

the writer CHARLES R. MORRIS, 1988

But it's a nice day, and the sea air is soporific, and I am far enough upwind to hear the droning airplane no longer, far enough away now to turn my back on the offensive advertising. It's time to think great thoughts. (This may sound grandiose, but it is really just a technique. Long ago, I developed a mental strategy for dealing with advertising jingles that kept running through my head: What I do is recall the Grand March from *Aida*, which triumphantly silences even the worst jingle.) What will it be, to displace the distasteful thoughts—shall I solve the origin of life, the balance-of-payments problem, or the fate of the universe? Let's see now. Perhaps I should solve the problem of *consciousness*—something like that, appropriate to the seashore.

The danger is instead lapsing into unconsciousness while contemplating the problem, given the sun and wind and sighing surf. Alas, unconsciousness doesn't provide a very satisfying definition of consciousness. Being asleep is very different from being in coma (readily arousable versus total lack of response to even painful stimuli), but neither has an opposite that tells you very much about higher consciousness.

The other reported danger is merging with the environment, participating in things so much as to lose one's identity. This too gets called consciousness:

The view of nature which predominated in the West down to the eve of the Scientific Revolution was that of an enchanted world. Rocks, trees, rivers, and clouds were all seen as wondrous, alive, and human beings felt at home in this environment. The cosmos, in short, was a place of *belonging*. A member of this cosmos was not an alienated observer of it

but a direct participant in its drama. His personal destiny
was bound up with its destiny, and this relationship gave
meaning to his life. This type of consciousness—which I [call]
"participating consciousness"—involves merger, or identification, with one's surroundings, and bespeaks a psychic whole-
ness that has long since passed from the scene. . . .

Plato's own psychological ideal was that of an individual
organized around a center (ego), using his will to control his
instinct and thereby unify his psyche. Reason thus becomes
the essence of personality, and is characterized by distancing
oneself from phenomena, maintaining one's identity. Poetry,
mimesis, the whole Homeric tradition, on the other hand,
involves identification with the actions of other people and
things—the surrendering of identity. For Plato, only the
abolition of this tradition could create the situation in which a
subject perceives by confronting separate objects. Whereas
the Jews saw participating consciousness as sin, Plato saw it
as pathology, the archenemy of the intellect.

the historian MORRIS BERMAN, 1981

CONSCIOUSNESS IS A VERY OVERUSED WORD, the same
string of syllables being used to designate a multitude of meanings. It's much worse than the multiple meanings of *brain*, which,
besides denoting the three pounds of nerve cells inside our heads,
is also used as a verb (to club, aiming at a head), as the opposite of
brawn, as a surname in England, as a term for a studious student
or the chief planner of an enterprise, and more recently to designate something as inanimate as a computer. Being a neurophysiologist, I tend to avoid the nonneurological uses of the word, but I
doubt that I'll convert the rest of the English-speaking world to
my more restrictive usage.

The multiple-meanings problem is an order of magnitude worse
for *consciousness*. Compounding the problem, there is a lot of
willful ambiguity here for some puzzling reason: People actually
go out of their way to muddy the issues. It is reminiscent of when
people intentionally confuse the letter *O* and the number *0* on a
telephone dial (try telling someone your phone number is "two-
three-zero-eight" and most of them will repeat it back to you for

verification as "two-three-oh-eight"). I'm not really worried about the inaccuracy, except insofar as it confuses foreign visitors confronting American telephones, but the perversity of insisting on ambiguity is indeed very much like discussions of consciousness that I've heard among scientists. You'd think that they wanted to keep things sloppy, to prevent clarity.

And since there is not a more restrictive meaning of consciousness among the professionals, it is very easy for everyone to talk at cross-purposes: There is no agreed-upon term equivalent to "zero" to which we can all retreat when consciousness confusion threatens, the way that we can retreat to using zero when reading off a mixed letters-and-numbers automobile license plate. While I have no ambition to propose a rigid definition (they seldom solve problems), attempting a definition usually allows one to sort things out better, set the stage for clearer thinking about the problem.

Are there any uses of the word *consciousness* that we can dismiss as trivial? Well, one person's triviality is another person's favorite subject, but I'd certainly spin off *nonunconsciousness*. Sleep and wakefulness are so important as to deserve their own terms, and their description can do nicely without *consciousness;* neurologists already tend to avoid the word and talk instead about a graded spectrum of *arousibility* from coma to stupor to drowsiness to wakefulness.

BUT THAT AROUSIBILITY USAGE is closely related to another one that is not so easily dismissed: *awareness.* I am conscious of the breeze blowing on my face. We talk of "consciousness-raising" when we want to sensitize a troglodyte to a problem to which he remains oblivious. A budget-conscious shopper is one particularly sensitive to price tags; we talk of being conscious of our heartbeats in times of stress, even though unaware of them normally. There is *selective attention*, including *altered states of consciousness* such as hypnotic trances, which limit awareness in odd ways. We cannot be conscious of our blood pressure at all (except with the aid of external instruments), and the same is true of a whole host of involuntary autonomic functions regulated by our brains such as body growth and digestion.

Awareness is a little tricky because we sometimes cannot report being aware of something, yet have our brain register the information and make use of it. The classic cases involve patients with damage to their visual cortex: While functionally blind according to the standard tests, they can navigate around obstacles much better with the lights on than with the lights off. Ask them to guess where a light is and—while denying that they can see anything—they'll guess pretty accurately. At some subcortical level, the visual information is accessible—but to the narrator of their conscious experience, if the usual connections from visual cortex don't have the information, they'll report it isn't there. Which may, of course, be why we cannot report on our blood pressure either—it's just not handled by cerebral cortex.

Consciousness is said to be about the nonroutine aspects of our mental life; as Karl Popper noted, posing alternatives seems especially "conscious":

Much of our purposeful behaviour (and presumably of the purposeful behaviour of animals) happens without the intervention of consciousness. . . . Problems that can be solved by routine do not need consciousness. [The biological achievements that are helped by consciousness are the solution of *problems of a nonroutine kind.*] But the role of consciousness is perhaps clearest where an aim or purpose . . . can be achieved by *alternate means,* and when two or more means are tried out, after deliberation.

We are unaware of most of the things that go on in our heads, and sometimes that's better, as in Zen archery. You sometimes even have to avoid thinking about a problem. When I try consciously to adjust my stride to step over an approaching puddle of rainwater, I usually foul it up; if I instead take note of the puddle from afar and then go on to think consciously of something else, my stride adjusts automatically so as to place one foot at the leading edge of the puddle and the other foot at its far edge. Heaven forbid that I should attempt to tell my liver what to do; I'd turn yellow within minutes.

Consciousness involves our operating on the margins, against the enormous background of automatic things. It's something like civilization, where we can drive a car without understanding a carburetor, use a radio without being able to build one, improvise jazz without being able to tune a piano, create electronic music without understanding the innards of the black boxes. Consciousness doesn't always involve creativity and choice, but they're close relatives, much more so than mere awareness.

Indeed, *aware* is perfectly adequate in most cases where one says *semiconscious* or *conscious of* or *losing consciousness* or *consciousness-raising* (and the word *aware* is even shorter—though I predict that the "zero-oh" type of perverse replacement of "aware" by "conscious" will persist).

There are, however, some variants on the theme of awareness that have a big following among psychologists and neuroscientists who comment on consciousness. I am conscious of that sea gull watching me—I caught him staring at me this time (I probably brushed away a fly and so disrupted his lookout routine). I recognize him as a particular kind of bird. I recognize his search routine, and the significance of its interruption. I know that if I stand up, he'll be conscious of me. *Perception, cognition* (those mental processes we are "conscious" of), and *selective attention* aren't trivial at all: Figuring them out is a major problem, as each is likely to be more complex than the sleep-wakefulness spectrum.

Perception/cognition are processes shared in large part by that meditating sea gull, by that inquisitive ant exploring my big toe, and by those primitive *Limulus* wandering around offshore, trying to keep from getting tipped over by a wave crashing ashore. We can even argue about whether that wildflower poking out of the sand dune is "conscious of" the sun: It does, after all, unfold in the morning, follows the sun around the sky pointing as surely as a bird dog, and then folds its petals back up just before sunset. There are some higher aspects of cognition that a flower surely doesn't share with me, such as my ability to tell a Picasso from an Edward Hopper or a Winslow Homer painting, but recognition abilities do seem to lie on a plain-to-fancy spectrum. Having learned something from Descartes's mistake, I wouldn't want to define consciousness as uniquely human, but the term should capture something of our advanced abilities rather than covering the commonplace.

I go along with Julian Jaynes on this one: He says that the narrator of our personal experience is the really nontrivial aspect of consciousness, and that perception/cognition ought to be pared off from the problem just as sleep/wakefulness is. In comparison to the narrator who spins scenarios, choosing between alternative future courses of action, I think that perception and cognition will prove easy to understand mechanistically. But I have a hard time believing that hallucinations were the primitive form of consciousness (as Jaynes postulates for the pre-*Odyssey* mentality in *The Origin of Consciousness in the Breakdown of the Bicameral Mind*) or that "participating consciousness," the identification of self with the environment (which Morris Berman in *The Reenchantment of the World* tends to treat as essential to reintegrate somehow) was either. Identifying too closely with the environment, or listening to a burning bush "speaking" to you, tends to result in being eaten by a predator, or falling off a cliff. It seems more likely that animism and its descendants are cognitive mistakes to which we are prone when agriculture removes us from the wild environments in which we evolved (Homeric times, about 1200 B.C., were nonetheless 7,000 years after agriculture started up at the end of the last Ice Age).

Yet the limits of self—how much you consider yourself a part of your environment when making choices—is surely an important element of the consciousness discussion, even if one treats animism and its descendants as naive mistakes to be avoided. The Australian aborigines see themselves as stewards of their land in ways that go considerably beyond the shortsighted European settlers who are displacing them. The inventor of the throwaway Styrofoam cups that litter this beach will hopefully be considered seriously retarded by the standards of some future consciousness, because of fouling his own nest. Even if we limit our use of the word *consciousness* to choosing between alternative futures, the biodegradable movement's "consciousness-raising" still qualifies.

The three great elemental sounds in nature are the sound of rain, the sound of wind in a primeval wood, and the sound of outer ocean on a beach. I have heard them all, and of the three elemental voices, that of ocean is the most awesome, beautiful, and varied. For it is a mistake to talk of the monotone of the ocean or of the monotonous nature of its sound. The sea has many voices. Listen to the surf, really lend it your ears, and you will hear in it a world of sounds: hollow boomings and heavy roarings, great watery tum-

blings and tramplings, long hissing seethes, sharp, rifle-shot reports, splashes, whispers, the grinding undertone of stones, and sometimes vocal sounds that might be the half-heard talk of people in the sea. And not only is the great sound varied in the manner of its making, it is also constantly changing its tempo, its pitch, its accent, and its rhythm, being now loud and thundering, now almost placid, now furious, now grave and solemn-slow, now a simple measure, now a rhythm monstrous with a sense of purpose and ele-mental will.

the natural historian HENRY BESTON, 1928

TIME TO GET UP AND STRETCH, walk a little farther down the beach; the sea gull will just have to get along without me. Now I was aware of that decision to stand up before I actually moved—or was I? My fellow neurophysiologist Ben Libet has, to everyone's consternation, shown that the brain activity associated with the preparation for movement (something called the "readiness potential," a tiny electrical wave that one can measure atop the frontal lobes starting more than a third of a second before a movement actually can be observed) starts a quarter of a second before you report having decided to move. You just weren't yet conscious of your decision to move, but it was indeed under way; the techni-cian watching the brain waves probably became aware of your decision to move about the time that you did.

Is this voluntary-movement aspect of awareness-type con-sciousness something that we can get our teeth into, something a little closer to the "little person inside the head" than mere pat-tern recognition, bridging the gap between the lower conscious-ness of arousibility and awareness and the higher consciousness of narrators and subconscious scenarios that we use to plan shopping trips and careers?

This intriguing issue is all mixed up with the sticky subject of time, what physicists since Einstein have called the simultaneity problem, because the theory of relativity shows that there is no such thing, or at least no way to measure if two events are truly synchronous, without worrying about how long messages take to get from here to there. The brain has simultaneity problems in a big way, if only because messages move faster in some directions than others. Unlike electrical signals in a computer, which travel at nearly the speed of light (about 300,000,000 meters/second), neural messages propagate using a burning-fuse effect, which is very slow in comparison (the faster-conducting nerves use a string-of-firecrackers scheme; just imagine the firecrackers daisy-chained). When I start to move my right leg, a message starts out from my left frontal lobe. It travels down to my back and then out the nerves to my leg, usually taking more than a tenth of a second just in travel time. The same message is also sent over to my right brain, just to keep it informed about what's going on.

But the speed at which the two messages travel is very different: Messages between regions of cerebral cortex travel much more slowly (1–5 meters/second, even using the firecracker-chain scheme) than messages down to the spinal cord (more like 20 meters/second, but sometimes 100), even if they just involve two different branches of the same nerve cell. Like the common-place observation that it takes about as long for the postal service to deliver a letter on the other side of town as it does for it to deliver a letter on the far side of the country (sometimes it takes four days either way), so a neural message takes about as long to travel from one half of the brain to the other as it does to travel all of the way down to the leg (nearly a tenth of a second either way)! I call this the *paradoxical postal principle* of the central nervous system, and it may explain some of the apparent paradoxes of consciousness, such as being unable to report decision-making until the neural antecedents of the movement are already under way.

I try not to think about this too much as I stand up and brush off the sand, for fear of falling flat on my face. I remember that cautionary poem:

> *The centipede was quite happy*
> *Until the toad in fun*
> *Said "Pray, which leg comes after which?"*
> *Which brought its mind to such a pitch*
> *It lay distracted in a ditch*
> *Considering how to run.*

SHORT-TERM MEMORY as a basis of consciousness? That's Marvin Minsky's claim ("agents that are engaged in using and changing our most recent memories . . . lie at the roots of consciousness"). Again it doesn't seem to have much of the qualities that make the ant a fancier form of life than the Venus's-flytrap (that carnivorous plant indeed has a form of short-term memory). And which make us fancier than the ant.

There are all sorts of advantages to a memory system that allows one to analyze the past, as Minsky points out in *The Society of Mind*, especially for an animal like us that does a lot of non-routine problem-solving. But metabolism is essential for consciousness too, and I put memory in a similar low-level category. What constitutes an appropriate level of explanation? When one says *basis* or *foundation* and is talking about a presumably hierarchal system like the brain, one usually means the immediate subjacent level, not the utility basement—certainly physics is *a* foundation of biology, but biochemistry is the immediately subjacent level whose analyses are more relevant than quantum mechanics. Indeed, these levels are sometimes seen as a way of defining consciousness as the ultimate level:

> "Causal decoupling" between the levels of the world implies that to *understand* the material basis of certain rules I must go to the next level down; but the rules can be *applied* with confidence without any reference to the more basic level. Interestingly, the division of natural sciences reflects this causal decoupling. Nuclear physics, atomic physics, chemistry, molecular biology, biochemistry, and genetics are each independent disciplines valid in their own right, a consequence of the causal decoupling between them. . . . Such a series of "causal decouplings" may be extraordinarily complex, intricate beyond our current imaginings. Yet finally what we may arrive at is a theory of the mind and consciousness—a mind so decoupled from its material support systems that it seems to be independent of them—and "forgot" how we got to it. . . . The biological phenomenon of a self-reflexive consciousness is simply the last of a long and complex series of "causal decouplings" from the world of matter.

the physicist HEINZ PAGELS, 1988

SCENARIO-SPINNING is more promising as a foundation for consciousness. It fits in well with another defining-by-variants aspect of consciousness that I've barely mentioned: subconsciousness. *Preconscious* and *subconscious* and Freud's *unconscious* are most helpful in defining consciousness a little better, because they indicate that there is far more going on than just autonomic-type unawareness: There is really something creative happening in the background, something nonroutine and unique, of which we get snapshot glimpses occasionally. And movies every night: the *stream of consciousness* in glorious Technicolor, uninterrupted by commercial breaks as our censor jumps in to remind us that our dream's new story line is sheer nonsense, which is what happens to our daytime dreams we call thought. In dreams we have a series of "visual bursts" that we attempt to integrate into a story line.

An impressive amount of problem-solving goes on subconsciously. One of the classic characters of Woods Hole science was Albert Szent-Györgyi, who, among other things, discovered vitamin C. He commented:

> I have to think very hard about a problem but this thinking never leads me anywhere; it is but a necessary priming process. Finding myself unable to solve the problem, I let it sink into my subconscious. How long it stays there varies. Then, unexpectedly, the solution is passed into my conscious mind. My brain must have done as the Hungarian laxative which was advertised: "While you sleep it does the work."

Without memory of the past problems and solutions, we'd never get much better at problem-solving. But then, neither would the kitten who eventually learns about hidden objects that wiggle blankets or newspapers, learns to peer behind or underneath rather than just attacking frontally. Our mental life and our various powers involve a lot of processes. If we call them all *conscious*, we dilute the word into meaninglessness, one of those words like *thing* or *stuff*. We already have enough difficulties thinking about thought without the burden of self-imposed ignorance.

Personally, I would say that the only aspects of our mental

life that deserve singling out as peculiarly conscious are those associated with the narrator, with *self-conscious* and *subconscious* and *stream of consciousness;* the others are important in their own right, likely essential foundations, but not to be confused with "the real thing."

SO THERE YOU HAVE THE RATIONALE for why I am restricting myself to "What shall I do next" as the main aspect of consciousness that I will consider here. I don't mean it in the narrow sense of motor-systems neurophysiology (whose physics-addicted practitioners assiduously avoid the word *consciousness* for fear that someone might confuse them with psychologists), but rather in the broad sense stretching from the next second to the millennium. Hereafter when you see *consciousness* used in this book, it will probably mean planning for the future, spinning alternatives and selecting among them for one's next act.

It might be objected that this is an excessively "movement-oriented" view of consciousness, that it takes insufficient account of the "awareness" connotation of the word. Surely one can contemplate the sensory inputs without making movement plans? Or fantasize visual objects without movement? Well, maybe not—lots of things betray themselves by little movements, as when someone's eyes turn leftward when reacting emotionally to a "pure thought." My grandmother Calvin had a tendency to flex and extend her knee whenever she was "rearranging the truth a little" in telling a story (this involuntary movement was known to the whole family). And one of the lessons of sensory-systems neurophysiology is that the movement-directing nerves descending from brain to spinal cord also have little branches to the ascending sensory pathways, serving to adjust sensory bias or communicate an expected sensory input from the about-to-be-ordered movement (so-called efference copy) for comparison purposes.

There's a lot of feedback from muscle tension and limb position into consciousness that affects our "will"; I remember how surprised the neurologist Oliver Sacks was when he had his shoulder muscles electrically stimulated—whereupon he felt as if he wanted to shrug his shoulders expressively, as in "So?" The electricity was interfering with his will! His own movement-production system, by tensing those muscles in the usual way, could have perhaps achieved the same effect. The sensory and movement systems are a good deal less independent than we originally thought; while movement-planning language may not serve as a universal description of what's going on in consciousness, it seems less prone to the tangles in which sensory-oriented descriptions land us (see the tortured debates on "representations" in any cognitive science treatise).

THE NARRATOR ASPECT brings me up short, because the little person inside the head is a fallacy that psychology and neuroscience have long tried to combat. We tend to imagine the eyes as some sort of television camera projecting onto a screen inside the brain—watched by . . . ? *Who* is doing the watching? Before I make the narrator's neural machinery into the seat of consciousness, I had better watch out for the pitfalls of all such "central viewpoints," as they have led a whole series of thinkers, including Descartes, down blind alleys.

In my first year as a physiology instructor, I taught a discussion group for a large lecture course. And when we covered the optics of the eye, a medical student asked the question that was probably on everyone else's mind too: If the floor is projected onto the top of the eyeball, and the sky onto the lower part (in the usual inverted image, just as in your camera), then "how does the image get turned back right side up, so the world doesn't appear upside down to us?" In an instant camera's photograph, you just turn it over with a flick of the wrist, probably without ever realizing that the photograph was upside down in the first place. In the wiring connecting the TV camera with the TV screen, camera top is simply connected to screen bottom, and vice versa, without anyone noticing the switch-around. So where in the brain is the wiring switched around? (If this concern seems excessively quaint, remember that even Leonardo da Vinci worried about this problem, tried to figure out an optical scheme to reinvert the image using the clear jelly that fills the eyeball).

Now the usual professorial answer to this philosophical question about "why isn't our visual world inverted?" is to say that it's all a matter of convention: You can "get used to anything," as when someone wears inverting spectacles and eventually learns to move around in the upside-down world (and gets so used to the inverted perspective that, upon his removing the inverting prisms several weeks later, the real world seems inverted!). But the real problem is the assumption of a central viewpoint, a *place* where something does the viewing, as if we had a voyeur-puppeteer hiding out in a central cave, pulling our strings. The little-person-inside problem is so old that it has a Latin name: the *homunculus fallacy*.

> *What controls the brain?   The Mind.*
> *What controls the Mind?   The Self.*
> *What controls the Self?   Itself.*

> a parody related by MARVIN MINSKY

What we usually say is that the brain as a totality produces the illusion of a central viewpoint, a *virtual center*, just as the physicist can often represent the earth's gravity as an attraction to the center of the earth rather than the more complicated problem of dealing with the separate attraction of the many individual atoms, some nearby, one in the center of the earth, and some on the opposite side of the world. As Minsky points out, "the idea of a single, central Self doesn't explain anything. This is because a thing with no parts provides nothing that we can use as pieces of explanation." The Romans even coined a slogan out of this notion: *Ex nihilo nihil fit* ("You can't make something out of nothing"). But, nonetheless, we have a unity of conscious experience; even if comprised of many functional sub-units, our mental life somehow arrives at the virtual equivalent of a narrator. Sometimes even more than one, as in the case of multiple personalities.

It's not an easy explanation, with what we replace this center-of-it-all concept. And neurophysiologists are themselves always falling prey to overenthusiastic reductionism—as when we fall once again into a trap we call the *Grandmother's face cell fallacy*. I'm not sure that I'm up to explaining this fallacy on such a nice day as today, especially if even Minsky feigns incomprehension of it. Yet I'll have to do it sometime, if only to convince people that a narrator's unity of consciousness can be produced without a physical center of it all, a seat of the soul. I'll first have to digress into some nuts and bolts (we neurophysiologists prefer to call them synapses and nerve cells), step back, and survey the parts that we can use as pieces of explanation.

Only human beings guide their behaviour by a knowledge of what happened before they were born and a preconception of what may happen after they are dead; thus only human beings find their way by a light that illuminates more than the patch of ground they stand on.

PETER B. MEDAWAR AND JEAN S. MEDAWAR, 1977

—— 5 ——

THE ELECTRICALLY EXCITING LIFE OF THE INHIBITED NERVOUS CELL

Men ought to know that from nothing else but from the brain come joys, delights, laughter and sports, and sorrows, griefs, despondency and lamentations.

HIPPOCRATES (460–377 B.C.)

How is it that I am a collection of a hundred billion nerve cells, yet I think and act as one?

the neurophysiologist RODOLFO LLINÁS, 1986

Several centuries ago, we were remarkably ignorant of how the brain worked, this despite the brain being identified as the seat of thought and feeling by each of the four great ancient civilizations: Mesopotamia, Egypt, India, and China. Or at least by some of their best thinkers (Egyptian embalmers still threw out the brain but attempted to preserve the heart and liver). The brain as "where all the action is" didn't become part of the everyday concepts of educated people until much more recently.

With the Enlightenment and the Industrial Revolution came a gradual improvement in knowledge about the brain; by the end of the nineteenth century, many of the major neurological disorders had been identified, and the brain was seen to be made up of a great many cells organized in spectacular ways. Here, surely, were the parts from which one could construct an explanation for the major mental phenomena.

Such *fin de siècle* figures as Sigmund Freud show us how frustrated the basic scientists were, trying to understand how brain components related to the higher mental functions and their disorders; Freud finally switched from studying stained nerve cells under a microscope to listening carefully to his neurotic patients for indications about how higher levels of functioning became disordered. Trained in the mechanistic physiology of Helmholtz, Freud would probably have been one of the first to suspect that his disorders of id, ego, and superego could be better described as the disordered activity of certain regions of the frontal lobe and subcortical structures; he would have loved to look at the rainbow-colored images thrown up on modern computer screens displaying the excessive metabolic activity of the inferior medial surfaces of the frontal lobes in obsessive-compulsive patients. Yet he too would have soon asked himself the question: "*Ja*, but why are those regions so active?" What causes them to "spin their wheels" and go nowhere?

In earlier centuries, sages would probably have said that these poor individuals were simply "born under the wrong star" or that they (or their parents) had "sinned and were being punished by the gods for their transgression." But those who look more carefully, painstakingly developing the tools needed to get answers, have been finding that most brain disorders are either (1) incidental consequences of strokes and tumors, (2) disordered development of the brain *in utero* (essentially, gross miswiring by the standards of modern human brains) that manifests itself in later life as mental and neurological disorders, or (3) more subtle and labile disorders in the chemical systems used to communicate between nerve cells, also likely to be part of the variations thrown up by evolution.

Indeed, part of the local history of Woods Hole is all tied up with this gradual improvement in our understanding of ourselves; you see reminders when walking around town.

Discovery consists of seeing what everybody has seen and thinking what nobody has thought.

the biochemist ALBERT SZENT-GYÖRGYI, 1962

OUT TO SEE THE SEA, or at least semiprotected Vineyard Sound. A few blocks east of Eel Pond and the Marine Biological Lab, one passes the Little Harbor, complete with coast-guard station. Looking down on it from the shore is the Woods Hole Library. Little Harbor opens out onto the choppy Woods Hole channel (locally called "the Hole") that connects Vineyard Sound to Buzzards Bay.

Along this main road toward Falmouth is the headquarters of the Woods Hole Oceanographic Institution, where much basic research is also done (and applied research: One sometimes trips over television camera crews on Woods Hole sidewalks, if one of the WHOI ships is just back from exploring the deep-water wreck of the *Titanic* by remote-controlled "robots").

Then one turns down Church Street. It is so named because it has a church on it, just as School Street has a school on it (Water Street once had water along it, until they built a platform out over the water on stilts—and then paved it!). Not far down

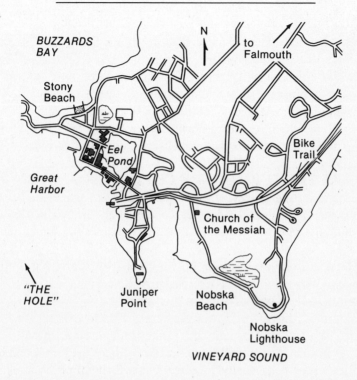

BUZZARDS
BAY

N
to
Falmouth

Stony
Beach

Eel
Pond

Bike
Trail

Great
Harbor

Church of
the Messiah

"THE
HOLE"

Juniper
Point

Nobska
Beach

Nobska
Lighthouse

VINEYARD SOUND

Church Street beyond the wooden bridge, one comes to the church
and surrounding graveyard.

The Church of the Messiah is, like Woods Hole Library, a
stone structure pieced together from all the local glacial debris,
weathered down to a certain softness. This church is where the
Woods Hole Cantata sings its annual concert every August (I've
been listening to them practice up in the Meigs Room). Except for
the distant drone of a lawn mower, the church is silent today, as
is the graveyard alongside.

I wander among the tombstones, looking for familiar names.
There is a prominent new tombstone: ALBERT I. SZENT-GYÖRGYI,
1893-1986, NOBEL LAUREATE, followed by an inscription in Hun-
garian. And many surnames familiar to a neurophysiologist are
found here, as if the local families had contributed more than their
share of brain scientists. Other names are scientists who moved
here, often escaping from Hitler's mad designs.

Otto Loewi is buried here, just downhill from the back of the church. The modest red tombstone says that he died in 1961 at the age of 88, the same year that I was taking my first physiology course. I never met him, but his discoveries were not only central to understanding the brain but important to me personally. I've since found out quite a lot about him, both from the people around Woods Hole and elsewhere (I ran into Loewi's one-time bottle-washer in California, now the novelist Ramón Sender Barayon).

BACK AT THE TURN OF THE CENTURY, it was known that nerves ran on electricity of some sort—and so, presumably, did that enormous collection of nerve cells we call the brain. But the anatomists were still arguing about a particularly fundamental issue: Are the nerve cells really independent, as much so as the individuals in our society—or do they constitute one big web of interconnected cells, where (at least functionally) it is hard to tell where one cell leaves off and another starts?

You don't have to go to a coral reef to find examples of the latter arrangement: Our hearts are like that. So it wasn't a trivial issue: The electrical current generated by one heart cell spreads to neighboring cells easily because the cell membranes stick together and open up holes that connect the inside of one cell to the inside of its neighbors.

Various prominent histologists and neuroanatomists at the beginning of the twentieth century said brains were reticulated webs something like that. However, the great Spanish neuroanatomist Santiago Ramón y Cajal (1852–1934) essentially said that nerve cells were more like the individuals of our society lightly touching one another via outgrowths ("Holding hands with one another" was the way he put it)—but not kissing continuously. It's something like the holistic versus reductionistic arguments, the whole brain acting as an indivisible whole versus acting as a collection of independent agents, each different.

And Loewi (pronounced rather like "Levi") is the fellow who settled the argument in Cajal's favor (at least to most physiologists' satisfaction; the anatomists weren't really convinced until 1953, when Sandy Palay's electron micrographs demonstrated the narrow synaptic cleft separating nerve cells). Loewi was the German physiologist and pharmacologist who discovered the key feature of how nerve cells interact with each other; he demonstrated that nerve ends release chemical "neurotransmitter" molecules that act as a messenger substance rather like a hormone. That's how most nerve cells affect the next nerve cell in a chain: They release a little puff of molecules that diffuse a short distance and stimulate the next cell into electrical action, rather as the perfume advertisements claim that the barest whiff of their scent will stimulate social electricity. We now know that some nerve cells are tightly linked in the heartlike manner; indeed, many cells are, at one stage or another of prenatal development (that's one of the things that my wife studies at Woods Hole, the electrical coupling of the 16-cell stage of squid), but most nerve cells lose it later and substitute the perfume trick.

Loewi originally wanted to be a historian of art, but he dutifully went to medical school, bowing to family pressures (similarly, Ramón y Cajal's plans to become a painter were thwarted by his father). Discouraged with the poor therapies of his day, Loewi later went into pharmacology research. He was one of the first people to propose that cells talked to one another with little whiffs of scent (well, more formally known as the chemical theory of synaptic transmission). Back in 1903, that was an interesting idea, but several decades later it was in general disrepute, no one having been able to design an experiment that would really force one to believe or disbelieve in it. Most interesting ideas aren't ever disproved: They just fade away.

One night in 1921, just before Easter Sunday in Graz, Austria, Loewi fell asleep while reading a light novel. Some hours later, he awoke suddenly with this marvelous experimental design for proving that chemical transmission existed between the vagus nerve and the heart. Not trusting his memory, he wrote it down on a thin scrap of paper. And went happily back to sleep.

He awoke early the next morning and remembered that something important had happened, but he couldn't remember what. Then—happy relief—he discovered the note that he had written himself. But the brief message was incomprehensible. Loewi went around distracted all day, trying to remember what the idea was, mystified as to the meaning of the cryptic note that he had written to himself. Finally, he went to bed, in hopes that the dream would recur.

And indeed the dream did recur, and he awoke again at three in the morning. This time, he didn't write himself a note. Instead, he climbed out of bed, got dressed, and immediately went to his lab. And performed the critical experiment that forces everyone to accept the fact of chemical intermediaries at the gaps between cells, transforming an electrical signal into this "whiff of perfume" and then back into electrical signals again.

There are two major classes of chemical messengers, excitatory ones and inhibitory ones. Loewi did his work on the inhibitory connection to the heart, studying how the vagus nerve coming down from the brain manages to get the heart to beat slower. It had been known that one could mimic the brain's activation of this nerve by simply shocking the nerve repeatedly: These "jump starts" inelegantly produce nerve impulses identical to those started in the brain by more conventional means. The electrical impulses travel down the nerve rather like a burning fuse (or a string of firecrackers, in the case of the faster-conducting nerve fibers); when they arrive in the heart, they somehow slow down the beat. And it wasn't some roundabout effect: Loewi could take out the heart of a brain-dead frog, complete with attached vagus nerve, mount it in a lab dish, let it pump an oxygen-saturated blood substitute (just a fancy concoction of salt water called "Ringer's solution") to keep it supplied with oxygen, and show that the heart temporarily slowed its rhythmic beat whenever a few stimuli were given to the nerve.

Otto Loewi's middle-of-the-night experiment was simplicity itself: He took a second heart removed from a second frog, but left behind its vagus nerve. He took the blood substitute coming out of the first heart and used it as the "venous blood returning," the input to the second heart, a kind of artificial transfusion. The second heart thus pumped the same "blood" that the first heart had just expelled a second earlier.

Both hearts sat there beating away (their own internal pacemakers keep them going, unlike many muscles). Then Loewi stimulated the vagus nerve to the first heart. The first heart slowed down its beat. And just as Loewi had guessed, the second heart then slowed down too, just as soon as the blood substitute reached it from the first heart. The fluid was carrying along the inhibitory messenger substance that vagal-nerve impulses had caused to be released into the first heart. Evidently, so much was released that there was enough left over to slow the second heart as well.

He not only proved that a chemical messenger (now known to be acetylcholine) was used to slow down the heart rate, but he later proved with analogous experiments that the cardioaccelerator nerve to the heart used a chemical (now called epinephrine or adrenaline) to speed up heart rate. It now seems particularly appropriate that his dream facilitated the discovery of acetylcholine's role as a neurotransmitter—it turns out to be used by the neural system in the brain that facilitates dreaming!

DESIGNING EXPERIMENTS is just a particular art form related to the scenario-spinning that we use to plan shopping trips and careers. And so it is tempting to engage in a little dream analysis to see if we can understand how Loewi's subconscious stage-managed this elegant insight. Despite the "Eureka!" aspect, one can see that all the pieces of this simple but elegant experimental design had been present for years before 1921, in the possession of many physiologists around the world (especially the English school working hard on reflex organization); all that Loewi's subconscious finally did was to piece them together. Loewi had uttered the chemical messenger idea 18 years earlier (he didn't publish it, but an English physiologist who visited Loewi's lab in Austria remembers him having mentioned it in 1903). The chemical intermediary possibility was common currency among researchers after about 1904. Later, in 1918 and 1919, Loewi had used the blood substitute method for studies on how ions (especially calcium) affected the heartbeat. When Loewi switched the solution from the normal salt concentration to the altered composition, the heart would speed up or slow down as soon as the new solution reached it. What Loewi's unconscious had linked together in 1921 was using this method to investigate the chemical transmission hypothesis; rather than the calcium of his blood substitute affecting heart rate, perhaps the stuff released by the vagus nerve would affect the second heart's rate? (Acetylcholine was originally called *vagustoff* by Loewi, literally "the stuff from the vagus.")

His elegant demonstration that the nerve's electrical message was mediated by the release of chemicals won him the Nobel Prize in Physiology or Medicine in 1936 (along with Henry Dale, who discovered acetylcholine in 1914). But the Nazi government extorted the prize money from Loewi as a condition for allowing him to leave (he was considered undesirable because of having chosen the wrong parents). He first fled to Brussels, and then to Oxford. In 1940, he became a research professor at New York University and started spending his summers in Woods Hole at the MBL. People who were around MBL in those days recall how Loewi liked to go for a swim at Stony Beach; they'd see him floating out there in Buzzards Bay, his pipe sticking up in profile against the skyline.

Later it was shown that the slowing action of acetylcholine could be blocked by a drug called atropine. You set up the frog heart, stimulate the vagus repeatedly until the heartbeat stops. But before the next trial, after the heart has recovered, you add atropine—whereupon you can stimulate the vagus nerve all you want, and the heart will take no notice of your stimuli. Atropine seems to have disconnected the vagus nerve from the heart! That's very impressive to demonstrate to students.

IT'S EVEN MORE IMPRESSIVE when it is one's own vagus nerve and own heart; it certainly gets your attention. The "flu" does some funny things to nerves on occasion. Just when I thought that I was getting over a mild case, I started having heart trouble: Blood pressure and heart rate were fluctuating all over the place. And so I went to see my physician, who promptly sat me down in a wheelchair and had me rolled across the street to the hospital's cardiac ICU. I protested all the way, not feeling shaky. When they finally got me installed in the hospital room and hooked up all the monitors, I was resigned to a day of hospital routine. But I was very impatient, not having brought anything to read. The nurses tried very hard to get me to lie back in bed. Finally, I did, if only because they insisted on hooking up an oxygen tube to my nose. And technicians kept coming around to take blood samples, or to hook up a venous catheter "just in case" they needed to rapidly inject a drug.

It was in the midst of one of these blood-letting sessions that I suddenly felt funny, tingling sensations coming from both my hands and feet. I knew that arterial punctures could be unpleasant, something like a bee sting, but this was clearly systemic in a big way. Whatever it was, it didn't feel so good—and so I told the technician to call the nurses. But they came on the run anyway, because the cardiac monitor had set off an alarm. Almost immediately I had six people surrounding me, half looking at the EKG display over my head and the others doing things like propping up my legs, or increasing the oxygen flow, or checking my blood pressure repeatedly.

I was all but unconscious: The world was slowly fading out amid an incredible barrage of tingling in all extremities. You know how, when you're traveling abroad, trying to listen to the BBC or the Voice of America on a shortwave radio, and you hear the static level rising and the announcer's voice fading out simultaneously? And you never get to hear the rest of the newscast? That, insofar as I experienced it, is how consciousness ends.

Talk about Primal Questions: How does one stay tuned in?

THAT I REMAINED CONSCIOUS (or should I have said "retained awareness"?) through it all was only because they were giving me pure oxygen to breathe—otherwise a blood pressure of 60/45 will cause one to faint and miss all the excitement, that crescendo of tingles. My heart hadn't stopped completely, but it wasn't for lack of trying by the vagus nerve: The regular pacemaker at my sinoatrial node was completely silenced by massive amounts of vagal inhibition. This caused a backup pacemaker in the atrial-ventricular node to start beating. But it was generating heartbeats at too slow a rate to maintain a decent blood pressure.

I didn't know all of this at the time. All I knew was that I suddenly began to feel much better, and that the world started to come in loud and clear again. The tingles stopped. I wasn't ready to hop out of bed, but it was quite clear that I'd been snatched back to a safe harbor.

What the cardiology resident had done when she saw the EKG (it was missing the little initial bump called the P-wave that indicates the S-A node is initiating the heartbeat) was to inject some atropine into a vein. The atropine stopped the acetylcholine from inhibiting the heart pacemaker (the pacemaker cells have little "locks" in their membrane to which acetylcholine acts as the "key"—except when the "keyhole" is plugged by atropine). And so the S-A node started beating again, and at a normal rate that could maintain a normal blood pressure. That's when I began feeling better.

And why had my vagus nerve been acting as if it were being repeatedly stimulated in the manner Otto Loewi treated those frog vagus nerves? Was my brain telling my heart to shut up, emphatically?

No. It was a false message, inserted into the nerve. The nerve had run amok in very much the way that other nerves do when they cause muscle cramps. What happens is that the nerve endings begin producing nerve impulses on their own, "jump-starting" themselves rather than being faithful followers of what the brain tells them to do.

In the case of a leg muscle, this causes sustained contraction of the muscle, so much that it becomes painful. There is no voluntary way to relax the muscle, as the extra nerve impulses are coming from the nerve endings embedded in the muscle, not from the brain or spinal cord in the manner that impulses usually do. In the case of the vagus-nerve "cramp," the barrage causes complete inhibition of the heart pacemaker. Instead of feeling pain, one faints (except when oxygen is provided). Such an intense barrage eventually depletes the stockpile of acetylcholine, so that the heart's pacemaker may eventually resume even if the impulse barrage continues.

So the problem wasn't with my heart, but with the vagus nerve endings in the heart. And like muscle cramps, the problem usually goes away in a few days, probably because some disrupted insulation on the nerve is repaired. They kept me around the cardiac ward for a few more days to run tests to be sure that there wasn't something else wrong. But nothing else happened after that first hour. Eventually, they kicked me out.

That's a story that is repeated every day in one modern hospital or another, but most patients can't reconstruct what happened. They're just very happy that the physician knew what to do, and why. That knowledge came from basic research by physiologists and pharmacologists experimenting on various animal species (most heart research requires dogs). Most of the research achievements aren't as easy to communicate as Otto Loewi's story, but they all have similar elements: an idea about how it might work, a clever experimental design that provides a believable answer, and then a new wave of developments that make use of the now-known mechanism to solve additional problems like the atropine blockage.

My great relief that day when I was brought back from Tingleland was due to that research, most especially Otto Loewi's. And so Professor Loewi is remembered by far more people than happen to see his gravestone at the Church of the Messiah in Woods Hole—hundreds of thousands of medical students have learned about Otto Loewi and the discovery of neurotransmitters. Some have even heard about the workings of his subconscious.

IN A NEWER SECTION OF THE CHURCHYARD, there is a small, flat stone, overgrown by the grass, for Stephen W. Kuffler, who died in 1980. He was a teacher of mine, when I took the neuroscience course at Harvard Medical School back in 1962, and I've probably read most of the scientific papers that he wrote before and since.

Steve was a follower of Otto Loewi in a number of ways: He also escaped the Nazis, worked on acetylcholine and inhibition. Born in Tab, Hungary, he was reared on a farm and had no formal schooling until he was ten years old. After graduating in pathology from the University of Vienna in 1937, he went to Australia during the war and there became involved in basic research on nerves, showing that acetylcholine sensitivity in muscles occurred only in a specialized region close to the nerve endings. And he did the classical analysis of how an inhibitory synapse actually works when the downstream cell is a nerve cell rather than a heart pacemaker.

In 1971 he showed how the vagus nerve actually slows down the heart by activating an intermediate nerve cell. Hidden in the heart wall, right in the thin septum between the two upper chambers of the three-chambered amphibian heart, are some tiny nerve cells. They're what the vagal nerve ends upon, not heart muscle directly. These little "parasympathetic ganglion" cells are what actually release the acetylcholine that slows the heart pacemaker—when the vagus nerve tells them to do so by releasing acetylcholine. Kuffler searched and searched (I remember him saying that he spent six solid months in the Harvard Medical

School library), trying to find an animal whose neurons were embedded in a transparently thin muscle, so that he could put that sheet of muscle under a microscope and see the nerve cells at the same time that he maneuvered electrical-recording leads in their vicinity. The frog had a particularly thin septum, and a dozen parasympathetic nerve cells clearly visible. This 1971 experiment that he did with Jack McMahon marked the beginnings of a new standard in "seeing what you're doing."

They could cut the vagus nerve a few days earlier and show how these cells "got lonely" when deprived of their contact with the outside world; the denervated cells turned up their sensitivity so high that they would respond even without vagal input, a cellular version of the hallucinations one experiences if deprived of all sensory input. That kind of sensitivity adjustment is thought to be what happens in patients who experience phantom-limb pain, who report that their big toe hurts even though the leg was amputated in an industrial accident. We haven't yet discovered how to relieve such patients of their disabling pain, in the manner of atropine for the pacemaker standstill, but when we do, it will likely owe something to Steve Kuffler and his co-workers, who managed to see the sensitivity-adjusting process at work in those little nerve cells inside the heart wall.

Many of the major neurological and mental disorders (those that aren't due to strokes and gross developmental disorders) seem to involve neurotransmitters like those Otto Loewi found: There may be too much, or too little, or an effect lasting too long. And the number of keyholes in the next nerve cell can be too great, as seen in Steve Kuffler's denervated nerve cells inside the heart wall. Whatever, it disrupts the music of movement. Finally, a century after Freud abandoned his microscope, we have the concepts like synaptic regulation, and we have some tools such as the brain-imaging devices that can measure neurotransmitter and receptor distribution inside a living brain, that may allow us to understand schizophrenia, depression, obsession, and the variety of more common mental ailments that occasionally disable many of us.

EFFECT AND COUNTEREFFECT, as seen in all these examples of push-and-pull together, may sound a bit like Newton's

Third Law ("For every action there is an equal and opposite reaction"), what pushes rockets forward at the same time as exhaust gases rush backward. But principles in biology are mostly guides: If you see a process doing one thing, like exciting a nerve cell, look around and you'll probably find an opposing process, such as an inhibitory synapse. In the heart, the cardioaccelerator nerve's actions are opposed by the vagus's slowing actions.

Neurosurgeons made good use of this principle in developing surgical relief for Parkinson's disease: A virus destroys cells in the substantia nigra, part of a system that tends to inhibit a postural control system, and so patients get "uptight," excessively stiff. So the surgeons tried destroying a perfectly good piece of the brain (the ventrolateral thalamus normally has the opposite effect on the system), and so brought the system's excitation and inhibition back into balance.

But as a principle—well, the first thing that you find are exceptions to the rule. Look at our smooth muscle, or the leg muscles of insects, and you'll find "peripheral inhibition" like that of the vagus nerve upon the heart. But there is none in mammalian skeletal muscle. Our skeletal muscles receive only excitation, never inhibition. In our case, the push-and-pull balancing act is all done back at the motorneurons in the spinal cord that run the muscle; the muscle then just does what the motorneuron tells it to do (except in "cramps"!). As a result, the touch receptors in the skin overlying the muscle cannot influence the muscle except by the long trip into the spinal cord, where their recommendations are judged in the light of thousands of other influences on the motorneuron, and then a message is sent back out to the muscle, telling it to contract. It takes time for that long round trip, and sometimes that's important.

Still, all brain cells receive both excitatory and inhibitory synapses—about half and half, in most of the cells where they've been counted. And so each brain cell is a little computer, adding up an account balance of all the deposits and withdrawals, seeing how much interest to pay out to the cells it talks to. The brain is a society of billions of those little computers; occasionally the cells act together as a mob, but usually they all go their own way—and so do many different jobs at the same time. We need to learn the sociology of this society—we hardly even know the grossest phenomena, such as the mob actions of epileptic seizures, when we badly need to know its system of checks and balances. Perhaps when we learn the nuts and bolts—the job that Loewi and Kuffler started—we will be able to understand how new abilities emerge from the compounding of the parts.

BIOLOGY SHAPES UP ORDER since it provides a memory of the past via which genes survive and which drop out; each one of us, in each of our cells, is guided by the history of ancestor organisms extending back three billion years. Whenever I throw a baseball, I am aided by the successes and failures of my Ice Age ancestors who threw to hunt. Those memories are encoded in the gene pool; cultural evolution provides even more detailed memories. Whenever I think about a problem, I am aided by the successes and failures of untold past generations in dealing with various problems—Archimedes' still-successful analysis of floatation and Aristotle's attractive but nonsensical physics shape the way I think about cars and boats. Loewi and Kuffler speak to me still through their writings and my conversations with their students.

As I left the churchyard, I thought about how much of our modern world is due to a relatively few people pursuing abstract ideas, out of the billions who have lived on earth. Ideas that work. Until recently, most such long-term-payoff research was done by stealing time from teaching students or treating patients. But today, mostly in the last four decades, we see whole institutes devoted to basic research. They are the leading "industry" of Woods Hole. In the future, there will be people who owe major debts to the researchers who think and labor here, just as I am indebted to Otto Loewi.

I've been freed from the self
that pretends to be someone,
And in becoming no-one,
I begin to live.
It is worthwhile dying,
to find out what life is.

T. S. ELIOT

6

MAKING MIND FROM MERE BRAIN: TAKING APART THE VISUAL WORLD

Indeed they were very close to the Lighthouse now. There it loomed up, stark and straight, glaring black and white, and one could see the waves breaking in white splinters like smashed glass upon the rocks. One could see the windows clearly; a dab of white on one of them, and a little tuft of green on the rock. A man had come out and looked at them through a glass and gone in again. So it was like that, James thought, the Lighthouse one had seen from across the bay all these years; it was a stark tower on bare rock.

VIRGINIA WOOLF, 1927

Our brain is domineering when it comes to coping with reality, and so we sometimes see things not as they really are, sometimes invent categories that do not exist in nature, sometimes fail to see things that are really there. Romanticizing things is the least of the problems.

It's not so much that we only see certain wavelengths of light, only hear a limited range of frequencies, have an impoverished sense of smell compared to most mammals. But once accepted by the sensory receptors, information may be forced into a Procrustean bed created by our expectations. We may force reality into a certainty and definiteness that it doesn't naturally possess. If the information is probabilistic, we make it definite. You see this at the level of physics (the discoveries of quantum mechanics have backed us up somewhat, out of excessively rigid human categories for nature), and you certainly see it in how the brain processes the information that gets in.

We also ignore repeated inputs, tend to respond only to the new and unexpected. Though our brain asks the questions, it is more interested in answers that are new and odd. We see contrasts and borderlines, hear changes and movements. Prevent the eye from moving, and it will see nothing unless the object itself is moving. What does that say about "consciousness" if an object can disappear, returning only if it moves?

While attuned to categories, our brain seems to seek gestalts (and sometimes finds them even if they aren't there!). It constructs scenarios, most of them sheer nonsense and discarded the moment they are compared to our memories of the real world; as we sleep and dream, that testing isn't very efficient, and so this fantasy is largely unedited. Awake, we shape up our scenarios by additionally testing them against reality. And these scenarios, when trying to explain the past by constructing a story about it, may also prove useful in predicting the future.

So why is the brain so simultaneously Procrustean, but also inventive of the categories into which the incoming information is impressed? The nature of reality, as we perceive it, depends on what it is filtered through.

It is, of course, filtered through the whole nervous system, a distributed collection of cells extending a meter and more in length. True, there are some systems that extend over only a tenth that distance, such as the 10 cm of the visual system. Within such systems are multiple maps, which compress half of a sensory world into about 1 cm worth of cerebral cortex. Within each map are distributed many networks, each contained in about a cubic millimeter of tangled nerve cells. Those cells, the neurons, stretch over various distances, though many are contained in about 0.1 mm. The synaptic connections between them are a hundred times smaller, and seem to be the sites of modification, where memories are recorded. And all this is effected by molecules at least 10,000 times smaller than a synapse, some of which form structures such as membranes (and channels through the membranes), others of which move like messengers through the membranes.

So where in all this does my memory of a lighthouse reside? Or my plan to go there? Or my one-foot-in-front-of-the-other subprogram?

> *[What] you are describing is not an object but a function, a role that is inextricably tied to some context. Take away the context, and the meaning also disappears. . . . When you perceive intelligently, as you sometimes do, you always perceive a function, never an object in the . . . physical sense. . . . Your Cartesian idea of a device in the brain that does the registering is based on a misleading analogy between vision and photography. Cameras always register objects, but human perception is always the perception of functional roles. The two processes could not be more different. . . .*
>
> the mathematician STANISLAW ULAM, about 1970

IT IS CURIOUS HOW DISTRACTING little black lines in the sky prove to be, as if they had some privileged access to our brains—like visual equivalents of advertising jingles hung from utility poles. And they do have privileged access, another discovery that Steve Kuffler had a hand in.

Leaving the Church of the Messiah, one walks east along a winding road in Woods Hole that would be beautiful except for the proliferating poles stringing the skyline with metastasizing threads of metallic tumor. It's an area of expensive homes whose owners could afford to pay for burying the utility wires, but only people get buried around here. In another block down Church Street, the wires thin out and the view opens onto Vineyard Sound, a long, sandy beach stretching into the distance. At the end of the beach, a white pillar rises into the blue sky, capped with black. It is surely the Nobska Point lighthouse, and it looks somewhat familiar.

A lighthouse is a version of the scarecrow, but meant to warn off sailors. And just as the scarecrow is a human mimic of sorts, so the lighthouse stands as a surrogate human, erected to send a human message in times of need. As lighthouses get "smarter" with the addition of automatic fog sensors that trigger their fog-horns, they come to be more and more like a stationary robot. Their foresightful designers have endowed the lighthouse with ways of forecasting trouble, and appropriately responding. Light-houses lack the versatility to be considered conscious, but the air-traffic control system might someday evolve into a partially conscious robot, constantly trying out "what if" scenarios and so heading off collisions between airplanes in much the same ways as human controllers now attempt to do.

WALKING UP THE BEACH IN THE WET SAND just above the lapping waves of Vineyard Sound, I saw various people from the MBL and WHOI, talking science. Bankers from Boston can also be found on this beach, though they do not draw diagrams of cells in the sand, so far as I know. The diagrams may be washed away by the next high tide, but the new concepts linger on. This beach has seen a lot of science happen, as has Stony Beach near MBL, which Lewis Thomas immortalized in his essay "The MBL," in *Lives of a Cell:*

> It is so crowded that one must pick one's way on tiptoe
> to find a hunching place, but there is always a lot of standing

up anyway; biologists seem to prefer standing on beaches, talking at each other, gesturing to indicate the way things are assembled, bending down to draw diagrams in the sand. By the end of the day, the sand is crisscrossed with a mesh of ordinates, abscissas, curves to account for everything in nature.

You can hear the sound from the beach at a distance, before you see the people. It is that most extraordinary noise, half-shout, half-song, made by confluent, simultaneously raised human voices, explaining things to each other.

This beach on Vineyard Sound is instead spread over two blocks and has a higher proportion of sand castles than graphs. The lighthouse down at the end of the beach, as one walks closer and the perspective changes, evokes ever stronger sensations of *déjà vu*—I seem to have some mental image that this picture is triggering.

And then I remember the art museum where I've seen it before: It's a close relative of the lighthouse that Edward Hopper painted. And painted again and again, though they might be different lighthouses, because the coast guard built a number of them from the same 1870s design; they can be found all around Cape Cod and the offshore islands. This lighthouse looks even more solid than the painted versions, ready to take whatever the weather dishes out next.

I HAVE AN EDWARD HOPPER SCHEMA somewhere in my head, not to mention a Picasso schema, and a Henry Moore schema, and so on. A schema is a mental image. While *schema* was initially used to avoid using *memory trace* (another term invented to try to pin down an elusive concept), a schema is not just any memory. A sensory schema is a schematic outline that fits most of the likely variations that Hopper constructed; it fits in a fancier way than a cookie-cutter fits a Christmas cookie, but that's the general idea.

A collection of schemas—say, my collection of mental images of artistic styles—is something like a family of cookie-cutters, each shape being tried out on a particular Christmas cookie to see which comes closest. The collection of schemas seems to sit there in your head, constantly on the lookout for something that fits it. So that when you see a fragmentary Picasso sketch, and something shouts "Picasso!" inside your head, you've heard a schema speaking.

I also have a lighthouse schema, equally well activated by English lighthouses and Hawaiian lighthouses. It is only the lighthouses that are in the local 1870s style that additionally activate my "Edward Hopper" schema, and then only when seen from a perspective similar to the ones that Hopper favored (aerial photographs won't do). Such an "Edward Hopper schema" is a collective memory, containing something of the "essential" features of his style and subject matter that come through whatever variations are present in a particular example. For every word in your vocabulary, you probably have one or more schemas—though I certainly have some schemas for which there is no word in my vocabulary, such as people that I've seen before but whose names I haven't learned yet. And some schemas aren't objects but movements: When we construct a sentence or spin a scenario, the units that we are chaining together are primarily sensory ("noun") and movement ("verb") schemas. You, me, food, rock—as well as run, walk, gallop, shuffle, touch, bend, break.

EPICURUS AND LUCRETIUS considered mental images to be simulacra, and Aristotle compared them to "the imprint left by a seal on a wax tablet." They hadn't seen cookie-cutters. And now we have some even better analogies—indeed, potential mechanisms. The lighthouse beacon winking on and off (even in broad daylight, the 150-watt light bulb looks bright because of that old 1825 Fresnel lens that focuses its photons) reminds me of another Steve Kuffler classic. His 1953 work was on how nerve cells in the eye respond to such lights winking on and off; I'm unlikely ever to forget it, as reading it about six years after it was published was one of the major reasons that I had forsaken physics for physiology. It is still a classic, required reading for the aspiring graduate student. It demonstrates a cellular version of the schema—or at least one of its building blocks.

The story starts even earlier, in 1938, when H. K. Hartline studied frog retinas and their response to winking lights. He found that each optic-nerve "wire" responded to far more than

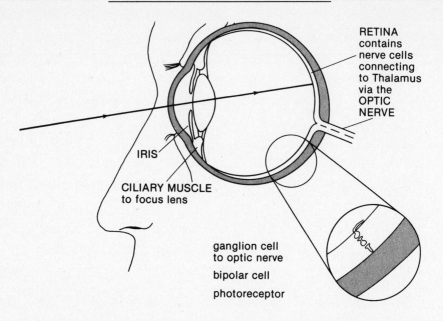

RETINA contains nerve cells connecting to Thalamus via the OPTIC NERVE

IRIS

CILIARY MUSCLE to focus lens

ganglion cell to optic nerve

bipolar cell

photoreceptor

just one spot on the retina—it was a whole patch (which he called the cell's "receptive field"). It would fire a train of spikes in a staccato manner whenever the light was turned on, but then settle down, not acting much different than in darkness. But when the light was finally turned off, it gave another burst of activity, a cellular version of "Hey! Who turned the lights off?" This OFF-response was a puzzle, though not unrelated to the problem of feeling your wristwatch's absence just after you remove it from your wrist and all those flattened hairs start popping back up.

A friendly caution: You are approaching some conceptually difficult material in the remainder of this chapter, and at places in the following two chapters. Ordinary mortals will likely, at some point, feel disoriented—and for good reason. Everyone who has learned this material has complained too. Graduate and medical students traditionally stumble on "receptive fields"—but then, like art students who finally learn how to "see" a particular painting, recover and soon sort out a mental picture of how a brain cell sees the world.

The "viewpoint" turns out to be all-important, both the

cell's viewpoint and the scientist's varied viewpoints used to analyze the cell's properties. We're still debating how a committee of cells, like a jury of critics, can have a collective viewpoint!

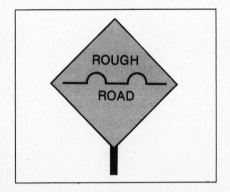

None of this material is essential, in that you could skip over it and still understand the rest of the book, but I include it because so many of those who come to understand it are, let us say, inordinately impressed. It provides a nice, concrete example (almost too nice!) of how the brain goes about its business. Indeed, to those familiar with business accounting, the time history of the cell (such as those OFF-responses) is like cash flow tracking, and the Mexican hat "receptive field" represents another way of looking at much the same data, showing where the income and expenses originated in a given time period and how much profit was paid out to shareholders. Anyone familiar with accounting practices may have a better background for appreciating this material than the typical neurobiology graduate student.

This "Somebody turned the lights off" report (an OFF-response) is an exaggerated aspect of "temporal contrast" a sensitivity to changes in light level rather than absolute light level. It is why flashing or moving lights grab your attention better than steady lights. Keffer Hartline (another luminary of MBL) also noted in passing that the background was important in influencing the vigor of these staccato responses, rather as the brightness of the sky behind the lighthouse affects how bright the beacon seems. Robert Barlow (once Hartline's graduate student, and now a veteran of the Woods Hole science scene) noted this spatial-contrast effect in 1953, as did Stephen Kuffler. *Temporal contrast* and *spatial contrast* turn out to be the major building blocks of visual perception, with *color contrast* an important added feature in some animals such as the primates. Our ancestors made their living by being able to spot ripening fruit high up in the trees against a background of waving leaves; that green spot you sometimes see from the Nobska lighthouse alongside the setting sun is one of the collateral consequences.

Kuffler dug deeper and wound up showing the underlying mechanism of spatial contrast: Each of the cat's retinal ganglion cells (which are typically third in the chain of cells between photoreceptor and brain) was receiving input from thousands of photoreceptors (via intermediate cells called bipolar cells and amacrine cells), rather as a funnel collects raindrops from a wide area and concentrates it into a narrow stream. There has to be some funneling, as there are about a hundred photoreceptors for each "wire" back to the brain (the retinal ganglion cell axon; about a million of them constitute an optic nerve). And it isn't a matter of a hundred photoreceptors connecting to each ganglion cell: Messages from thousands of photoreceptors are funneled into each ganglion cell, except some cancel out the actions of others.

Each of those little "wires" in the optic nerve sends messages akin to a bank statement when it tells you how much interest was paid this month. You have to imagine, instead of an eye, a giant bank that is busily mailing out a million statements every second. What maximizes the payout on a single wire? That depends on the bank's rules, and how you play the game.

The plus-and-minus, push-and-pull arrangement (which neurophysiologists tend to call "excitation" and "inhibition" instead) is not unlike the deposits to and withdrawals from my bank account. The output (the interest paid out) is naturally proportional to the net balance. There is often a minimum requirement ("5 percent interest paid on all balances over $1,000"). Nerve cells don't compound interest (since they pay it out each time)—but they have other nice features that bank accounts lack. I sure wish that my bank account paid an "adaptation bonus" whenever I resumed depositing money after a fallow period! Some nerve cells even have "OFF-responses" as a rebound from inhibition, equivalent to a bank paying a bonus when you stop a long series of withdrawals. I must remember to suggest that to my bank; they can advertise it as "the brain's way of doing business."

Kuffler discovered the parts of the retinal mosaic from which "deposits" and "withdrawals" each originated, something that

Hartline couldn't resolve in frogs. A single retinal ganglion cell really receives two funnels, a wide funnel and a more potent narrow funnel; one inhibits and the other excites the retinal ganglion cell. It's not unlike the sources and sinks of a checking account: We usually funnel into our account a small number of large deposits, and write a much larger number of small-amount checks.

A uniform illumination of the back of the eye, such as one gets from looking at the blue sky, stimulates both funnels, and the messages cancel much of the time. A small spot of light such as the lighthouse beacon might fill the small funnel but only half fill the larger one. If the large but weak funnel was connected with inhibition, and the small but potent funnel with excitation, the net difference would cause a vigorous response. Fill up more of the large but weak inhibitory funnel by using a larger spot of light, and the excess of excitation over inhibition would decline and the staccato response would decrease to a whimper.

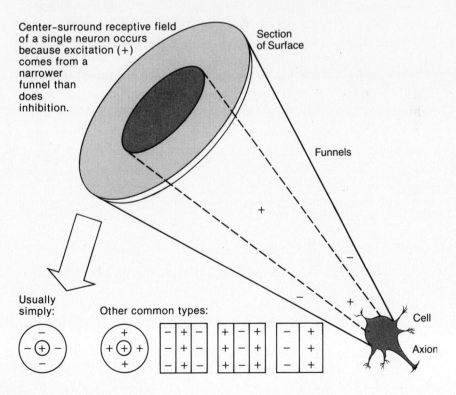

Center-surround receptive field of a single neuron occurs because excitation (+) comes from a narrower funnel than does inhibition.

Section of Surface

Funnels

+

−

−   +

Usually simply:

Other common types:

Cell

Axion

The overall result after subtraction looks something like a doughnut, with a center and a surround. An even better analogy is the Mexican hat, peaked in the middle and flanked by wide shallow troughs: That's the size of the interest paid out for a small spot of light at each position in space. When you adapt to darkness (your night vision improves after about 20 minutes in the dark), that wide inhibitory funnel is disconnected from the retinal ganglion cell as a way of "running wide open," getting maximum sensitivity by not subtracting anything. Again I wish that my bank would let me boost my interest payments by simply not making any deposits for a few months. Disconnecting the inhibitory funnel in dim light doesn't similarly result in big problems later, unless you count the momentary blindness that occurs when you turn on the bathroom light in the middle of the night (bathroom lights were not a big problem as humans evolved during the Ice Ages).

So such a cell is a specialist in small spots of light—indeed, the diameter of the optimal spot is about the size of the hatband in that Mexican hat analogy. Such a cell discriminates against larger spots, hat-brim width or more, sometimes refusing to tell the brain about them at all. But that's all right, as there are other nearby cells specializing in big spots, having a somewhat different arrangement of funnel sizes, just as there are hats with narrow brims for fat heads. We tend to start thinking about such cells as

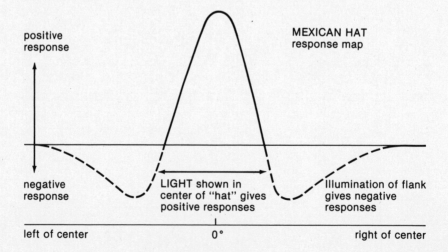

positive
response

MEXICAN HAT
response map

negative
response

LIGHT shown in
center of "hat" gives
positive responses

Illumination of flank
gives negative
responses

left of center   0°   right of center

specialists like cookie-cutters of a certain size, just sitting there trying out each new spot of light to see if it's the right size. But the Mexican hat arrangement is the better analogy, as it tells you what would happen to spots that weren't quite the right size.

Now some bank accounts don't have the few-deposits-but-many-checks characteristics of my checking account; they're more like a small business that receives many mail orders and has only a few suppliers to pay. Some retinal cells are like that, with their funnels hooked up just the opposite of the previous examples. Their weak but wide funnel is excitatory, and their narrow but potent funnel is inhibitory. And so they seem to specialize in black spots on white backgrounds rather than white spots on darker backgrounds; they're better at detecting the insects on the sand beach (and the black periods ending sentences) than the white spots such as lighthouse beacons against the night sky. This yields an inverted Mexican hat curve: A black spot imaged onto the inner of the two-funnel arrangement doesn't cause any inhibition, and so the excitatory response from the white background imaged onto the larger funnel has nothing to balance it. Thus one gets a vigorous staccato burst to a black spot on a lighter background.

The map (such as the Mexican hat) of what's connected to a single cell is what is now called the "receptive field" of that cell—but one can also think of it as a template, the cell always being on the lookout for images that fit its favored template. Just as cookie-cutters the size of the smaller funnel won't fit a larger cookie, so receptive-field centers (the hatband size) tend to represent the optimal size of a stimulus spot. Specialists in small black spots on lighter backgrounds are sometimes called "bug detectors," because they spring into activity when the image of a fly is presented to them. But they also respond pretty well to thin black lines and usually to edges that cover only half of a funnel. So they are not exclusively "bug detectors": The moving black bug is simply their optimal stimulus. If you think of the bug as the "essence" of the cell's function, you miss out on the whole range of less optimal, but still effective, stimuli that also run the cell.

In 1959 it was reported by Maturana, Lettvin, Pitts, and McCulloch that frogs were even more discriminating. Their retinal ganglion cells didn't bother telling the frog's brain about anything that wasn't moving food like flies, or a tilting horizon, or some other key feature of their environment. Presented with a novel visual feature like a house or car, they often didn't bother mentioning it at all to the brain (unless, of course, it was moving quickly toward them, something that every visual system manages to sense). The frog's retina seemed to be a special-purpose computer, not a TV camera that indiscriminately reports everything it sees. That was troubling: Why was the frog throwing away all that more detailed information?

Doesn't he realize that he'll need it to read with, when he "grows up" evolutionarily? This is, of course, our point of view; the frog is interested in more immediate things, like catching flies for dinner, and has apparently tuned up his eye to maximize the detection of little moving black spots. Our point of view might seem pretty parochial to the frog too. It would have a hard time understanding our reductionist preoccupation with taking things apart into ever-smaller pieces: Discriminating between the fly's wings and feet might seem a little excessive to the pragmatic frog.

> *Much of today's public anxiety about science is the apprehension that we may be overlooking the whole by an endless, obsessive preoccupation with the parts.*
>
> the physician and essayist LEWIS THOMAS

> *Behind the holists' very proper concern with the need to consider the system as a whole lies also a fear that reductionism attempts not to just explain but to explain away; that by reducing humans to an assemblage of working parts, their humanity has been in some measure also reduced. This is an important fear, and one which should be treated with respect.*
>
> the neurobiologist STEVEN P. R. ROSE

SPRINGY SAND? Walking on the sand beach on the eastern side of the lighthouse can be like walking on a forest floor carpeted with pine needles where the floor gives and rebounds a little. But here on this sandy beach one positively bounces. Why?

The "underlying mechanism" is not hard to discover, since it is literally underlying and can be uncovered by digging down a little with one's toe: Great masses of seaweed have been washed ashore during a recent storm, some stuffed with little air bladders that keep them floating up near the light just under the ocean's surface. Then a windstorm washed sand up the beach to cover up these mats of cushioned seaweed. And so one bounces along the sand like some improbable ballet dancer.

Eventually, the seaweed cooks beneath the hot sand. Vegetation that gets buried deeper can turn into oil; our cars are propelled on the cooked vegetation of great tropical swamps that got themselves buried many millions of years ago. That some of the great oil fields are now located up above the Arctic Circle shows you how much the continents drift around, as all that oil was originally buried when it was within about 20° of the equator.

This also shows you what scientists mean by "reductionist" approaches: Springy sand attracts a scientist who wants to know what the resiliency is all about. Its underlying mechanism, discovered by "digging deeper," is buried seaweed. Then the agenda shifts: Why is the seaweed bouncy? Its underlying mechanism is little air bladders. And why is that? It's due to the way light is filtered by water, making things dark in the ocean depths: If you want to photosynthesize, you want to stay as close to the surface as possible. And hence built-in flotation devices. Why photosynthesize . . . ? And so forth, with a constantly shifting agenda that maintains little of the original question about resiliency (which, after all, was answered right off).

There are a lot of scientists who started out hoping to understand the mind who haven't been able to answer such questions right off, and so have gotten distracted by underlying mechanisms and the subtle meandering of the agenda. The only way to understand something thoroughly is to investigate all its parts, but sometimes that isn't enough: Sometimes you have to figure out how they work in committees, as when they regulate your body temperature or blood pressure to remain within a narrow range of desirable levels. And so "understanding how we see something" may involve a lot of analysis of the parts, but also figuring out how new properties emerge from combinations.

Understanding emergents is generally harder than understanding the pieces, and an imperative of science (or at least of scientists continually faced with raising money and training graduate students) is to "make progress" via asking answerable questions. And some of our most respected scientists are the ones who switch from subject to subject, constantly exploiting the new techniques for "looking deeper." Only if they are disabled from laboratory work by illness or retirement do they ever get around to "trying to piece things together." Yet the history of science is written by both types, the experimenters like Hooke, Franklin, Boyle, and Faraday, *and* the great synthesizers like Newton, Mendeleyeff, Einstein (Neils Bohr had to think for years before coming up with the model of the atom that proved so successful). In eighteenth- and nineteenth-century biology, the great synthesizers were even more prominent: Linnaeas, Lamarck, Darwin. Neurobiology is young, and its history is mostly the history of the meandering reductionists.

The important thing in science is not so much to obtain new facts as to discover new ways of thinking about them.

the physicist WILLIAM LAWRENCE BRAGG (1890–1971)

Many students of animal behavior have become so fascinated with its directedness, with the question "What for?" or "Toward what end?" that they have quite forgotten to ask about its causal explanation. Yet the great question . . . "How?" [is] quite as fascinating as the question "What for?" —only they fascinate a different kind of scientist. If wonder at the directedness of life is typical of the field student of nature, the quest for understanding of causation is typical of the laboratory worker. It is a regrettable symptom of the limitations inherent to the human mind that very few scientists are able to keep both questions in mind simultaneously.

the ethologist KONRAD LORENZ, 1960

VISUAL PERCEPTION MECHANISMS had been a mystery before all the wire-tapping neurophysiology on frogs, cats, and monkeys; optics had yielded to investigation, and some shrewd guesses (particularly Thomas Young's 1802 trichromaticity theory) had been made about underlying color vision mechanisms, but no one had shown how the brain went about taking apart an image into its component parts.

Now we had an impressive explanation of how the nervous system went about that, breaking the image into components via how the excitation and inhibition were wired up. And a flurry of new research started, analyzing the next stages of analysis back in the brain proper. We were particularly interested in a visual area at the back of the head, which is where those messages in the optic nerve seemed to be addressed. If that area, called "primary visual cortex" or "Area 17" or sometimes just "V1," wasn't working because of damage, people seemed to be functionally blind.

Two of Steve Kuffler's immediate followers were the young ophthalmologists-turned-neurophysiologists, David Hubel and Torsten Wiesel. When Kuffler went to Harvard Medical School in the late 1950s, he hired the pair—and then went back to studying his first love, synapses (in 1961, together with Josef Dudel, he discovered a major new principle we call presynaptic inhibition, which results in a percentage-type computation more like multiplication or division than the usual excitation-inhibition analogous to addition-subtraction).

Kuffler had worked on the third layer of cells in the chain between photoreceptors and brain (he'd have worked on the photoreceptors and second-order cells, but they were too difficult with 1953 techniques). Hubel and Wiesel discovered a gold mine when they started looking at the brain structures farther along in the visual pathways, the fourth-order cells in the thalamus, and the fifth- and higher-order cells in the cerebral cortex. Other neurophysiologists were busy investigating how sensations from the skin and ears were analyzed in the brain, but the same techniques applied to the visual pathway had an important advantage: The visual system, more so than any other of our senses, has been streamlined by one evolutionary adaptation after another. And we humans tend to think visually, compared to most other animals, giving human neurophysiologists an advantage in trying to understand such stages of analysis of what the eye initially "sees" with the first-order photoreceptors.

We understood how cameras worked, and how television cameras worked, and some of us probably expected the eye to produce a picture of what it saw for presentation to a viewer back in the brain somewhere. Though we knew that the fine mosaic of about 100 million photoreceptors receiving the optical image had to repackage some of that information, because there are only a million "wires" leading back to the brain, we somehow still expected that a faithful image would be recreated at the other end, much as a television tube recreates what the TV camera saw and encoded in radio waves.

But there was that troubling result from the frog studies, all that more-detailed-than-a-fly information that was simply thrown away. Kuffler had fortunately studied the cat's retinal ganglion cells rather than the frog's (he needed a big eye because of the size and complexity of the experimental apparatus); clearly, they were at least reporting the boundaries between all objects. Potentially, the cat's brain ought to be able to read a newspaper. And as Hubel and Wiesel soon showed, a monkey's retinal ganglion cells were rather like a cat's, except for being better at fine resolution and at color. What, however, happened in the brain cells to which the optic nerve reported? The main line from eye to brain goes through the

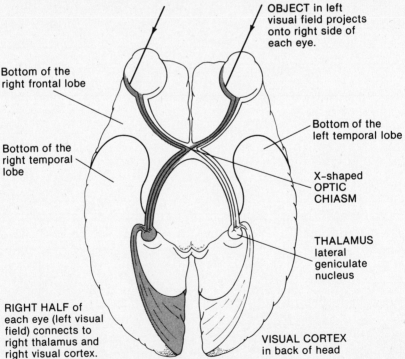

OBJECT in left visual field projects onto right side of each eye.

Bottom of the right frontal lobe

Bottom of the left temporal lobe

Bottom of the right temporal lobe

X-shaped OPTIC CHIASM

THALAMUS lateral geniculate nucleus

RIGHT HALF of each eye (left visual field) connects to right thalamus and right visual cortex.

VISUAL CORTEX in back of head

thalamus, whose lateral geniculate nucleus is an elaborately layered structure (bent knee-like, hence *geniculate*) that had long intrigued neuroanatomists. Surely something fancy happened there.

Hubel and Wiesel recorded from those geniculate cells. And at first glimpse and even second glimpse, they were indistinguishable from the retinal ganglion cells upstream from them—nothing new seemed to be happening, as if they were just some sort of relay station (this terminology is borrowed from the old Pony Express, where tired horses were exchanged for rested ones, the messages in the saddlebags passed on unaltered). The geniculate's receptive fields were the same center-surround doughnut shapes as the dual-funnel arrangement had produced in the retinal ganglion cells. About all that the first-pass analysis of the geniculate showed was that diffuse light was an even poorer stimulus than it was to the retinal cells: Excitation and inhibition tended to totally cancel out in the geniculate cells, whereas retinal cells often had some net excitation or inhibition when simply looking at an unbroken field like a cloudless blue sky. Not until one uses colored lights as stimuli does one discover the geniculate cells doing something that retina doesn't do: In some cells, the center-surround organization disappears.

When Hubel and Wiesel looked up in the cerebral cortex at some of the still higher-order cells in the processing chain, things were obviously quite different than in the retina or geniculate. Cortex was no relay station; the messages were rearranged here to make new patterns. Most obviously, the circularly symmetric receptive fields of the cells feeding into the cortex were somehow modified to make elongated receptive fields. The optimal stimulus for retinal and geniculate cells was a white spot on a dark background (or in other cells, a black spot on a light background) of a certain size—but round, always round. In the cortical cells, round spots might evoke a response, but the best stimuli were lines and elongated edges.

Now given that switching from spots to lines and edges *decreased* the responses of the geniculate cells forming the input to the cortex (compared to the optimal spots), better responses to lines was a surprise. But a given cortical cell arranged those inputs so as to sum together the activity of many input cells whose receptive field centers were not all in the same place:

Indeed, they were all strung out in a line, thanks presumably to the genetic instructions that had wired up the thalamus and cortex during prenatal development.

While some cortical cells obviously preferred horizontal white lines, others preferred vertical ones. And others preferred various in-between angles, so long as they stayed within about 5 to 10° of their optimal angle. As the tilt of a line shifted (as, for example, the horizon tilts when the Vineyard ferryboat rolls in a wave), one group of cells fell silent but another group sprang into activity. Each cell seemed to be a specialist in a particular tilt.

And while some cells were best at edges such as the sea-sky boundary, some preferred narrow black lines, and others liked narrow white lines (just as one might predict from the two major classes of their input's Mexican hat arrangements, regular and inverted). So the cortex had a lot of variety, but it was orderly: Neighboring cells tended to have the same preferences for tilt, until suddenly reaching a neighbor that liked a quite different tilt. In all of the layers of the cortex, the tilt preference was the same—so if one sampled one neuron after another, they would all like the same tilt. But sometimes the recording probe would stray into an adjacent "column" that preferred a different tilt—and so we began to talk about "orientation columns" in the cortex.

Because a cell would respond somewhat to a small spot of light, one could patiently explore its receptive field, making a "map" of it from which one could predict the optimal stimulus: a narrow black line at 45°, or an edge oriented vertically, and so forth. And when they tried out the predicted optimal stimulus, the cell indeed sang in its loudest voice. But some cells refused to respond to small spots, and so Hubel and Wiesel tried lines and edges— and they'd usually work, once they twisted them around to the preferred tilt. It was as if these cells simply had a high threshold, as if they require a $10,000 balance before paying interest. Spots simply aren't big-league hitters by the time that the information gets to the cortex, according to this interpretation.

Then they got another surprise: Some such cells would respond to the line even if they moved it sideways somewhat. For every cell in retina, geniculate, and (so far) cortex that had been examined, that maneuver would cause the cell to become uninterested, shutting up because the stimulus had wandered out of its receptive field center or off onto a weak portion of its periphery. While they couldn't move the tilted line simply anywhere on the retina and have it work, there was a region perhaps 10 to 15° wide where the cell still responded to the line. But try tilting the line away from its favored orientation, and the cell would promptly shut up, no matter where the line's center was located. Hubel and Wiesel called these "complex cells," and the ones with the predictable maps "simple cells."

This was an exciting development, as the complex cells appeared to be "generalizing" on the concept of "line tilted at 45°" regardless of location. Psychologists had long been pushing generalization as a difference between lower and higher animals: Some species will learn to treat an erect and an upside-down triangle as "the same thing," and other species will always treat them as different, refusing to "generalize on the concept of triangle." Complex cells were generalizing, not about triangles but about one of the parts of the triangle, a tilted line.

So were there higher-order cells in the brain that specialized in triangles, no matter what their size or tilt, no matter whether black-on-white or white-on-black, no matter whether the center was filled or not? Were there triangle detectors in higher animals' brains, just as frogs had good "bug detectors" even out in their retinas?

We know already how to hear isolated cells among the millions of elements in the system. I cannot imagine a more important task than the reconstruction of the symphony.

the neuropsychologist HANS-LUKAS TEUBER

STEPHEN KUFFLER NEVER WON the Nobel Prize, despite his involvement in this string of successes in uncovering one fundamental aspect after another of how inhibition is used. The betting among the neurobiological community in the late 1970s was that the next Nobel Prize in matters neurobiological would go to the triumvirate of Kuffler, Wiesel, and Hubel. But Nobel Prizes are never awarded posthumously, and Steve Kuffler died while working at his desk in his Woods Hole home on October 11, 1980, at the age of 67. As was his custom, he had been swimming at Stony Beach that morning.

In 1981 Hubel and Wiesel did indeed receive the Nobel Prize in Physiology or Medicine. And as in all such matters, they were particularly noteworthy representatives of a whole community of successful scientists. Neurobiology grew up in those years: There was no such word in 1959, just various neurophysiologists and neuroanatomists and neuropharmacologists and developmental specialists, etc., coming from backgrounds in medicine, biology, psychology, and the physical sciences. Today, students can find a variety of graduate programs in neurobiology, and there are even a few places with undergraduate majors in neurobiology. But mostly we remain a diverse group of emigrants from other fields, something of a melting pot. Everyone learns the reductionist techniques, as they remain the best way to train graduate students, but a few wander off into trying to piece it all together, to see the big picture, maybe discover some emergent properties.

What we get on the retina, whether we are chickens or human beings, is a welter of dancing light points stimulating the sensitive rods and cones that fire their messages into the brain. What we see is a stable world. It takes an effort of the imagination and a fairly complex apparatus to realize the tremendous gulf that exists between the two.

Consider any object, such as a book or piece of paper. When we scan it with our two eyes it projects upon our two retinas a restless, flitting pattern of light of various wave lengths and intensities. . . . But we are never conscious of the objective degree of all these changes unless we use . . . a peephole that makes us see a speck of color but masks off its relationships. Those who have used this magic instrument report the most striking discoveries. A white handkerchief in the shade may be objectively darker than a lump of coal in the sunshine. We rarely confuse the one with the other because on the whole the lump of coal will be the blackest patch in our field of vision, the handkerchief the whitest, and it is the relative brightness that matters and that we are aware of. The coding process begins while en route between the retina and our conscious mind.

the art historian E. H. GOMBRICH, 1959

7

WHO SPEAKS FROM THE CEREBRAL CORTEX? THE PROBLEM OF SUBCONSCIOUS COMMITTEES

The map is not the territory.

the early semiotician ALFRED KORZYBSKI, 1933

[Jorge Luis Borges] talked of a country that prided itself on its cartographical institute and the excellence of its maps. As the years went by, this institute would draw maps of greater and greater accuracy until at last the institute achieved the ultimate, the full-scale map. And, Borges says, if you wander through the desert today, you can see places where portions of the map are still pegged to the region they represent!

The point of all this, of course, is that our job as cognitive scientists is only to chart *the territory of mental life to establish the major phenomena and their relationships, not to provide the full-scale map, not to replace a life richly lived by the running of some computer program. . . . Our job as scientists, irrespective of our job as philosophers, is twofold: not only to provide explicit accounts where we can, but also to understand the limitations of those accounts. And so we must always exist in that tension, between the uncharted and the unknown.*

the brain theorist MICHAEL A. ARBIB, 1985

Is the road to consciousness paved with Mexican hats? Or at least lateral inhibition? Probably, as lateral inhibition is all about competition between adjacent cells for dominance, all about finding maxima and minima—and so it provides a way of judging the best choice among alternatives. But some other properties of cells in the aggregate need to be mentioned before returning to consciousness per se—such as sensory "maps" in the cerebral cortex.

Each cell in the visual pathways has a receptive field, one of whose properties is a "center"—a point in space toward which that cell's attention seems focused. Its neighboring cells are usually focused on about the same spot—but there is a drift, so that cells farther away seem to concentrate upon more distant points in space. This drift is generally orderly, so we can make maps, e.g., simplifications that plot only the centers. Cortical maps tend to be distorted because the cells are more interested in some things than others—rather like those maps of the world that show the continents resized according to their population, or gross national product.

THE SUNRISE WAS HAZY THIS MORNING, thanks to all the humidity of the sea air. Since the sun rises in the northeast in midsummer, it is over Cape Cod, as seen from Woods Hole, rather than hanging over the Atlantic Ocean as you'd expect. The Cape is shaped somewhat like the arm of a strongman flexing his biceps. The cocked wrist out at the northeast end is where Wellfleet and Truro are, with Provincetown the clenched fist. Eastham is on the forearm, Chatham is on the south side of the elbow looking down toward Nantucket. Hyannis is about the triceps, Dennis the biceps. The armpit would correspond to Falmouth and Woods Hole, and the head would be up along Cape Cod Bay about Plymouth Rock (where the Pilgrims landed), towered over by Boston and Cambridge, as befits their institutions of higher learning.

The armpit image of Woods Hole might have once been accurate, back in the days before the Marine Biological Laboratory and the Woods Hole Oceanographic Institution were founded. In the late nineteenth century, Woods Hole was industrial and a railroad terminus for the train ferries between Boston and New York (the great parking lot for the Vineyard and Nantucket ferries was once a railroad switching yard, and a pall of coal smoke often hung over it).

But the most potent smell came from a fertilizer factory that mixed local fish called menhaden with bat guano mined from cave floors in the tropics. Nine whaling ships operated out of this port between 1815 and 1860, and they smelled pretty bad too. The Pacific Guano Company went out of business in 1880; the whaling ground to a halt because of greed (they foolishly helped to exterminate entire species of whales).

The stench may be gone now, but Woods Hole isn't exactly the virginal salt marsh that it used to be. Earth-moving machinery has remade its landscape, sculpting the fill dirt into a bulldozer operator's idea of landscape aesthetics. Too bad they didn't straighten out those diabolical twisting roads while they were at it, though half of the blind corners could be fixed with hedge clippers. Perhaps blind corners are the local equivalent of a hair shirt.

The shape of Cape Cod suggests that it might have been the terminal moraine of an Ice Age glacier. Those of us who live in glacier country get used to seeing moraines. Hiking around Mount Rainier each summer, one sees glaciers melting back, exposing the big piles of rubble that they had plowed in front of them as they advanced. If you want to hike up to inspect the snout of a retreating glacier, you will likely climb up over a series of tongue-shaped "terminal moraines" on the way up the valley, recording the fitful advances and withdrawals of the snout.

Cape Cod is also tongue-shaped, and glaciers came down this far south (indeed, others made it to Central Park in New York City, where one can see the parallel scrape marks made by rocks trapped under the advancing front of the glaciers; Long Island is another moraine). The lowered sea level during the glacial periods (as much as 30–40 stories) exposed a lot of the Continental Shelf off the Atlantic coastline to habitation by land-loving glaciers.

The New England fishermen are always complaining about another leftover of the Ice Age melt-off: The shallow bottom around the Continental Shelf is littered with big boulders that ensnare nets and lobster pots. They're the submerged equivalent of the "glacial erratics" that New England farmers try to clear out of their fields, using them to build rocky fences. They were carried along by the glacier, but the melting ice dropped them on the spot. And in the case of those at lower elevations, the rising ocean eventually covered them.

There may have been a series of terminal moraines south of Boston. The Nantucket Shoals, where the Atlantic Ocean is only one story deep in places, may represent the southernmost rubble pile. The offshore islands of Martha's Vineyard and Nantucket, and the shallow waters in between them, may be the terminal moraine of an advance that followed the meltback from the shoals. Cape Cod itself may record, in part, the shape of the tongue of the glacier during its last advance. One might expect that the next Ice Age will rearrange all this scenery, another glacier plowing it all into a new terminal moraine. It's literally a case of *sic transit gloria mundi*.

THE BIKE TRAIL follows along the shores of Vineyard Sound from near Nobska all the way past Oyster Pond and into Falmouth. The Shining Sea Bikeway is an old railroad right-of-way reclaimed for the public; now, you can now walk or bicycle nearly six kilometers without having a car sideswipe you, once you get away from the ferry parking lot at Woods Hole.

Most people walk, though some masochistic runners are also in evidence. Bicycles come in all flavors, but mostly this is a slow lane, not a fast one; people look around at the flowers, the forest. Little paths lead off through the brush here and there. Then a pond pops into view, complete with a pair of majestic swans.

One long stretch of the trail borders the ocean, and you can look south between Martha's Vineyard and Nantucket to the open sea. And this sea really does shine; since you look to the south and the sun is in the southern sky above it, a lot of sunlight gets reflected back into your eyes. Katharine Lee Bates, whose home in Falmouth is a National Historic Something hereabouts, wrote "America the Beautiful." Every time that I hear that lovely phrase "From sea to shining sea" commemorating the East and West Coasts (where the sea only shines at sunrise or sunset), I think of this south-facing beach where the sea shines all day.

Your view is unfortunately interrupted by the most obnoxious utility line yet seen. This is a trunk line of some sort, tennis-ball thickness in most places—more a sagging pipe than a wire. Every few poles, it expands to football fatness, the tumors representing splices where a break has been repaired. A pipe in the sky. It is so heavy as to require utility poles almost as closely spaced as fence posts in places. And these utility poles march right along the beach, their guy wires causing you to detour as you walk along near the lapping waves. At least the monstrosity is exposed to all the vagaries of wind and tide; one can hope such insidious influences will undermine it even if human planning doesn't eliminate it.

I can see it's time to think great thoughts again. I need a version of the Grand March from *Aida* to deal with visual irritations. Perhaps imagining Russian dolls, one inside another, *ad infinitum*, would be sufficiently compelling. Or perhaps the little person inside the head, he who is viewing the vision seen by the eyes?

VISUAL CORTEX probably isn't the center for our perception of the faces and cars and trees that we readily recognize. The utility-pole schema certainly doesn't live there, because none of the cells in this region of brain can handle objects much larger than 2° (the sun and the moon are both about 0.5°, just for reference).

The so-called visual cortex may get the information first from the thalamus, but there are many other "secondary" visual areas in the back half of your brain. And they sometimes seem to do fancier things. Perhaps triangles can be found there, and even the shapes of swans. Or my schema for tumor-infested utility poles.

V4 is a patch of cortex where a complete map of the opposite half of the visual world was found (as you might guess, V4 was the fourth one discovered in cortex). The left hemisphere's V4 has a map of the right half of your visual world; the center of the retina is on one side of the V4 "patch" and the periphery on the other, the cells in between specializing in the intermediate locations. The map is similar to one of those telethons where the people answering the calls from the various states are stationed at desks that are spread out over the floor of a basketball court in the shape of the United States, the "Maine desk" up in one corner, the "Texas desk" at the bottom, etc.

In Daniel Hartline's metaphor, each brain cell is like a general getting verbal reports from the battlefield that he cannot see directly. And so a brain map resembles a command center with specialists in each battle sector. I remember those movies about World War II where England's air defenses were coordinated from England-shaped plotting tables, different officers specializing in each sector.

The receptive fields of V4 cells are often very similar to those found in V1. So why is there this near-duplicate of V1? Is it like those backup command posts, there in case the main command post was bombed? Of course, V4 isn't the only extra center with a complete map: In monkeys, we've discovered several dozen so far. There are unlikely to be fewer in humans, and I wouldn't be surprised if we had hundreds. That's why I call each half-map a "patch": The whole convoluted cortical surface looks like a patchwork quilt when unfolded and flattened out, each patch having a texture within it representing the fine-grain "grid."

Dozens or hundreds of "duplicates"? That's a lot of backups, so I doubt they are in fact redundant spares in the manner of the airplane's three systems for lowering the landing gear. Even if you argue that we have paired kidneys to insure against loss of one, then why not a spare heart? For one thing, evolution by natural selection shapes up extras very slowly, as the Nth spare would come under natural selection only on those rare occasions where all N-1 had failed simultaneously. Evolution is full of good-enough solutions, where makeshifts are never replaced; it seldom gets around to pair-and-a-spare.

But redundancy isn't just for backups: It can be a way of ganging up on a problem, as when a dozen people get together to push a car out of a ditch. Having lots of separate centers doing the same job can sometimes solve a precision problem, thanks to the Law of Large Numbers.

CONSIDER DUNKING FREE THROWS in basketball: You've got to be able to estimate how far away that hoop is, if you are to drop the basketball through it cleanly. The distance is about five paces, and the room to spare inside the loop is only a few fingers' width—so that's about 1 percent of the total. While I doubt that basketball success played much of a role in hominid evolution, hunters had the same problem when throwing at a small animal: About half your chances of hitting a rabbit with a thrown stone occur hitting its front profile, but about half involve the stone landing atop the animal. Hunters with good depth judgment will be twice as successful as those with crude judgment. So how do I tell that the 20-cm rabbit is between 8.0 and 8.2 meters away, and not between 8.2 and 8.4 instead? That's again a judgment with a tolerable error of about 1 percent.

We humans have a number of ways of estimating distance. Up close, we can see how much we have to accommodate our eyes (squeezing that lens to bring the object into focus). Farther away, the relative size gives one clue, as we know about how big adult rabbits are—but you could be fooled by an immature rabbit closer than you think. Texture is another clue: If we can see the ruffles in its fur, it is closer than if we cannot. But the best method for distances under about 10 meters is the range-finder effect: We converge the two eyes to look at a close object, but make their axes parallel to look at a very distant object. And some V1, V2, and V4 cells are very good at making use of this.

In both V1 and V4, most cells receive inputs from both eyes. And it is a very similarly organized input: A receptive field mapped with the left eye shut is shaped the same as the receptive field obtained looking only through the left eye. Looking with both eyes together usually gives the most vigorous response. Now in V1, the best responses occur when the axes of the two eyes are parallel, staring off at a distant object. But in V4, the two eyes' receptive fields are slightly staggered, their centers not quite in the same place. And so the way to get an optimal response out of the cell is to converge the two eyes slightly until the centers overlap perfectly. Thus the cell, while responding to objects at various distances, responds best to those in a certain range of distances, say between 7 and 9 meters away. Another V4 cell might prefer 2 to 3 meters because its centers are even more

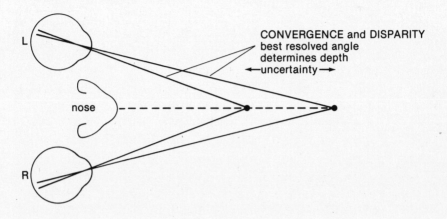

CONVERGENCE and DISPARITY
best resolved angle
determines depth
←uncertainty→

offset and thus require more convergence to overlap. But V4 cells are never sharply tuned, say, for 8.0 to 8.2 meters only and no other distance.

Should you average together the responses of a great many V4 cells, you can get a much better estimate of distance. And usually these matters improve with the square of the number of cells: With 25 times as many cells, you can improve your estimate by a factor of 5; a hundredfold redundancy usually gives you a tenfold reduction in uncertainty. While the Law of Large Numbers places some restrictions on the types of neural circuits that will provide this square-root-law improvement (the noise in the various cells must be statistically independent, each cell must make a small contribution to the total so that they function as democracies rather than oligarchies, the summation must be fairly linear rather than some binary logic, etc.), many types of neural circuits can succeed in using the Law of Large Numbers to solve precision problems. While I have worked it out in detail only for the case of differential depth discrimination and the case of timing precision, it would appear that many types of precision discrimination behaviors could profit from many-fold redundancy: Precision color discrimination (for telling ripening fruit from the surrounding leaves), precision spatial discrimination (many animals exhibit "hyperacuity" in a sensory system, where an individual's performance is better than the best receptor's resolution), "perfect pitch," and so forth.

And so the prospect of several dozen extra visual maps immediately suggests a fivefold improvement in some aspect of resolution, not several dozen backups in case of frequent failures. It can be sensory performance that is improved, or it can be movement skills such as throwing. Those basketball stars who always sink their long shots have probably learned to get a lot of their brain cells to gang up on the depth discrimination problem and another group to gang up on releasing the grip on the ball at just the right instant.

BUT THE SECONDARY VISUAL AREAS also differ from V1 when you look at optimal stimuli. Often the differences are subtle, as when some V4 cells turn out to like different degrees of convergence of the two eyes. Other V4 cells are much better at colored lights than are V1 cells. In some distant secondary areas such as the medial-temporal (MT) area, receptive fields are organized strikingly differently from those of V1 or V4 cells; an MT cell will prefer dumbbell or four-leaf-clover shapes rather than lines or corners. And so combinations of such elements can come to specialize in irregular shapes such as the outline of a hand or the shape of a face. Indeed, some such temporal lobe cells are said to like the shapes of faces better than anything else—maybe not exclusively your grandmother's face, but at least faces in general. So does one have several dozen specialized subcenters?

Still, they overlap more than they differ, just what you'd expect if most had evolved by a simple duplication: the same genetic instructions used a second time to make an extra map, with some subtle modifications made later to subserve an additional function such as color or depth discrimination. Duplication-then-diversification is a big principle at the gene level, a handy way of improving a program while still running the reliable version a while longer, just as a computer programmer always tries out modifications on a duplicate of the functioning program. It seems likely that cortical map duplications were promoted by their usefulness when ganged together (on occasions when real precision was needed), but that the duplicates later diversified a little and so became useful for another function.

MORE THAN A QUARTER-CENTURY after Hubel and Wiesel found those line-orientation specialists in visual cortex, no one has yet found a generalized triangle detector in any species' brain. Nor are there many primate brain cells specializing in any of those features that the frog's eye seemed to find so compelling in 1959. Why?

Well, perhaps someone will eventually find a generalized triangle detector cell, but we humans remember so many different facts from our lifetimes that there may not be enough cells in our brains for each cell to be a specialist in just one fact; just because computer memories store each fact in a pigeonhole of its own doesn't mean that there aren't other ways to accomplish memory and recognition tasks. Just because I can remember the profile of my grandmother's face doesn't necessarily mean that I have a cell somewhere in my brain that responds only to that shape and no other. Registering "that's a picture of my grandmother" could instead be accomplished by a committee of cells, each of which also belonged to other committees (such as the one for my father's face *and* for four-leaf clovers).

Expecting a specialist cell (or "labeled line") for each schema (Marvin Minsky, take note) is called the *Grandmother's face cell fallacy* by neurophysiologists. It isn't that we're sure that such a specialist cell doesn't exist (we haven't examined every brain cell yet!)—it's that we are sure that some properties emerge from combinations of simpler parts, that the whole can be created by a sum of the parts. The parts may just be line specialists, and the whole created from lots of little segments.

GESTALT PSYCHOLOGY emphasized, early in this century, that all experiences consist of *gestalten*, integrated structures or patterns that must be apprehended as wholes rather than as their disconnected parts. The notion that the whole is sometimes more than the sum of its parts goes back to Aristotle—but if it's not going to be just another leap of faith (what scientists call hand-waving), if we are to understand more when we finish the explanation than when we started contemplating the parts, then we need to surmount a difficult conceptual hurdle. Surprisingly, it is closely related to another puzzle: how a function like perception and cognition need not have a location, a place to which you can point and say, "There, Grandmother's face lives right there."

Happily, there is an excellent example of awareness based on committees and reducible no further. This example has been learned (and then usually forgotten) by every neurobiologist, probably in grade school. It is the lesson of color mixing, the first "emergent property" that we came to appreciate. An emergent is a more-than-the-sum-of-the-parts property that *emerges* from the collection of parts, and is incapable of meaningful reduction.

This sterling example dates back to 1802. It was discovered by the English scientist Thomas Young, whose descendant John Zachary Young is one of the foremost neurobiologists of today. J.Z. is well known around here, having discovered in 1936 the squid's giant axon (which is what attracts so many scientists to MBL during the early summer's "squid season"). He went on to analyze memory mechanisms of the octopus, write some of the major textbooks (you'll see *The Life of Vertebrates* on many an MBL desk), give some of the earliest popular lectures on neurobiology (the 1950 Reith lectures on the BBC), and write influential critiques of neurobiology (such as *Programs of the Brain*).

Thomas Young discovered one of the great "you can't reduce it any further" themes of neurobiology which stands as a warning to reductionists: Just as the Nobska lighthouse warns that "you can't go any further and still float," so Thomas Young's analysis of color mixing now serves to warn that you can't go any further than sensor committees without changing the agenda. Here, at least, reductionism isn't everything: Committees are the real thing, at least if color is your agenda. Or taste, for whether something tastes salty, bitter, acid, or sweet seems to be a matter of irreducible combinations of activity in the chemical sensors embedded in the tongue; there are no labeled-line specialists in one taste or another in your tongue.

Thomas Young got his start on this with the realization that we can see many different colors (say, a hundred for the sake of argument) at each point (say, 1 billion) in our visual field. Young suspected that the retina didn't have a hundred different sensors at each point in the visual field, each labeled with a hue; he theorized that there were instead only three types of sensors at each point and that it was the differing combinations of activity in each of the three that communicated color sensations. A century and a half later, it was shown that he was exactly right: We now call them the blue cone, the green cone, and the yellow cone (those colors being the peak sensitivity of each photoreceptor type, not its exclusive specialty). Hermann von Helmholtz in 1860 suggested that for each colorful stimulus, there is a ratio of responses across these three sensor types that is specific to that color—and that suffices to represent it. Right again.

THAT A PARTICULAR SHADE OF RED is simply a 3:1 ratio in the activity of the yellow and green cone types, with the blue cone mostly inactive, nicely accounts for the many different ways we can produce the sensation of that reddish hue, one of which is with a pure 600-nanometer wavelength. But that a single wavelength is usually the simplest way of producing the sensation is misleading: Some hues, such as purple, cannot be produced by any single wavelength.

Purple corresponds to a pattern of activity in the yellow and blue cones (with green mostly inactive) that cannot be achieved by any single wavelength, that indeed can only be evoked by a combination of long and short wavelengths that would individually appear red and blue. Violet, in comparison, is simply a lot of activity in the blue cone pathway, less in the green cone pathway, and very little in the yellow cone pathway; it can usually be

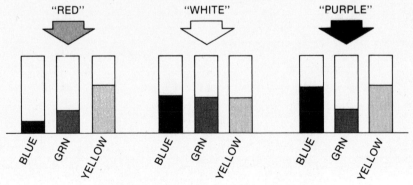

Ratio of responses in the three cone types
determines the hue perceived.

mimicked by a single short wavelength between "blue" and "ultra-violet," such as 400 nanometers.

Evolutionarily, we should not expect pure wavelength specialists anyway: Color is used to distinguish one surface from another and, except for monochromatic gratings, all surfaces reflect a combination of wavelengths. My proposed *Purple Principle* says that the need is for detecting combinations (of which the two extreme ends of the spectrum together, but little of the middle, is merely a rare example), not for detecting part of a rainbow (which is about the only time in nature that we come close to seeing a single wavelength in isolation).

Of course, one can and should play reductionist games and analyze the component parts; knowing that there are indeed three different kinds of cones, each with a different pigment and thus wavelength sensitivity, is invaluable information. So is the fact that certain retinal ganglion cells and geniculate cells specialize in color contrast. Some of these so-called P-cells might even turn out to be far more sensitive to purple than anything else, and thus qualify as purple specialists. But the existence of such narrowly tuned cells will not obviate the fact that color is an *emergent* property of a *committee* of photoreceptors, capable of being expressed as the activity of many broadly tuned cells as well as a few narrowly tuned cells. They serve to drive home the fact that color hue is fundamentally a *pattern* and not a pure specialty with its own cubbyhole somewhere in the brain whose activity signals purple to the mind.

What is so surprising is that, as Robert Erickson points out, neuroscientists are always "rediscovering the wheel" while searching for labeled lines: The people working on skin sensation rediscovered Young's principle; so did the people working on motor cortex's control of movement. Young's patterning principle has been called many things by its reinventors: population codes, parallel processing, distributed functions, ensemble coding, and across-fiber pattern. It bears a strong resemblance to the holistic side of the reductionism versus holism dichotomy. And to the developing distinction between the categories of cognitive psychology and the distributed networks of computational neuroscience (to be discussed in Chapter 10).

Neurons are the anatomical units of the nervous system, but are not the structural elements of its functioning. [The latter] have not yet been defined, and it will probably be apparent when they are that they must be expressed in terms of invariants of relative activities between neurons . . . and not in terms of separate anatomical entities. . . . Unless [the observer] explicitly or implicitly provides a theory that embodies the relational structure of the system, and conceptually supercedes his description of the components, he can never understand it.

the neurophysiologist HUMBERTO MATURANA, 1980

The power of Young's logic is that the pattern is the message; it is the brain's sensory code in its final form. This means that the population of neurons can never be divided into separate neurons for, say, each discriminate color at each point in the visual field.

the sensory physiologist ROBERT P. ERICKSON, 1984

THE MOST FUNDAMENTAL REASON why labeled lines (another name for Grandmother's face cells) aren't needed in sensory processing, however, has just occurred to me (though, before fans of alliteration start calling this Calvin's Coactivated Committee Concept, we'll have to see how many other people also recognized this minimalist principle during the last century). We don't need a single cell specializing in "purple" simply because it takes many cells for me to pronounce "purple" (or act on the purple-coded information in other ways). Many-to-many will suffice without a many-to-one-to-many hourglass-shaped bottleneck.

Sensory processing is all about coupling sensation to action in a manner that is reliable. And actions all require a motor program that orchestrates a number of muscles, creates a spatiotemporal pattern of cell firing something like a fireworks finale. An action always involves many muscles—and therefore many motorneurons. This usually involves some motorneurons firing first and others later.

Triggering this ensemble into action need not require a single "command neuron"; it only requires a committee of interneurons active in some characteristic pattern. It is the difference between starting an automobile engine by pushing the Model A's old-fashioned starter button and the modern procedure: turning the correct key in the ignition lock where each tumbler has to be set just right. It is the correct notching pattern that starts the engine of a modern car, not a single push on a single button.

The analogy is deficient in that it is the activity in a single information channel (the wire from ignition switch to starter motor) that really starts the car. Manufacturers who want to slow down thieves use a ribbon cable from switch to effector, fixing it so that a pattern of information in many wires is required rather than touching a single wire to the battery connection. A keypad outside a door, connected to the electrical door lock, needs to use a ribbon cable to foil thieves who merely rip the keypad from the wall and touch two wires together.

Animals seldom use the single-wire approach; the patterned activity in a ribbon cable is the more appropriate analogy for almost all motor programs. The classic exception is the Mauthner cell in the brain stem of fish: When it fires a single impulse, the fish executes a massive tail flip. One could put a label on the right side's M-cell saying "emergency on right, flip left" and another on the left M cell saying "emergency on left, flip right" and have true labeled lines.

It is only very simple motor programs with simple spatiotemporal patterns of muscle activity that can get by with the "Model A" approach to orchestration. The appropriate trigger for most motor programs is going to be a keylike correct *combination* of triggers in many cells; indeed, it will probably be just as important *which cells are inactive* as which are active. Therefore, one expects the ultimate stage in sensory processing to produce a pattern as the trigger. And it's not just a spatial pattern like the key notches: It is a spatio*temporal* pattern, like the fireworks finale, the *order* in which various neurons are activated, as well as *which* neurons are activated, being the key.

The sensation-to-movement transformation is many-to-many; there is no need for a many-to-one-to-many bottleneck unless the one cell has some special advantage for producing the spatial or temporal aspects of the movement subcommands (as does the M-cell). That's why purple doesn't require a specialist neuron: The correct combination of activity in yellow cone and blue cone channels (together with the absence of green cone channel activity) should suffice to pronounce "purple." That's why labeled lines and command neurons are so rare, why distributed sensitivity and committees are so common.

> *To categorize is human,*
> *to distribute, divine.*

> TERRENCE SEJNOWSKI, 1988

PATTERNS AS THE DETERMINANT, rather than absolute quantities of some one thing, are also a big feature of growth and development. The curling vines that one sees along the bike trail are good examples of this.

How does nature produce a nice, graceful, regular curve? Or a spiral? Largely by making one side of the stalk grow faster than the other. Want to make a stalk bend to the south? Just let the north side grow faster than the south side. Want it to grow in a corkscrew? Let the east side at the base also grow faster than the west side. Want it to spiral upward, tightly coiled like a telephone cord? Just keep the upward growth rate low compared to the north-south and east-west differences. The final shape is "specified" by the *relative* magnitude of those rates, not by individual magnitudes.

Forms can result from such simple rules involving differences and ratios in growth rates. The genes do not contain an image of a spiral: They contain a set of codes for enzymes. Those enzymes control growth rates. One pattern of enzyme quantities results in a tightly curled spiral, another pattern in a stem that merely tilts south. It is another example of the Purple Principle.

The curved surfaces of our bodies are due to such differential growth rates too, a surface layer of cells dividing faster than a deeper layer of cells and so bending the sheet. The shape of a dog's face, whether pointed like a setter or flat like a pug, is a matter of differential developmental rates too: Puppies tend to start off flat-faced, and some grow the elongated noses of setters while others have their growth terminated before ever getting to that stage. When the development of sexual organs proceeds faster than general somatic development, the body form often gets arrested in a juvenile form, since puberty tends to slow down further somatic development to a crawl. Animal breeders have, in effect, selected for those variants with markedly different sexual versus somatic developmental rates in breeding for the pug.

And so it makes remarkably little sense to ask "where" the stem's shape is stored in the plants' genes or where the face's shape is stored in a mammalian chromosome. It's going to be a *pattern*, like purple.

CLOSELY RELATED to the Grandmother's face cell fallacy is the little-person-inside-the-head fallacy, the notion that there is some ultimate emperor to whom all those specialized command centers report. It's reminiscent of those Russian dolls that come apart, only to reveal a slightly smaller version of the doll inside. It too comes apart. . . . Now, at some level, there will be too few atoms left for the shape of a doll to be maintained; you can keep taking it apart into protons and neutrons and electrons, and then into all their quark components—and that is proving very interesting—but you're no longer talking about miniature dolls. You've changed the agenda.

I've long been suspicious of an infinite regress: It always reminds me of something that happened when I was about 6 years old. One snowy Saturday morning in winter, my father took me down to the local barbershop for a haircut. I'd always liked the barbershop, which was full of new smells and absorbing rituals. In those days, it was something of an all-male club, at least on Saturdays, when fathers brought their sons in. It was a father-and-son sort of thing, something like following the fire trucks to see a fire (my father was an executive of a fire insurance company, and so I learned how to tell the sirens of the fire trucks from those of the police cars from those of mere ambulances; for my birthday each year, I'd get to go to the local fire station and ring the brass bell on an old fire truck, once for each year of age).

The barbershop was long and narrow: You saw a long row of barber chairs down one side of the room, with waiting chairs and magazines down the opposite side, the shorn and the unshorn facing one another. The shorn towered over the unshorn. Young boys sat especially high up in the chair, boosted up by a special board placed across the arms of the old-fashioned chairs so that the barber didn't have to bend over. And so you had this commanding view over everyone's heads: and the view was overwhelmingly of yourself.

Down each wall were mirrors, big plate-glass mirrors. No matter which way the chair rotated, there was the mirror reflecting back your image—as well as the image of the mirror in back of you showing you what you looked like from the rear. But of course it too contained a somewhat reduced-size image of your front. Since someone had carefully made the mirrors parallel to each other, there was an infinite regress of ever-smaller images of your front, back, front, back, front, back. . . . I had marveled at this Russian-doll-like succession during my first visit to the barbershop, but later tired of it.

Then came one quiet Saturday of winter when it was softly snowing outdoors. I was perched atop the chair, getting bored. There was some commotion outdoors, but I couldn't see anything because I was a few chairs down the long corridor from the front window, not in the first chair as I liked to be. Various people disappeared to see what was going on, and I became even more impatient for the barber to finish. A siren or two was heard, but then nothing. An accident of some sort, according to the people (including my father) who'd looked out the window. And there I was, trapped in this glorified high chair.

This haircut seemed to take forever. The barber tried to get me to count my images in the mirror, saying that there was a prize for the boy with the sharpest eyes who could spot the smallest image in the center of it all and see if the smallest one was different. And so I diligently counted this infinite regress, but they all looked the same to me: None was different—all were me—except for being a little smaller each time. So the barber told me to count them again.

There was much fussing with talcum powder, even some fancy-smelling hair tonic that I'd never had before. Finally, I was unwrapped and helped down off of my high perch. My father paid the barber, thanking him more than usual. Then I was wrapped up again, this time because of the winter cold. Eventually we went outside into the fresh snow. I'd almost forgotten about the earlier commotion.

The barbershop was near the end of the trolley line. A big circular loop track allowed the cars to turn around and go back into the city; I had often watched the trolley cars clanging their way around this circle, warning the pedestrians who took short-cuts across the tracks. Now, a cluster of people gathered around an abandoned trolley car, and a crumpled figure lay on the ground covered by a blanket. A smaller object lay a few feet away, covered by someone's coat. His leg. The dark reddish-brown stains in the snow were not at all like the catsup-red of blood in the make-believe of movies. All was being slowly covered by fresh snowfall. It was, the people said, a sad case of suicide.

Each time that I encounter another infinite regress, I wonder whether it is just another time-consuming exercise. And if it will lead to another dead end, literally at the end of the line.

> *[If] a command to move originates in prefrontal cortex, that command should be considered a product of multiple inter-actions of prefrontal cortex with other cerebral components, cortical and subcortical. Thus the quest for a prefrontal executive is pointless. Only by reasoning this way do we avoid an infinite regress of ever higher executives or the implausible notion of prefrontal cortex in a pontifical posi-tion.*

> the neurophysiologist JOAQUIN FUSTER, 1981

PHILOSOPHERS TRADITIONALLY COMPLAIN about infi-nite regresses and tautologies, but practical people like electrical engineers aren't anywhere as worried. My old friend John DuBois points out that most oscillator circuits tend to chase their tails; you just have to use the right types of phase plane reasoning in order to analyze such feedback circuits (as an undergraduate, he tried pointing this out to his philosophy professor but got no-where). Cause-and-effect reasoning sometimes isn't very good when it comes to open systems with energy to spare. Might a semi-infinite regress subserve consciousness, some sort of frontal lobe circuit that chases its tail?

We like to ridicule bureaucracies whose committees do nothing but "shuffle papers," making endless recommendations to one another but never acting. "Paper chasing paper in a circle." Yet the cautious bureaucracy may be a good analogy for our subconscious. The problem is: At what point does one act, do something in the external world? What's a good analogy to decision-making?

Homunculi are only bogeymen if they duplicate entirely the talents they are rung in to explain. . . . If one can get a team of relatively ignorant, narrow-minded, blind homunculi to produce the intelligent behaviour of the whole, this is progress.

the philosopher DANIEL C. DENNETT, 1978

---8---

DYNAMIC REORGANIZATION: SHARPENING UP A SMEAR WITH A MEXICAN HAT

[How] we come to analyze the world, without postulating the presence of a non-material central agent or homunculus . . . is a problem that is rarely faced by neuroscientists. . . . Perhaps the reason for this serious failure is that neuroscientists mostly think about individual units but not about the population of neurons and their connections, the synapses of the brain.

the neurobiologist J. Z. YOUNG, 1988

To learn is to eliminate.

the neurobiologist JEAN-PIERRE CHANGEUX, 1983

Surely there is something bet-
ter than an infinite regress of little people inside the head. Or the
infinitely regressing agendas of "reductionism forever," constantly
changing so that one never answers the interesting questions
about how the mind works.

Well, one thing that's better is the bookstore. The Shining
Sea Bikeway is the only path I know that has excellent bookstores
at each end, both in Falmouth and in Woods Hole. No matter
which end you start from, you can take a break in the middle of
your round trip by sitting down and browsing through the new
books. A truly enlightened trail, with some foresightful soul having provided park benches every mile and, not far from each end,
a truly civilized bookstore with a readers' table and chairs. And
J. Z. Young's new book, *Philosophy and the Brain*.

"Jay Zed," after providing the membrane biophysicists with
the squid giant axon (he and Keffer Hartline did the first recordings from it here; Hartline was surprised, never having seen such
a large electrical signal before, and suspected faulty equipment
initially), went on to study the other familiar cephalopod mollusk,
the octopus. It is the most intelligent of the invertebrates, sometimes compared to a laboratory rat in its behavioral versatility.
And after modeling the octopus's visual memory, he suggested
that memory may work, in part, by eliminating some neural
connections—by carving away material, in the same way those
carved figureheads for old sailing ships were created.

This was somewhat heretical: Everybody was used to thinking of growth and memory as a process of adding on material, the
way children with modeling clay are likely to make a figurine by
padding it out. Neurobiologists are like everyone else, always
filling up one file cabinet after another, and when we said that
memory was a cumulative process, we usually meant it in both
senses of the word. J.Z.'s proposal had the interesting property of

suggesting some limit to how much information could be stored with such a process: After all, a carver who doesn't know when to stop soon runs out of wood. If you lived long enough, you might run out of brain! And surely consciousness before that. You can see why the idea didn't immediately catch on.

Because new memories had to be somehow superimposed on old memories, one imagined smaller figures being carved into larger ones, as in graffiti on a wooden figurehead; from a distance, it would loom like one thing, but focusing up closer would tell a different story. So adding on new memories had to conform in some way to the old memories: After all, carving a whale does make it hard to superimpose the form of a giraffe on it. Reorganizing your memories, in the manner that I periodically reorganize my file cabinets, might be a little hard if the information was stored by carving. Certainly neural carving raised the possibility that some experiences could produce irreversible effects.

Much to my surprise, carving connections has provided one of the key insights required to understand how consciousness committees function, and for why one doesn't need labeled lines to get Grandmother's face recognition. It's all because of the Mexican hat—what was originally called *lateral inhibition* by its neurophysiological discoverers, Georg von Békésy, Keffer Hartline, Floyd Ratliff, Stephen Kuffler, Robert Barlow, and such.

To begin personally, on a confessional note, I was at one time, at my onset, a single cell. . . . I do not remember this, but I know that I began dividing. I have probably never worked so hard, and never again with such skill and certainty. . . . At one stage I possessed an excellent kidney, good enough for any higher fish; then I thought better and destroyed it all at once, installing in its place a neater pair for living on land. I didn't plan on this when it was going on, but my cells, with a better memory, did.

Thinking back, I count myself lucky that I was not in charge at the time. If it had been left to me to do the mapping of my cells I would have got it wrong, dropped something, forgotten where to assemble my neural crest, confused it. Or I might have been stopped in my tracks, panicked by the massive deaths, billions of my embryonic cells being killed

off systematically to make room for their more senior suc-
cessors, death on a scale so vast that I can't think of it
without wincing. By the time I was born, more of me had
died than had survived. It is no wonder I can't remember;
during that time I went through brain after brain for nine
months, finally contriving the one model that could be hu-
man, equipped for language.

the physician and essayist LEWIS THOMAS, 1987

IRREVERSIBILITY has been an important idea about human beings for a long time. The Jesuits thought that they could produce lifetime obedience with suitable indoctrination of little boys; Charles Darwin noted that "a belief constantly inculcated during the early years of life, while the brain is impressible, appears to acquire almost the nature of an instinct." Defense attorneys invoke such reasoning to attempt to excuse their clients' actions, saying that their behavior was all the manufacturer's fault, i.e., the school system and "society" in general. Some psychologists claim that the child's brain is infinitely malleable by the environment in which it grows up—but usually recognize that adults are more likely to become set in their ways as they grow older. Whatever the extent of the plasticity in various periods, it certainly seems likely that something so important will be carefully regulated, probably on a day-to-day basis (or night-to-night—one proposed function of sleep is to adjust what is passed from temporary to long-lasting memory).

Behavioral plasticity may be restricted to some "critical periods" in development; in certain respects, it really matters what your experiences are during some years. If the two eyes don't get a chance to work together within the first two years of life, chances are that one eye will become functionally blind; there will be nothing wrong with it optically, but it will act as if disconnected from the higher centers of the brain (this is the reason why cross-eyed babies need such early surgery).

Something as well learned as a schema becomes the modal schematic of a series of similar experiences: We no longer remember when we first encountered the letter *A*, or when we took our first step. A snapshot schema, however, is a record of a unique event (in my generation: what you were doing when you heard about President Kennedy being shot). Unless there is some way of freezing it (the way those infantile memories of binocular experience were frozen by myelination and synaptic editing), we might expect such memories to be malleable. We shape up schemas to be the average shape of a lighthouse or the defining character of a Picasso. The lack of "fixing" means that every time we reactivate the schema (as when we recall it "to mind" in the absence of the original), we stand some chance of modifying the memory.

History is what you remember, and if you don't think it's being revised all the time, you haven't paid enough attention to your own memory. When you remember something, you don't remember the thing itself—you just remember the last time you remembered it.

The Grateful Dead songwriter JOHN BARLOW, 1984

MALLEABILITY IS THE FLIP SIDE of irreversibility: Our memories are sometimes more modifiable than we imagine. Indeed, each time we recall something, we have an opportunity to modify that memory. This means that we can readily fool ourselves, unless we have disciplined ourselves to keep fantasy separate from reality. Even then, "brainwashing" techniques (of which some religious-conversion practices are the most familiar) may persuade us that the exact opposite is true. Ordinarily, human memories are pretty good, and we have come to insist (as a matter of social policy) upon one's responsibility for telling the truth—but there are no guarantees biologically, just as there are no guarantees against mental illness.

So how does this malleability, this plasticity, of memory arise—and how is it occasionally "fixed" to resist further change? There are no general answers yet, but a spectrum of phenomena has been uncovered, ranging from dramatic examples of carving during childhood to subtle modeling of interconnections during adult experience "permitted" by neuromodulators.

I was reminded of all this when I sat in on the neural systems course and heard Patricia Goldman-Rakic lecture on the frontal lobes (yes, indeed; frontal lobes have finally made it to MBL!). We usually think of the process of growing up as one of growth, of adding on to the body and filling it out with additional material. But development is also a process of removing some material. This isn't the familiar old saw about "you lose ten thousand nerve cells every day" (the experts now say that isn't particularly true in higher centers, that nearly all the cell death in cerebral cortex is accomplished before you are born, even though some subcortical structures such as the *substantia nigra* lose a lot of cells during life—and excess loss is a component of what we know as Parkinson's disease). But there is an evolutionary version of the carving principle, some neurobiologists now saying that new neural structures deep in the brain have been created by a process of removing intervening cells to define their shapes better, that this is how differentiation of "subdepartments" occurs.

Nerve cells also die during one's lifetime, of course, as when injured by a bruise or the loss of oxygen supply or by escaped hemoglobin (when blood cells rupture, and the arterial walls as well, the hemoglobin may come into direct contact with nerve cells and kill them). These local areas of damage may never be noticed, as adjacent areas take over their function so well. When large areas of brain start losing a lot of nerve cells, however, you start having problems with memory, reasoning, speech, and all the rest.

There was an old Garry Trudeau cartoon posted on the bulletin board in the student lab for the neural-systems course, from the series "In Search of Reagan's Mind," where the investigative reporter is wandering around inside the convolutions of a seemingly empty frontal lobe, shining his flashlight here and there and exclaiming, "Where is Ronald Reagan?" But neurologists don't find that so funny: Every day they look at magnetic resonance scans (those computerized pictures that seem to slice up the brain; they're particularly useful for judging the size of various structures) from patients who are losing a lot of frontal lobe and getting senile, exhibiting many of the signs and symptoms that Elaine had for a month and then got over.

Alas, the senile patients with such massive loss don't recover: Once brain cells are gone, they're not typically replaced (unlike the blood cells, which are totally replaced every 120 days, or the intestinal lining, which is replaced every 3 days). Neurologists look at the brain images and see the infolded cortex developing wide, unoccupied valleys, and they sigh regretfully. In a normal brain, those valley walls are pushed together so tightly that you cannot see down into the groove. Strangely, many magazine photographs of "normal brains" are really the brains of people who had senile dementia—that's because art directors like exaggerated features that reveal the deep folds, and so they pick the pictures that "look best." But those brains had been carved from within by the disease process that destroyed most of the cortical nerve cells and shrank the brain. You wouldn't want to have a brain like the ones that they, in their ignorance, like to picture.

Is the disease process an exaggeration of normal developmental processes, something like cancer? Cancer is wild proliferation of cells, adding on more cells uncontrollably to create tumors and infiltrate other tissues, the way that strip cities invade farmlands insidiously. Is this loss of cells in senile dementia a disorder of a later stage of development where editing, not addition, is the dominant feature? That is just one of the many reasons why so many people around MBL are studying developmental processes in biology, trying to learn the normal rules of the game so as to better understand how things go wrong.

When one sees a process in biology, such as cell proliferation, one is almost sure to see one or more additional processes, such as cell editing, that oppose it. Everything is usually a tug-of-war, with net movement occurring only when strengths no longer balance. Yet the two opposing processes are seldom symmetrical like the tug-of-war with a dozen people on each end of the rope: In biology you find situations more like a winch being used on one end of the rope, people on the other. Push and pull often come about in different ways, and it may not be obvious what is being "balanced."

We learn . . . that there's a utility in death because . . . the world goes on changing and we can't keep up with it. If I have any disciples, you can say this of every one of them, they think for themselves.

the pioneer neuroscientist WARREN S. McCULLOCH

EDITING CONNECTIONS during childhood is a much less destructive process than the loss of entire cells during prenatal development or senile dementia. What we are talking about here is not nerve cells dying, but selectively breaking half the interconnections between cortical nerve cells.

As we grow up, we lose close to half of all the interconnections in our cerebral cortex—we gained connections until about eight months after birth, but after that comes this net loss. It can be even worse for some long-distance connections; e.g., the connections between the monkey's left brain and right brain decline by 70 percent between birth and sexual maturity. Mammalian brains have connections from all areas of cerebral cortex to the spinal cord at birth but, by maturity, all have been withdrawn except for those from the usual somatosensory, motor, and premotor cortical areas.

That is a lot to lose; if you'd told me (or any other neurophysiologist) this fact maybe two decades ago, I wouldn't have believed it. Nerve cells seem to start out by making lots of connections with other nerve cells (not quite "everything is connected to everything," but much more widely than anyone thought)—and then something edits them, disconnects quite a few, shaping up the child's mind by whittling away. There's an important principle here: Make lots of overlapping connections, then narrow them down somewhat—but not all the way down to unique "labeled lines." The necessity for such a disconnection principle was recognized a quarter-century ago by a philosopher, Daniel C. Dennett, in his 1965 doctoral dissertation at Oxford; he even recognized the analogy to biology's pre-Darwin convergent selection:

> What is needed is for some intra-cerebral function to take over the evolutionary role played by the exigencies of nature in species evolution; i.e., some force to extinguish the inappropriate. . . . This would have the effect of pruning the initially unstructured connections along lines at least compatible with and occasionally contributory to the appropriate inherited links already endowed by species evolution. . . .
>
> The process is a repeated self-purification of function, gaining in effectiveness as more and more not inappropriate structure becomes established.

Least destructive of all would be simple modifications in the strength of the synaptic connections between cells, being able to diminish the strength to nothing without actually disconnecting it (a "silent synapse"). Maybe physical disconnection is one way of "fixing" the memories encoded by such reductions-to-nothing; if the connection remains physically there, some future retuning of the system might destroy the old memory that relied on the weak connection.

So there seem to be a variety of ways of editing brains: killing whole cells (as happens in prenatal development and senile dementia, and possibly in songbirds that learn a new song every year), disconnecting some interconnections between selected cells (as happens during the tuning-up to the environment seen in childhood), and simple increases and decreases in synaptic strengths (as certainly happens in short-term memory throughout childhood and adult life). Long-term memories, of the multitrial varieties we call schemas, likely involve both altered synaptic strengths—and sometimes the creation of additional synapses by an existing cell budding off a new axon branch and attaching to another cell.

New synapses? All that the childhood halving of synaptic numbers in cerebral cortex means is that there is a difference between the rate at which new connections are being made and the rate at which old synapses are being disconnected. Up to eight months after birth in humans, the creation rate exceeds the destruction rate; afterward, slightly more are disconnected than new ones are formed. But no one knows how many synapses are being destroyed in the average week: All we know is the cumulative difference between creation and destruction rates, which yields a 35 to 50 percent loss during childhood. We have no way of tracking individual cortical synapses over time in a given animal, though brain-imaging techniques that visualize proteins involved in making new synapses should eventually give us a clue about creation rates. Sprouting to make brand-new connections gives us an additional process to modify for memory's sake: We have little idea of how frequently this happens in adult life, or if there are favored sites for sprouting, or how it might be regulated.

Worrying about fixing snapshot schema may, of course, be needless: There is no evidence that humans were designed by evolution to be faithful recorders of events. It is true that one-trial learning exists, particularly for the tastes of foods that make you sick. But there is nothing about that which says that the memory must remain forever fixed. Modification is probably the rule, not the exception.

Nothing seems more possible to me than that people some day will come to the definite opinion that there is no copy in the . . . nervous system which corresponds to a particular thought, or a particular idea, or memory.

the philosopher LUDWIG WITTGENSTEIN (1889–1951)

Information is not stored anywhere in particular. Rather, it is stored everywhere. Information is better thought of as "evoked" than "found."

the cognitive scientists DAVID RUMELHART and
DONALD NORMAN, 1981

POINT-TO-POINT REPRESENTATION is the notion that maps are connected in orderly ways, as by a pipeline from the tip of your little finger to your somatosensory cortex's little finger region. Or from a photoreceptor on the retina to the corresponding place in the visual cortex's map of the visual world that "represents" that direction from the eye. I suppose that it was reasonable to expect this, but we've known for a long time that it wasn't that simple. For example, the visual world is represented by several *hundred* million photoreceptors in the two eyes, but they have to get funneled down into several million optic-nerve axons. So, we said, maybe the fine grain is only several million points instead.

But then it turned out that we can detect line spacings that are finer than the spacing between photoreceptors (what is called "hyperacuity"): We're even better than hundreds of millions! How can this be? It is because "Mexican hat" committees do the job, not pipelines. It is a population of cells at work, not just a single cell lighting up while the others keep quiet.

The only way to understand how information is stored in the brain may be to understand what the information is being used for; that's always been obvious for learning new skills but isn't so clear for our more detached kinds of knowledge such as words. Certainly for the more familiar kinds of computers, you need not understand the program to understand storage techniques—but processing and storage are all mixed up in nervous systems. The brain circuitry that analyzes the information is likely to be used to store it as well. So all that pruning of synapses is likely to subserve an analysis or performance function as well as a storage function. If many-to-many is the circuitry connecting sensory and performance regions of the nervous system, rather than many-to-one-to-many, we will simply have to learn to think in population terms—just as Darwin did when contemplating transformations of one animal species into another.

The most familiar transformations in our everyday experience are associated with hearing: the treble and bass controls on a radio that augment or reduce the high and low ends of the spectrum. Some hi-fi setups even have equalizers so that a half dozen different parts of the spectrum can be adjusted separately. You transform what's really there into an altered version that is more pleasing. The brain is doing such transformations, and adjusting them, all the time—but internally, without twiddling knobs.

Our nervous system is indeed in the business of transforming things, not in the TV camera's "faithful reproduction" business. Sometimes what you see doesn't correspond perfectly to what you feel touching the same objects (so which is "reality"?). What we "see" when we look at a seashore scene is not what a TV camera would record—it is subtly different because of the transformations taking place that help extract the information our brains need to make decisions.

Some of the differences from reality are simply called "illusions," as they are unwanted side effects of the processing: Look at a waterfall for a moment, at the waves of water tumbling down, and then look at the trees nearby. The trees will seem to be moving upward! Look between your fingers at a bright light: You will see some little black lines partway between your fingers. They are not interference fringes but illusions called Mach bands, a side effect of a contrast enhancement transformation that occurs at several levels of visual processing in eye and brain. When we say we "see" something, we are simply reporting on one intermediate stage of a multistage set of transformations—probably just the stage that is accessible to our language cortex.

The transformations aren't always the same: They are adjusted as conditions alter. In the moonlight, one can see pretty well (though in monochrome). But try to read a newspaper in such light and you'll discover that the type is indistinct, as if irredeemably out of focus. Try to catch a thrown ball at dusk, and you'll discover that your visual images are too slow to keep track of ball position. The retina has readjusted some of the inhibitory mechanisms in the retina that enhance both spatial and temporal resolution, choosing to improve low-light sensitivity at their expense. If you were missing those spatial and temporal transformations in the daylight, you wouldn't be able to either read or catch balls: What we normally "see" is enhanced in some respects, degraded in others, and has unrealistic features added. So much for "reality"!

And, of course, different animals are tuned up in different ways. Those primitive *Limulus* wandering around offshore have about 10 eyes, positioned at various strategic points around that horseshoe-shaped shell (including one on the tail that specializes in day-night rhythms!); most of the eyes probably use inhibition for contrast enhancement. And *Limulus* is extraordinarily good at detecting faint shadows even in moonlight, even when two stories deep offshore Stony Beach. Robert Barlow, a second-generation neurobiologist who studies lateral inhibition at MBL (in neurobiology, one can trace genealogies back to just a few pre-1940 workers: Barlow was a student of Keffer Hartline's, whereas my wife and I are third-generation neurobiologists, both students of another student of Hartline's, Charles F. Stevens), says he can swim around in scuba gear at the full moon, and when his dim shadow falls across a *Limulus* on the dark bottom, the animal will change course. He can make it crawl along a zigzag course by simply casting a shadow on its left side, then its right side, etc.

I JUST SAW A FISHING BOAT return with a whole class of MBL students packed into its stern, standing room only. I can't believe they collected anything, as they were only out one hour. And there wasn't room for any fishing gear on the stern, so tightly packed was it with students. Sightseeing? Well, at least they saw the salt water from a boat—that's more marine experience than most students get here these days.

MBL is an oddity among marine stations: The staple course taught by nearly all marine labs is comparative invertebrate zoology. But it's not taught at MBL anymore. At other marine research stations, the tide tables are prominently posted and the researchers are likely to go out and collect their own animals from one or another of a fleet of small boats tied up at the dock. Life at such labs revolves around the tides. One sees rubber boots, set out to dry alongside the special nets and traps, diver's tanks and weighted belts lying out on the docks, instructions posted about how to reach the nearest decompression facility in case struck by the "bends." But the Marine Biological Laboratory is rather urban: The animals appear in aquarium tanks, delivered by ex-fisherman employees. With the exception of some people such as Bob Barlow, if you asked the typical MBL researcher when the best low tide of the season was going to be, you'd draw a blank stare. Or maybe, "What tides?" The MBL is now "marine" only at one remove for many of the researchers.

Some of the research at MBL could now be done in the middle of New York City with the animals delivered by air freight in Styrofoam picnic chests—an option that was not available in MBL's formative years. There are still many notable exceptions to that statement, such as the biophysics done on the fragile squid and the developmental biology on various eggs of marine organisms, and that research remains the hard core of MBL biology. But there are certainly some researchers around here who could get by on ice chests and couriers.

So why do they continue coming to Woods Hole? MBL is an expensive item for most researchers, not only for their supporting budgets but personally, as the housing around here is (thanks to the better-paid Boston bankers competing for it) so expensive that researchers' savings accounts suffer. It can't be scenery—going to the beach is far easier and cheaper elsewhere on the East Coast, and the people who come here to work typically go elsewhere for serious vacations. So what is the real reason that so many researchers still go to all the trouble of crating up their labs, suffering with the rental truck, the sore back, and the equipment that inexplicably stops working when disturbed—and then repeating the tasks several months later?

It's that MBL is, scientifically, a very special place quite aside from the setting and the animal availability that were associated with its origins. You learn important things here in three weeks, things that you'd seldom learn back home or at a convention center meeting amid 10,000 milling scientists. People are set up and working here; you can get a demonstration of something 10 minutes after you hear about it, check things out in the extensive library after lunch, and try the modification out on your lab rig that afternoon. The rumor mill in techniques and preliminary results is a fundamental part of doing science, even if it is hard to document. Its buildings and animals are vital, but it is as a social institution that MBL is so influential in biological science. No other marine lab has a comparable level of free exchange of important ideas, certainly not built into its basic program of courses, conferences, and rich diet of special lectures.

One of the pleasures of summer in Woods Hole is the breadth of evening lectures not only on science but on art, history, and public affairs. There are concerts several times a week (the philosopher Geoffrey Hellman just played the Brahms Intermezzo in B minor last night as the encore to a superb piano concert of Mozart, Berg, and Beethoven). "Try to learn something about everything, and everything about something" was Thomas Henry Huxley's epitaph; he would have liked Woods Hole.

What Woods Hole has now is, I suspect, partly a legacy of generations of nonworking wives with a lot of time and energy to organize. This was a form of scaffolding, now largely removed as most educated women pursue their own careers, but historians may come to see educated nonworking wives (and the occasional nonscientist husband of an MBL researcher) as essential intermediaries for the present cultural milieu of Woods Hole, what makes the social life here more than a place to meet people, more than the usual buffer to diffuse fatigue and hostilities. They've created a milieu that makes learning something about everything extend well beyond its usual liberal arts boundaries, and often bridge C. P. Snow's two cultures with grace. The number of families around here with second- and third-generation scientist-physician-musicians is one indicator of its success.

Buildings are buildings, but this feat of social engineering was far harder to achieve. And it is potentially fragile, capable of being wiped out by empire-building government agencies who want to keep "their people" on a short leash tied to Washington, D.C., or by an economy-minded Congress bent on cutting costs by consolidating facilities for "efficiency." MBL has no institutional backing—it's an independent nonprofit corporation owned by its 700 scientist members, and its finances are always worrisome. But places like MBL are not defense contractors producing products, or even designers with a definable output in terms of blueprints—they are think tanks, first and foremost. In the physical sciences, think tanks require an office building, lots of salary money, and much computer time. MBL just happens to be a bioscience think tank that instead requires a small fleet of fishing boats and a battalion of librarians.

WHAT KINDS OF TRANSFORMATIONS take place in brains? Perhaps they will help us understand the brain's versions of blueprints and libraries and computing. The sensory-processing examples are the best known transformations: While vision's lateral inhibition is perhaps the best studied, the same principles are seen in skin sensation and hearing. Most exhibit a version of those Mexican hat arrangements where one region is excitatory but a surrounding wider region is inhibitory, leading to an optimal spot size—any larger and the cell becomes uninterested.

In the moonlight, such inhibition is turned off in some mammalian eyes (certainly cats and probably ours as well) to increase sensitivity—another one of the things that Stephen Kuffler discovered. After our eyes adapt to darkness, big spots of light are even more effective than the formerly optimal-sized spots—the cell can no longer tell what size a spot is. Which is why you can no longer read anything with a less-than-headline-sized typeface in the moonlight. After all, in such dim light, a photoreceptor has to give a detectible response to a single photon—whereas in daylight it is bombarded by a million times as many. Inhibitory surrounds are one way of regulating sensitivity over that millionfold range.

Originally we called this "surround inhibition." But then those inverted Mexican hat cells were discovered with excitatory surrounds and inhibitory centers—so we began to talk instead about "center-surround antagonism," or simply "lateral inhibition." Whatever you call it, it's seen at virtually every level of the visual system, from retina to secondary cortical areas. The skin senses use it. Hearing uses it; a cell maximally sensitive to middle C may be inhibited by tones a half-octave above or below. Lateral inhibition's contrast-enhancing transformations require a broad wiring, each cell receiving excitation from a wide area, and inhibition from an even wider area. Or vice versa.

So is this related to the "everything is connected to almost everything" wiring of prenatal development, with pruning of far-flung connections used to narrow the connections down to a cone? Probably. Certainly the basic center-surround architecture is present by birth in the primate visual system. For at least four stages of processing, each cell's view of the world is from a funnel of

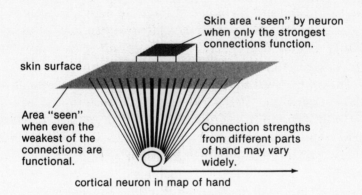

Skin area "seen" by neuron when only the strongest connections function.

skin surface

Area "seen" when even the weakest of the connections are functional.

Connection strengths from different parts of hand may vary widely.

cortical neuron in map of hand

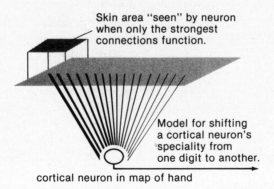

Skin area "seen" by neuron when only the strongest connections function.

Model for shifting a cortical neuron's speciality from one digit to another.

cortical neuron in map of hand

converging inputs. The same thing is true of skin sensation: a funnel of excitation, a wider funnel of inhibition. In theory, this should mean that the higher-order cells back in the brain receive from ever-widening areas of skin surface, and potentially can respond to half the body surface (if all the inhibitory surrounds are turned off at each stage!).

REMEMBER THAT CORTICAL MAPS are maps based on the estimated centers of cortical-cell receptive fields, not on their total size (much less their potential size!). If all the inhibitory surrounds are working full strength, receptive-field centers will seem small, and a center point easy to define. And so it won't be too much of an exaggeration to say that there is a point-to-point correspondence of the skin (or retinal) surface to the cortical surface—that we may, in short, talk meaningfully of a cortical "map" of the sensory surface. *But if all the inhibition were turned off, the "map" might be pretty hard to detect because of the gross smear of anatomical connections, almost half of the total sensory surface potentially converging upon each cortical cell.*

This widespread anatomical basis for the much narrower functional specialization is the reason why a cortical cell can shift function, coming to specialize in a different finger than it formerly did. Everyone thought that cortical maps were pretty fixed—maybe they are different in different individuals, but that they were fixed during the lifetime of an individual. But in the 1980s, we were all shocked to hear (from Michael Merzenich, Jon Kaas, Randy Nelson, and their colleagues) that somatosensory cortical maps were a day-to-day affair, changing size if the hand was exercised more; if a particular fingertip was regularly rubbed on something (say, a casino croupier always fingering the deck of cards with his forefinger), more cells in the somatosensory cortex would come to specialize in that finger. And conversely, the size of the average receptive-field center for a cell specializing in that finger would become smaller.

Usually when this happened, the new forefinger cells would come from cells that formerly specialized in adjacent fingers—but sometimes from cells that formerly specialized in the face! The face's connections to such versatile cells were turned down to

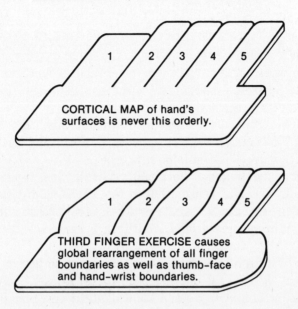

CORTICAL MAP of hand's surfaces is never this orderly.

THIRD FINGER EXERCISE causes global rearrangement of all finger boundaries as well as thumb-face and hand-wrist boundaries.

nothing, while the forefinger's connections were enhanced—and so a "retrained worker"!

But they also noticed that some changes in cortical boundaries seemed to occur spontaneously from week to week, even though the monkey wasn't being trained and was just moving about his cage. For example, the boundary between face and hand cells in cortex moved from week to week, back and forth— some weeks, the cells near the boundary were face specialists, other weeks the very same cells were thumb specialists. To neurophysiologists, this was approximately as if you had told us that the state line between California and Oregon was moving a few miles back and forth from week to week for no apparent reason.

When the researchers trained monkeys to hold one forefinger against a vibrating surface, they observed threefold increases in the number of cortical cells specializing in the tip of that forefinger. But the other finger boundaries shifted as well. When "California" was overly exercised, the California–Oregon boundary shifted—but so did the Oregon–Washington and Washington–Canada boundaries! The whole hand map rearranged itself to accommodate the fingertip exercise; the expansion wasn't just at the expense of the immediate neighbors in the usual boundary-dispute manner. Furthermore, it wasn't just the other fingers that were squeezed; much of the expansion was at the expense of the face and wrist representations, as the total "hand" enlarged. Historical trends may have remade the map of Europe over the centuries, but whatever remakes cortical maps can be much quicker. One almost has to think of maps as ephemeral, about as permanent as the arrangement of papers atop my desk.

So learning to play the piano probably does remake your brain, in a very real sense. But so too might almost any other activity that repeatedly stimulates a hand (or, presumably, foot). I told an anthropologist friend about this, because she always goes barefoot—her feet receive much more detailed sensation that way than when encased in a shoe. Does that increase her foot representation at the expense of other body parts? Does it decrease her other sensory abilities? No one knows yet. Is this plasticity why many stroke victims get much better in the weeks and months after their strokes, with uninjured regions of cortex taking over the jobs originally done by the injured cortex? Is this why blind people can hear more acutely? Tune in next year.

CORTICAL MAPS ARE EPIPHENOMENA anyway, since they serve no known purpose other than as guides to the neurophysiologist in the placement of recording electrodes. It is the nerve cells themselves, like the industries of a city, that are the functional pieces; while street maps do serve a function for strangers to the city, I cannot think of a comparable function served by the brain maps we produce. What is so interesting about these ephemeral maps is that they indicate that there is a lot of retraining of workers in the brain, that the number of cells assigned to a task (such as analyzing sensation from the forefinger) can be modified on a week-to-week (and probably a day-to-day) basis.

And most of the plasticity seems to be at the cortical level; the maps of the fingers in the monkey's thalamus, the relay station just before cortex, are not altered in a similarly dramatic way. The thalamic nerve cells specializing in the forefinger, however, seem to send axon branches all over the hand region of somatosensory cortex, not just to the forefinger's current patch of cortex. This is what probably allows the rapid retraining of a cortical cell: It just switches from suppressing everything except forefinger to suppressing everything except thumb. Those cells that switch back and forth between thumb and face presumably have anatomical connections from both, with one or the other set suppressed. The alternative explanation, that the thalamic axons sprout new connections and that the old synapses disconnect, is not ruled out—but the rapidity of the changes is faster than such sprouting processes usually happen in the nerves to muscle.

Dynamic remapping, going on all the time, suggests that there is an ongoing competition of some sort that results in the work getting spread around to the available workers. Rather than a lifetime structure, it may be more like a free-wheeling economy—perhaps a certain rate of neural unemployment is used to make sure niches are explored and filled. Are there monopolistic practices, used to seize power and keep down the newcomers? Is there some central direction, a circulating hormone that functions like a 5-year plan to steer migrant workers in some directions more than others?

And while economic analogies are perhaps more familiar, it seems likely that the true analogies are going to be to things even more primitive than economics: self-organization, darwinian evolution, and ecosystems. The familiar computer analogies to which we retreat when seeking an analogy for brain functioning seem totally inappropriate: Computers have a memory that is kept separate from the processor; they do what they are told to do, rather than seeking out new niches.

Ever since Darwin and Wallace, we've known that we need to understand evolutionary principles in order to understand how we came to be, that long road from monkey to ape to hominid to human. For almost as long, the analogies between ontogeny and phylogeny have made us aware that darwinian-like processes (such as all that prenatal cell death) are a major part of getting from fertilized ovum to an adult. But now it looks as if anyone who wants to understand day-to-day brain functioning (the nature of perception and cognition, the basis of memory, the organization of behavior) had also better bone up on Darwin.

What we call a mind is nothing but a heap or collection of different perceptions, united together by certain relations and suppos'd, tho' falsely, to be endow'd with a perfect simplicity and identity.

DAVID HUME (1711–1776)

Philosophy has succeeded, not without a struggle, in freeing itself from its obsession with the soul, only to find itself landed with something still more mysterious and captivating: the fact of man's bodiliness.

FRIEDRICH NIETZSCHE (1844–1900)

9

OF ARMS RACES
IN CHURCH GARDENS:
THE SIDE STEP
AND EVOLUTION'S
OTHER BYWAYS

What may be the only Roman Catholic church belltower in which the bells are named after biologists stands in a garden beside Eel Pond, the landlocked cove that, ventricle-like, is surrounded by the seaside village of Woods Hole on Cape Cod. One bell is called Pasteur, the other Mendel, and presumably they represent an attempt at a modus vivendi between St. Joseph's, the parish they belong to, and the four great marine biological institutions that stand nearby. . . .

the neurobiologist THEODORE MELNECHUK, 1980

The Bell Tower Garden is just a block from MBL, around the shores of Eel Pond. Two great bells ring out the Angelus three times a day: morning, noon, and evening (if you hear the bells at any other time, there's probably a wedding in St. Joseph's Church across the street). Surrounding the bell tower is a garden, a pleasant place in which to read or write, or just walk around trying to clear one's head.

The east end of the garden is patterned after the medieval church gardens of flowers and herbs that monks cultivated for their beauty and usefulness. Here grows *Digitalis purpurea*, which the Catholic Church calls "Our Lady's Glove," and most gardeners call foxglove. It is a medicinal plant, containing digitalis; it is used to treat heart failure, as it strengthens and deepens the beat if given in small quantities (in larger quantities, digitalis is a poison).

And, of course, its usefulness as a poison is what prompted its evolution, what with the perpetual arms race between the plants and the insects. I know that the Catholic gardeners who labor here probably tell the story of the plants in the garden rather differently, but it is also useful to tell the scientific story of them as, in part, deadly devices. Because that story leads to evolutionary mechanisms in general, the emergent properties of compounded mechanisms, and even to consciousness considerations.

To ward off the insects, many plants have developed defenses: sticky flytraps like amber (which have incidentally preserved 50-million-year-old insects, looking remarkably like modern species in some cases), heart-stopping or hallucinogenic drugs, agents that coagulate the blood (or, like garlic, prevent its coagulation), and all manner of diabolical devices. Except for the grasses (which mostly do without protection) and the fruits (which mostly want to be eaten, so as to have their seeds deposited several days later at some distance away, in the midst of a nice helping of fertilizer), most edible plants incorporate something disagreeable to some species that eats them. Cooking is the best invention yet for inactivating such toxins (the heat breaks up the proteins into shorter segments), though genetic engineering may have something to say on the subject soon (imagine stirring some enzymes into food during preparation that bind to the harmful molecules and render them harmless).

It is surprising in light of this evolutionary perspective that more people don't get sick from eating plants raw. Some "allergies" are probably just normal reactions that many people do not exhibit in florid form, causing them to be viewed as exceptions rather than rules.

But some plant defenses may just have delayed effects on reproductive fitness rather than immediate bad taste or sickness: It now turns out that the Guam and Rota Island variants of Alzheimer-type dementia, Parkinsonism, and amyotrophic lateral sclerosis (a degenerative spinal cord disorder) are probably all due to eating the seeds of the false sago palm (*Cycas circinalis* L.) pounded into flour, a traditional food that was eaten by some natives when rice was very scarce during World War II. And so researchers are now looking at the more common versions of Alzheimer's dementia, Parkinsonism, and other degenerative diseases to see if they too were triggered by foods. Thus, our environmental-contamination problems (all the lead, radon, carbon monoxide, etc.) may have to be viewed against the natural background of all the accumulated plant toxins that we consume. I do love spicy food, but spices would also top my list of potential neurotoxins that ought to be investigated.

The insects presumably suffered similar tribulations in their hard times when food was scarce and they ate 10 times more than usual of a plant toxin. The insects may not have invented cooking, but they have evolved other ways around the defenses: long feeding tubes that allow the insect to sup from a distance, digestive enzymes that inactivate the toxins, etc.

Then the plants up the ante, usually with a new toxin. Armaments races started a long time ago.

The social addiction to armaments races is not fundamentally different from individual addiction to drugs. Common sense urges the addict always to get another fix. And so on.

the anthropologist GREGORY BATESON, 1979

UNLIKE THE CURRENT HUMAN ARMS RACE, the ancient one between the plants and the insects is potentially very beneficial to humans. The insects have become a fascinating repository of knowledge: If one wanted to find a natural anticoagulant to use with stroke patients who have plugged up an artery, one might try to find a plant that uses a coagulant as its defense, then find the insects that still successfully feed on that plant and see what anticoagulants they produce. Some such insect anticoagulants may work only with that particular coagulating agent, but others may be more generally useful.

Of course, we are exterminating insect and plant species at a prodigious rate, which some future generation is going to want in order to solve such health problems, or the problems of agriculture. They're likely to view our thoughtless destruction of this genetic library about the same way as we view the book-burners of history.

THE PLANTS certainly did not acquire their toxins by foresight, analyzing the situation and then going down to the store and buying the right product. We humans "think things through," and so tend to assume that it is the only way, that some convenient god must have done the thinking for the plant.

But Darwin's explanation of evolution changed all that, made it clear how random variations that yield small advantages can shape up a new function over a long period to give some results similar to insightful planning. We call these "adaptations" to the environment. When some mammals such as whales and dolphins returned to the sea, they gradually lost their hair and gained a new layer of subcutaneous fat that replaced the hair's thermal insulation and also streamlined the waterfoil—those are adaptations that occurred simply because there were variations in hair and fat, and some variants produced more surviving offspring than others.

Some of us think that humans too went through an aquatic phase (maybe about 5 million to 7 million years ago, just before the savannah phase) where we lost most of our hair and gained an unapelike layer of subcutaneous fat. One likely way of producing such adaptive features would have been via making our living wading around in shallow waters looking for crabs and shellfish, and diving for them offshore in hard times. We certainly do have an unapelike fascination with shorelines, as witness the beaches and waterfront houses around here. And all those boats floating in Eel Pond, just beyond the boundary hedge of the Bell Tower Garden.

And a fascination with shorebirds. It seems that Eel Pond has only one cormorant for most of the summer, with a second one later in the season. The two current inhabitants are certainly friendly: I just saw them sharing a perch on the same buoy. One had its wings spread, the other standing unruffled—and from the angle I saw them, it looked just as if one had its arm around the other's shoulder. Then they both spread their wings to dry, and managed not to hit one another.

They seem to be the double-crested cormorant, *Phalacrocorax auritus;* apparently they go south for the winter, though perhaps only as far as New York. Finally, one left its post. This consisted of hopping into the water, swimming a short distance (and looking considerably more buoyant than earlier, when it cruised with only its neck out of the water), and then diving, producing only a few ripples to mark the spot it disappeared. Some cormorants dive from high cliffs when they spot a fish, others simply cruise underwater.

Despite a lack of oil glands of the kind that ducks use to preen their feathers with waterproofing, the cormorants look sleek. Small wonder that the cormorants have to spend so much time above water, drying their wings. On rainy days, when wings take a long time to "reset," they probably can't go fishing as often as on a sunny, warm day. Another little imperfection of evolution: Natural selection may have adaptively streamlined the shape of the cormorant's body, but missed out on waterproofing. Maybe the right variations never occurred; they are, after all, not totally random, but constrained by everything from where chromosomes break easily to the spatial and temporal matchups that occur during development.

But adaptations aren't the only way of changing functionality, though you'd think that was so from reading some of Darwin's latter-day followers ("ultradarwinists"). Yet Darwin himself emphasized two major ways in which species change without natural selection shaping adaptations up: sexual selection (the male peacock's tail was shaped up by female preferences, not environmental peculiarities) and "conversions of function" (where new functions emerge without anatomical change). And he noted that competition within the species may be minor after the discovery of what we now call a "new niche"—and that may allow a lot of drift away from the preexisting body form and behaviors.

The most powerful and prominent processes of competition in the real world may not be competition to occupy a fixed set of niches, but processes of specialization and niche elaboration. Hence we don't have to adopt a picture of the world that is all tooth and claw.

the computer scientist HERBERT A. SIMON, 1983

EVOLUTION is full of surprises. I don't mean the funny-shaped animals, like flounder or angler fish, that readily evoke an exclamation or laugh. I'm referring to the improbable ways that evolution has of doing things, the surprising paths taken by evolution that violate all the stereotyped notions about progress. Sometimes evolution isn't the slow grind, meandering along, continuously editing random variations into ever-better versions.

Slow but sure is the popular image of darwinism, but evolution really isn't very efficient. It's full of dead ends, which require backing up biologically in order to "make progress." Then there's coevolution, such as arms races. And most surprising of all, biological evolution sometimes takes a sideways leap to tread a novel path.

If all this is news to you, that's a commentary on the sad state of education. Such surprises are seldom conveyed by harassed schoolteachers, coping with creationist snipers and with compromising textbooks that endeavor to mention evolution in as few words as possible, perhaps in an optional section at the rear that is never reached before the end of the school year. Real biologists teach evolution integrated with all of biology, the common thread that unites molecules, microbes, monkeys, and men. Without that thread, biology can become an endless list to be memorized rather than the greatest adventure of all time. To a biologist, nothing makes any sense without evolution having occurred (but such professional opinion also seldom makes it into the laundry-list-like texts). If you've heard of any one of these surprises (none of which is particularly new; even Darwin emphasized the side-step-like "functional change in anatomical continuity"), count yourself lucky or well read.

Most people do, however, have a good working notion of how cultural evolution operates, just from watching the world around them change. And that provides a shortcut (albeit a somewhat hazardous one) to appreciating similar features of biological evolution such as backing up and sidestepping.

- We've seen novel words introduced into the vocabulary— and their typical fate, though some survive several decades.

- We've seen new products competing in the marketplace, many of them (breakfast cereals, soft drinks) simple variations on a theme in search of an advantage.

- We've seen old species of fasteners (anyone remember the diaper pin?) replaced with tape and Velcro. "Bailing wire and sealing wax" seem to have been replaced by battleship-gray duct tape.

- We've seen vestigial features (those nonfunctional buttons on men's sleeves without matching buttonholes; those buttonholes on their lapels without matching buttons) carried over from an earlier age when they were functional, giving us some analogies to the appendix.

- We've seen patent protection to allow the exclusive right to exploit a new invention for 17 years. There's no such law in biology, but since evolution is a little slow, a *new niche* (usually a specialized elaboration of an old one) is a wonderful thing: There's little competition for a while, and so the competition between members of the lucky species is greatly reduced, allowing various competitive "rules" to be broken—including ones that may have nothing to do with the new-niche discovery.

• We've seen cultural evolution *backing up* occasionally to explore a missed opportunity, as when the technology of ever-more-sturdy adhesives was mellowed to create removable notepaper suitable for temporarily posting reminder messages on doors and telephones. And strippable wallpaper, for those who like to redecorate regularly.

• We've seen cultural *combinations* that arise for one reason prove handy for other (sometimes diametrically opposed) applications. John Calvin imposed on sixteenth-century Geneva "a regimen which included getting up very early, working very hard, and always being concerned with good morals and good reading" (the emphasis on Bible reading instead of sacraments promoted education regardless of birth or wealth). Though more fiercely antiscientific than the Church of Rome (the scientist Servetus was burned at the stake in Geneva, in contrast to Galileo's house arrest), the Calvinist combination of education for all and hard work turned out to be conducive to science in the following century, the Puritans becoming staunch supporters of science.

• We can even see the *side steps* of cultural evolution, new uses for old things: computers invented for number-crunching becoming useful for noncalculating jobs (competing with typewriters and file cabinets, even running assembly lines and wristwatches), the old anti-inflammatory drugs such as aspirin becoming useful for unexpected applications (such as relieving pain and, more recently, preventing blood clots).

We can also see cultural examples of proximate versus ultimate causes: The *proximate* cause of the triumph of a new sugar-coated breakfast cereal may be our sweet tooth, but the *ultimate* cause of that triumph is the early primate's adaptation to eating fruit. When we say "smoking causes lung cancer," we are talking of a proximate cause; the ultimate cause has more to do with evolution not having prepared us for long-term insults (if we are going to aspire to live beyond menopause, we'll have to devise our own protections). People are always confusing levels of explanation—even scientists, as when *fin de siècle* geneticists claimed that it was mutations, not darwinian selection, that caused evolution—and so caused the eclipse of darwinism for nearly four decades until everyone agreed that both were involved. There are usually many causes—whenever you hear a choice posed ("It's either this or that"), remember it could be both or neither.

But, handy though cultural change may be for illustrating the *themes* of biological evolution, cultural analogies rapidly lead one astray when thinking about the *mechanisms* of biological evolution. It is downright hazardous to think of biological evolution using mechanistic analogies from cultural change, largely because biology doesn't pass on skills acquired during your life to your offspring.

Cultural evolution is very Lamarckian, but biological evolution isn't: Your muscle-building doesn't get passed on to your child (nor do one's sedentary habits; forget whatever you heard about legs becoming shorter because we sit around so much). At least not via the genes, only by the example you later provide for the growing child.

> *[There is a] need to distinguish two causations underlying all phenomena or processes in organisms. These have been referred to by earlier authors as proximate and ultimate causations. The proximate causes consist of answers to "how?" questions; they are responsible for all physiological and developmental processes in the living organism, and their domain is the phenotype. The ultimate or evolutionary causes consist of the answers to the "why?" questions, and provide the historical explanation for the occurrence of these phenomena. Their domain is the genotype. . . . Many famous controversies in various fields of biology have been due to a failure of opponents to realize that one of them was interested in proximate, the other in evolutionary, causes.*

the evolutionary biologist ERNST MAYR, 1988

THAT ISN'T TO SAY that culture doesn't influence biological evolution: Indeed, because brains are so innovative, the usual rule is that behavior invents and anatomy changes later. A squirrel may learn to leap between trees via either invention or copying others (that's culture); only later do the perils of leaping manage to select the flabby-skinned variants who stick their legs out to stretch the skin into an airfoil for more efficient gliding. Behavioral innovations thus paved the way for biological changes in flabbiness. Whoever invented sewing set the stage for later natural selection for even more nimble-fingered individuals, at least among those trying to survive winters where drafty clothing was a problem. The environment doesn't somehow "induce" flabbiness or sewing skills; it only selects from the novel variants thrown up by the combination of genes and culture.

Given the usual infant mortality, improved mothering skills are probably the cultural innovations that have had the most feedback into the gene pool for the longest time, enhancing those genes that somehow affect the tendencies to care for the child effectively. You can see the importance of a mother's skills in chimpanzees: Jane Goodall's group has shown that the infant mortality for first-time mothers is much higher than for experienced mothers.

Now chimps aren't noted for innovations (Goodall hasn't seen many new cultural traits arise in a quarter-century of following the Gombe chimpanzees), but you can imagine how an innovation in mothering techniques (say, protecting infants from falls, a significant source of infant mortality in chimps) would cause a big increase in the number of offspring reaching maturity from those mothers whose genes somehow helped them to adopt the innovation. Food-finding skills have strong feedback too (especially in those species that care for their young) but pain-relieving skills have probably had little feedback, since they mostly benefit people who are postreproductive. That weak feedback doesn't make pain-relieving skills unimportant: It just says that there isn't strong biological backup, should culture misplace that information.

Cultural evolution is quicker, but less stable, than the older biological ways of innovation. In biology, there are lots of inheritable variations produced (mostly by shuffling the chromosomes as new sperm and ova are made, rather than via new mutations);

some variants are edited out by the environment, some are passed on in average numbers, and some are associated with successful novelties. Since there is a long period of time between conception and the attainment of reproductive age (the developmental period) in which there is a lot of childhood-disease and happenstance mortality, culture can readily bias which biological variants survive best. But that doesn't pass on culture, only the propensity to be born with certain abilities that could reinvent the cultural practice.

Understanding the interrelation between culture and biology requires appreciating the mechanisms of biological evolution at least as well as those of cultural change. But the popular notions of biological change are largely myths that mislead most people (and often scientists as well).

NATURAL SELECTION is often mistaken for the whole darwinian process. Darwin pointed out that in every generation there is a great overproduction of offspring; only a small fraction can possibly survive to reproduce themselves. Second, all those individuals differ in their genetic endowment, and some will survive better than others in the environment into which they are born. And third, some of those individual differences (though not all) are heritable. Hence a drift to body styles that "fit" the environment (increased fitness, we call it).

While selection plays the role of eliminating the less fit (or giving only the most fit an opportunity to reproduce), the combination of variation and selection, back and forth, is quite creative; it is what is called darwinism. Selection is an optimization process, but without programming; it is simply opportunistic. It only shapes up a local "good enough" optimum, as Darwin noted when he observed that the native flora and fauna of New Zealand, never exposed to much competition in their isolation, had been rapidly replaced by European types brought in by settlers. Darwin saw quite clearly that a fixed type, a Platonic essence, cannot evolve either. Most philosophers, as well as most nonbiologists, have been obsessed with essences and determinism and designers; biology just doesn't work that way.

I have long been an admirer of the octopus. The cephalopods are very old, and they have slipped, protean, through many

*shapes. They are the wisest of the mollusks, and I have
always felt it to be just as well for us that they never came
ashore. . . .*

the anthropologist LOREN EISELEY, 1957

EVOLUTION IS NOT particularly efficient. The eye, often cited
as an example of how a series of adaptations can shape up a truly
magnificent instrument, has a number of stunning flaws that
evolution has not succeeded in fixing, not even over hundreds of
millions of years. Since nearsightedness is so maladaptive in a
considerable percentage of people, why hasn't better focus evolved?
And squeezing the lens in order to focus—that is a truly absurd
scheme compared to the way the octopus lens is moved fore and
aft, just as in a camera (after about 45 years, the human lens
cannot be successfully squeezed into a fatter shape, which is why
I now have to wear half-moon reading glasses). I ask you now—
have you ever seen an octopus who had to wear reading glasses?

And the retina, that hair-thin sheet at the back of the eye
containing the first few way stations of the brain's processing
machinery: The retina is inside-out by any rational design criterion. The light has to travel through four layers of not-so-
transparent nerve cells before ever reaching the photoreceptors
that change light into the first neural messages. Imagine what a
few layers of grease, smeared over the surface of the film in your
camera, would do to the quality of the pictures. The octopus again
does things the right way, the photoreceptors pointing out toward
the pupil with no biological wiring in the way to blur the image.
Vertebrates probably got started doing things the wrong way
when the environment was so muddy that a little additional blurring in the eye wasn't noticeable—and so, like a bureaucratic
procedure that can no longer be modified without changing everything else, we're stuck with the blurring and can only try to work
around it somehow. Fortunately, a fancier brain can correct for
much of the blur—and since the same neural machinery can be
used for other tasks as well, the early wrong-way-round mistake
might be said to have engendered some improvements in overall
abilities of the brain. (Alas, I cannot think of any bureaucratic
equivalents, where starting out with an awkward procedure—say,

for assuring that merchants collect and forward sales tax—has generated an unexpected bonus in the long run.)

Evolution is also not an inevitable consequence of natural selection: Every little bit *doesn't* count. Just as most pain and suffering have little effect on cultural evolution, so most of the episodes of climatic change have had surprisingly little effect on a species' biological evolution. This is at odds with the popular notion of darwinism: gradually getting better and better. Species may be stubbornly stable (this is why "living fossils" are still with us): Even if temporarily perturbed, they can return to their old body forms once the perturbing influence passes.

Complex systems exhibit far more spontaneous order than we have supposed, an order that evolutionary theory has ignored. But that realization only begins to state our problem. . . . Now the task becomes much more trying, for we must not only envision the self-ordering principles of complex systems but also try to understand how such self-ordering interacts with, enables, guides, and constrains natural selection. . . . Biologists are fully aware of natural selection, but have never asked how selection interacts with the collective self-ordered properties of complex systems. We are entering virgin territory.

the biophysicist STUART KAUFFMAN, 1984

Most natural selection is of no lasting consequence—unless quickly followed by an episode that isolates the newly shaped-up gene pool from its relatives, as when the sea rises to make a peninsula into an island, or when a concomitant change in mating habits makes it unlikely that new-fangled and traditional groups will successfully interbreed. Preventing dilution of the new gene pool by others with the traditional genes is the major way in which change is "made permanent" (and, paradoxically, also more likely to quickly succumb, as extinction is the fate of most new species and other small groups). As stock-market investors know, big entities are more stable but also less likely to "strike it rich" via developing new products (multinational merger mania is a prescription for governmentlike rigidity in ever-bigger "big business").

And the other popular notion about evolution is "upward to perfection." This myth was fashionable a century ago, fed by wishful thinking (how to make traditional religious notions "scientific") and by the first two myths. But evolution seems full of dead ends. Indeed, most terminal branches of the evolutionary tree of species lop themselves off.

Yet a closely related observation may, in fact, be true: Organisms get fancier and fancier, capable of dealing with varied environments rather than just one. This seems to be a consequence of evolution being too slow to "track" effectively the frequent back-and-forth changes in climate—and so those variants that are capable of dealing with both old and new climates, with both old and new diets, with both old and new predators, are the ones that survive better. The classic example is intertidal animals, under daily waves of selection for their ability to tolerate both water and air habitats, and so eventually (about 450 million years ago) able to live on land full time—and with a heritage of aquatic-only organs "freed up" for conversions of function.

Another way to accumulate mechanisms is through an arms race. When we discover that the black widow spider's venom contains a whole spectrum of toxins, a baker's dozen, capable of killing us by many different routes, we are glimpsing a bit of the spider's evolutionary history, of adding on additional armaments as a prey develops new defenses. From this, one learns to go looking at the spider's usual and accustomed prey (humans are merely thoughtless intruders, as when a camper forgets to shake out the shoe before inserting his foot) to see how they successfully defended against the first dozen toxins and so prompted the spider to evolve yet another toxin. Such examination of ancient arms races may allow us to mimic their successful defenses, but by using a vaccine or medicine. Evolutionary thinking about such coevolution can be of great practical use.

Progress in science is achieved in two ways: through new discoveries, such as x-rays, the structure of DNA, and gene splicing, and through the development of new concepts, such as the theories of relativity, of the expanding universe, of plate tectonics, and of common descent. Among all the new scientific concepts, perhaps none has been as revolutionary in its impact on our thinking as Darwin's theory of natural selection.

the evolutionary biologist ERNST MAYR, 1988

HOW IS AN EVOLUTIONARY ADVANCE stabilized? Not all are backsliders, at any rate. And in particular, how are side steps stabilized?

Side steps often confer some selective advantage (though not always, e.g., music) and when they do, some streamlining occurs— just as when those ungainly protobirds first started gliding, and then the ones with the more streamlined airfoils got to the food first. This is, of course, why side steps are so hard to see "in action": They are obscured by the streamlining that follows their crude beginnings. Language surely has some selective advantage now, even if it got its start via a side step from secondary uses of something else (a ballistic movement sequencer is my favorite candidate). And the same argument is made for consciousness.

Biology has this roundabout way of doing things that promotes stability in some cases. Unlike culture, which remodels its structures and transmits acquired characteristics directly to the next generation, biology instead builds upon some mixture of the original blueprints—while scrapping the old models (such as you and me; "planned obsolescence" was, alas, invented by biology before Detroit adopted it). Information stored in the genes is more secure against catastrophe, though much less can be stored than via culture's methods.

Information "stored" in everyday practices is terribly dependent on having a teacher, and so some techniques are totally lost when an epidemic sweeps through a small group. Documents, and ways to learn from them, do tend to carry along information over the vicissitudes that cause backsliding in preliterate societies— but just remember what happened to the library at Alexandria, and how the accomplishments of the ancient Greeks were almost completely lost by book-burning. And how most of the documents of the New World were destroyed by the pious Spanish explorer-priests. The folly of a single generation can wipe out culture (and, these days, biology too).

Both cultural and biological evolution "make progress" largely because they happen upon inherent stabilities that reduce backsliding: Jacob Bronowski liked to call this *stratified stability* to emphasize that there were a series of them, each building upon the foundation provided by a previous one. Language was an early human invention of such major proportions; writing's invention 5,000 years ago built upon this foundation by associating a written symbol with an object, as in hieroglyphics, and later with a speech sound. Writing prevented some of the cultural backsliding associated with word-of-mouth errors and "out of sight, out of mind" forgetfulness. In biology, stratified stabilities occurred with replicating molecules, cell envelopes, sexual recombination, and the invention of brains, to name but a few ways. The formation of a new species by a one-month shift in mating season is a prime example of how to prevent backsliding by subsequent dilution as I explained for the Grand Canyon squirrels in *The River That Flows Uphill*.

Understanding how evolution proceeds is important not only for understanding ourselves and from whence we arose, but in assuring that the things which we value in our culture are protected against future backsliding. It looks as if morality has little biological underpinning, and even high cultures (consider how accomplished pre-Nazi Germany was in science, philosophy, theology, history, literature, and the arts—not to mention technology) seem able to lose some essential ingredients rather rapidly. Any underlying principle concerning how innovations become sturdy foundations, capable of supporting new superstructures, is obviously a matter of much importance if other societies are to avoid such backsliding.

THE BREEZE SWITCHED AROUND AGAIN, and that gaggle of sailboats in Eel Pond just followed it around. Societies are sometimes like that too, ready to follow the wind. But usually we act and think individually, or as members of small groups. Sometimes those groups are particularly effective because of the combinations of individuals. Most of the labs at MBL are groups working together, and they get far more done than they would have accomplished individually; other times, personalities will clash and they'll get little done. Picking your co-workers is very important in science; it's hard to imagine how institutions function when they treat co-workers as interchangeable parts, army-fashion.

EMERGENT PROPERTIES may be one of the major sources of innovation in nature. They seem rather unpredictable, obeying no regular rules. But sometimes two mechanisms in combination turn out to have a property that neither had separately.

Some combinations are associated with diminished functionality: For example, having three versions of chromosome 21 rather than the usual two is bad news (*trisomy-21* is better known as Down's syndrome). For most of our genes, we have two identical versions— but for some we are heterozygous, having a different one from each parent. For some genes, such as the Major Histocompatibility Complex, having two different versions from which to choose seems particularly useful (two differing versions probably allows the immune system to fight off a much wider variety of invaders).

And sometimes the particular combination of near-identical genes gives a whole new property, as in the gene combinations that fend off malaria. Most of us have two identical versions (called *SS*) of a gene that affects the shape of red blood cells and thus their fragility. Some people from Africa have the regular dominant one *S* and a recessive version called *s* (so their genotype is called *Ss*), and others inherit *s* from both parents (becoming *ss*). It turns out that the mixed genotype *Ss* is good news (for the individuals carrying it, but not necessarily their children), and that *ss* is bad news, namely sickle-cell anemia (the red blood cell membrane tends to rupture, diminishing oxygen-carrying capacity).

In trying to figure out why the *s* version is still around, given that the people with a double dose of it often die without passing on their genes, biologists discovered that the heterozygous carriers *Ss* were protected against malaria. And so they were better able to grow up and have children, nurture them along up to reproductive age. Half of the offspring from parents who are both *Ss* will themselves be *Ss*, a quarter will be *SS* (and unprotected against malaria), but a quarter will be *ss* (and tend to die of sickle-cell anemia).

So the combination of both *S* and *s* has this emergent property, of protecting against malaria. The *s* is surely another one of those random variations that turned out to be less functional than the original *S*. Most variations are less functional than the original (if they are spectacularly less functional, and thoroughly gum up the works, they may find a role as a toxin in an arms race). But in combination with the original, and then only in places where malaria-carrying mosquitoes live, the combination *Ss* has an unexpectedly nice function.

HYBRID VIGOR is likely another example of combinations of genes being unexpectedly useful. When crossing two species to make a hybrid, many more genes become heterozygous. Again, this is usually bad news: Spontaneous abortions are very frequent in cross-breeding, and so one may get a false impression of vigor just because the bottom half of a distribution never gets born, giving the ones that do a higher average. But sometimes the combinations themselves have new functionality. Like mules (and some of the plants in this carefully tended garden), the hybrids may be sterile and so continue only by continued crossing.

But mostly hybrid vigor is seen when different subpopulations of the same species come to breed again. The "mixed race" individuals are seldom sterile, and their offspring continue to receive gene mixtures. But like genius, which is probably due to a fortunate combination of genes in a single individual, hybrid vigor is difficult to pass on because the combinations are broken up: When sperm and ova are made, the DNA deck is shuffled first, guaranteeing that you get some genes from each grandparent, not just one or the other's chromosomes. Mostly the chromosomes are broken at natural places during the crossing-over phase of meiosis, such as at the end of one gene's DNA sequence, and many genes move as a group (like sticky cards when a deck is shuffled; this increases the chances of inheriting a group of traits together). But newfound combinations of genes, one from each grandparent, usually do not have a newfound stickiness, and so are not reliably passed on together. Thus genius, and many similar inheritability phenomena, is often ephemeral.

The cross-fertilization of ideas is a cliché these days: Suffice it to say that hybrid ideas are easier to form than hybrid species—and that consciousness, insofar as it generates new alternatives and selects among them, is the supreme example of hybrid vigor.

IF MAJOR INNOVATIONS ARE SURPRISES from new combinations rather than predictable-from-the-environment streamlining, then we have to look at nature rather differently from our usual mechanistic approaches. There has always been a certain tension between scientists who reduce everything to properties of the component parts (reductionists), and the people who emphasize that there are different levels of explanation and that the whole is often more than the sum of the parts (in the extreme, called holists).

Though some manage to shift back and forth, alternating viewpoints for a more complete picture, many scientists work completely within one framework or the other. I was trained in a biophysical approach to neurophysiology, which led me from behavior to look at brains, from neural circuits (such as reflexes) to look at individual nerve cells, from looking at cell properties (such as action potentials) to membranes (where dozens of different channel types combine to produce action potentials). Look even closer, and there are electrical gates and molecular sieves controlling the channels, etc. And so on to quantum mechanics.

MBL specializes in such reductionistic science; delving deeper and deeper has produced a lot of valuable insights in the past and it surely will continue to do so. It is also downright addictive: Let a new technique come along that allows finer resolution, and our fingers get itchy. The surest topic for jamming a lecture hall around here is describing a new type of microscope, or a new computerized television system for improving the traditional images. You sit there and say, "I wish I'd thought of that" and then you add, "I've just got to get one of those setups."

Many psychologists were instead trained in a tradition that said the parts were unimportant, that one could treat the brain as a black box. There remain many cognitive scientists today who would claim that it really doesn't matter how the brain implements the algorithm or stores the information, that what's really interesting are the combinations that subserve higher-order pattern recognition (what I use to tell a Winslow Homer painting from an Edward Hopper). Philosophers too tend to ignore the machinery and how it evolved; Gilbert Ryle's *Concept of Mind* manages to avoid the word *brain* entirely.

However, both psychologists and philosophers have the same

tendency to subdivide the problem as physiologists do; they just don't use the natural subdivisions of biology. And so they wind up with separate departments of thinking, feeling, and willing (translated into Freudian terminology: ego, id, and superego). These separate units of mind become enshrined in textbooks as separate chapters on sensation, perception, association, memory, intelligence, reasoning, motivation, imagination, instinct, emotion, personality, etc. When they attempt, if they ever do, to put them all together, they are likely to say something like "consciousness emerges from the sum of all the parts." And the physiologists are likely to jump on them for being vague. Hopefully, we can do better by looking at evolutionary theory and basic neurophysiology, attempting to reformulate the problems in more natural terms.

Still, for all their insistence on "something more" than the "sum of the parts," holists of various stripes (some of which are "more holistier than thou," says Richard Dawkins have been generally unsuccessful at getting a handle on how emergent properties emerge. Surely there are some rules, if only we can find them. The compounding of mechanisms is the clearest aspect: Evolving two different digestive enzymes for breaking down two different plant foods likely gives rise occasionally to an ability to eat some novel third food. But brains are far better at "new uses for old things" than any other organ of the body, thanks to nerve cells having the propensity to reduce everything to so many millivolts and thus establishing a currency for comparing unlike things. Once the new functionality emerges, it will be streamlined by natural selection, and so when we look at it today, we'll see adaptations and not realize their innovative origins.

I suspect that emergents are the crux of brain evolution, and our brain mechanisms for imagination and choice are highly likely to have been shaped by such secondary uses. But having said that, I still have this physiologist's urge to take it apart and understand the pieces too.

SO MY PRIMAL QUESTION about the homunculus at the center of it all isn't likely to be satisfactorily answered by a generality about the narrator emerging as some surprise, as a lot of parts combine to give a new property. Yes, emergents happen; yes, they're probably the real stuff of brain evolution. But the generality—even if proved correct—doesn't save us from understanding the parts and how they work together to produce the emergent narrator. And that will surely involve clarifying how they evolved, the primary uses from which the secondary uses arose.

Was it some sort of arms race in cleverness? Or was the arms race primarily for armaments, and the cleverness secondary? No generality is going to answer this primal question, only a long (and very interesting) story.

I have developed a view of the growth of knowledge—of human knowledge more specifically, but also of animal knowledge—which differs greatly from nearly everybody else's. According to this view, our knowledge is not in the main derived from experience, not even from experience as I see it: the elimination of bad guesses. Most of our knowledge, and animal knowledge, and even vegetable knowledge, is rather the result of sheer invention. . . . All organisms are professional problem solvers: before life, problems did not exist. Problems and life entered the world together, and with them problem solving.

the philosopher KARL POPPER, 1984

10

DARWIN ON
THE BRAIN:
SELF-ORGANIZING
COMMITTEES

Contrary to what I once thought, scientific progress did not consist simply in observing, in accurately formulating experimental facts and drawing up a theory from them. It began with the invention of a possible world, or a fragment thereof, which was then compared by experimentation with the real world. And it was this constant dialogue between imagination and experiment that allowed one to form an increasingly fine-grained conception of what is called reality.

the molecular biologist FRANÇOIS JACOB, 1988

The darwinian competition of ideas, which the nineteenth century identified as a basis of thought, suggests that we might gain some insight about thinking from a study of evolutionary mechanisms that usually operate on long time scales. But in ideas, we are always dealing with a string of words or more elaborate concepts. How do we compare strings? How do masses of nerve cells interact to shape up new concepts from random noise? How do a group of nerve cells get together to initiate a movement?

It's actually not too different from how fancy tools can be shaped up by random bashing about. And how we devise "logical" shortcuts when we want to repeat a success.

DARWINIAN TOOLMAKING is probably the simplest way of making simple stone tools. I just hauled back some potato-sized rocks from the Oyster Pond Beach, all so that I can demonstrate the late Glynn Isaac's toolmaking technique. John Pfeiffer (whose books *The Emergence of Humankind* and *The Creative Explosion* are among the most widely read of anthropology books) is always around MBL in the summer, and we fell into reminiscence the other day about Glynn. John first met him in East Africa when visiting Louis Leakey, and found Glynn in charge of the archaeology (the search for cultural artifacts such as stone tools, as opposed to bones).

Some of the earliest toolmaking methods, even back 2 million years ago when hominids had ape-sized brains, seem based entirely on producing randomness and then selecting the useful. Glynn Isaac used to demonstrate early toolmaking techniques during his archaeology lectures by pounding together two potato-sized rocks, not delicately but furiously: Chips would soon be scattered all over the floor of the stage. After a minute, he would stop and sort through the dozens of stone flakes. And he would pick up some excellent analogs of the single-edged razor blade, just the thing for incising the tough hide of a savannah animal, or amputating a leg at the joint.

The half-potato-shaped fragments left over after the first round of brute bashing will have some sharp edges too, and the smooth part of the remaining rock will serve as a handle, enabling real pressure to be brought to bear, handy for carving harder stuff. All this without notions of design: It serves as a far simpler toolmaking method than our usual notions of careful craftsmanship. Make lots of random variants by brute bashing about, then select the good ones. Careful craftsmanship probably developed where the raw materials were scarce; before then, a different ethic prevailed. Just try to imagine this sign posted in a modern factory:

THE MORE WASTE, THE MORE PROGRESS!

Yet that was probably the philosophy at one time, before planning ahead was well established (and we started throwing away the finished product after only one use!).

Of course, you have to recognize the sharp fragment as useful in order to accomplish the selection step following the random one. So how did hominids get the idea of a sharp tool, so they could select the variant? If this is like the "faces in the driftwood"— children at the beach are always finding driftwood with familiar shapes, such as faces, and are hard to convince that the shape simply happened, wasn't created for their amusement—then we haven't gained much.

But there is clearly a simple way of developing the mental image of a sharp edge as useful. Even baboons and chimpanzees use rocks to hammer on tough nuts, to crack open their shells. And sometimes the rocks split open instead. Thus flakes and handle-sized sharp rocks might be available, just lying around during further nut-cracking. And some might be used as probes á la termite-fishing—but in nut-cracking, one can use them to pry open cracks in tough nuts and so get at the soft innards without the danger of pulverizing the soft innards with further hammering. It seems but a small step from such serendipitous use to the purposeful toolmaking of the kind that Glynn Isaac discovered had been practiced in East Africa—and used at some stage to carve up large chunks of grazing animal—to make protein portable.

Randomness plus selection is powerful, but multiple rounds of it are much more powerful as they can shape up the raw materials into things that look very nonrandom, very purposeful, even designed. Perhaps another round of brute bashing resulted in a flake splitting, two sharp edges intersecting in a point. *Et voilà*, a pointy instrument handy for gouging and other noncutting uses of knives. Among other uses, such intersecting edges make formidable weapons. One naturally thinks of arrowheads, but they came along very late, only during the last Ice Age or perhaps the one before last—but that's because hafting, the attachment to a shaft or wooden handle, seems to have been invented late. So for more than a million years, hominids instead held on to a half-potato-shaped remnant sporting two intersecting sharp edges, and probably treated such a stone dagger as a prized possession.

And given apelike tendencies to imitate, it probably wasn't long before other hominids were making their own stone knives and daggers, lots of handy rocks being sacrificed to the cause. Whether one calls it an arms race or just consumer mimicry not unlike the microscope mania one sees at MBL, it surely generated a lot of rounds of bashing and selecting.

SO IF TOOLMAKING AND BRAINSTORMING look, in their simple forms, like darwinism at work, maybe we had better see how darwinism applies to everything else that the brain does. While species evolution has a millennia-to-eons time scale, perhaps the brain has adopted darwinism in a big way on a seconds-to-days time scale. But what about the details—how does something fancy and logical arise from something random?

Certainly the familiar mechanistic example of darwinism outside of species evolution is how our body's immune system crafts a defense against foreign invaders. Most of us have two different versions of the gene that serves to get the immune system started; additionally, there is probably a lot of gene shuffling during development, which creates a wide variety of templates (attached to antibodies) for recognizing foreign molecules (called antigens) by their shapes. When an antigen comes along, one or another of the specialized B-cells most attuned to that molecular shape will bind it. And this stimulates the B-cell to produce more antibodies: not just clones of itself, but a variety of variations on the same theme. Some of these will be even better at detecting and binding the foreign molecule. And so another generation of variations on the better theme will be produced, some of which will be even better. Pretty soon all of the foreign invaders are bound, and taken out of circulation so they can't do further harm; if the antigens are attached to the surface of a cell like a bacterium, the cell too is destroyed.

And a population of circulating antibodies specialized for that particular foreigner remain in circulation, just in case it comes back. That's how we acquire immunity, why we don't get childhood diseases a second time (or not at all, provided that a vaccine has already stimulated the immune response with a harmless bit of the antigen sometime in the past).

So variation and selection can work fairly quickly to explore the possibilities, even if this antigenic molecule is a completely novel one, never seen before in nature. It's essentially a successive approximation method that homes in on a molecular shape. It is very reminiscent of the Puzzle Principle that Minsky reminds us about:

> We can program a computer to solve any problem by trial and error, without knowing how to solve it in advance, provided only that we have a way to recognize when the problem is solved.

The disappearance of the antigen signals the solution of the problem. We can also think about a problem using similar mental trial and error and, given enough time (which means knowing enough shortcuts!), solve it without knowing in advance how to proceed.

At the mechanistic level, might the brain do something similar to the immune system's variation-and-selection game in a matter of seconds? To fit a schema never seen before? Memorize a telephone number? Explore a creative thought? Or make an awkward movement into a skillful one? Darwinism (particularly the darwinism of committees) turns out to be involved not only in memory, but with how you move your hand—indeed, with how you *decide* to move your hand.

I'm holding my hand out in front of me. It's amazing! I can open and close it! Just like that. No problem. I just decide to do it, and it's done. There's something very strange going on here!

JOHN HOAG, 1987

You move it unconsciously, of course. The interesting thing about that is that you could learn to move it consciously if you went to a lot of trouble.

HOWARD RHEINGOLD, 1987

Well, I remember how hard *it was to get my hand to make fine motor movements. Remember making little circles with a pencil, in first grade? You think it's marvelous that you can move your hand just by wishing to do so, but actually that's the culmination of years of practice and training.*

CORINNE CULLEN HAWKINS, 1987

SAYING THAT THE "MIND" COMMANDS the hand to move really doesn't buy you much of an explanation. It has taken us a while to realize, however, that such a statement is little better than saying, "God did it," when there is an earthquake. Whether one believes in a vengeful, absentminded, or nonexistent deity, there are going to be a series of explanations at different levels. With an earthquake, there is fault-line slippage, which in turn is due to stored energy; that is due in turn to continental drift; due to the molten core of the earth circulating in "cells" not unlike the trade winds in the atmosphere; due in turn to radioactive heating and tidal forces from the moon; due to . . . God? Those are all "explanations" but at different levels.

In the case of this mind drama, we have a series of semi-autonomous actors in the brain, nerves, and muscles. Each has some capacity for spontaneous action, versus some capacity for being told what to do by some upstream agent. Take a muscle fiber: It can spontaneously fire (and thereby twitch), but such pacemaker activity is rare (at least in skeletal muscle; the smooth muscle in the gut walls uses autonomous pacemakers all the time).

Mostly a skeletal muscle fiber simply stays silent until commanded to twitch by its motorneuron, which resides back in the spinal cord; when the motorneuron "fires," an impulse speeds down to the muscle and tells the muscle to twitch. Muscle cramps result from the nerve-muscle junction developing an ectopic pacemaker.

Motorneurons can be pacemakers, too (eyelid "tics" and similar fasciculations; the thumb flexor muscle often develops them as you get older), seemingly doing their own thing despite your attempts to tell them to shut up. Since only one motorneuron does this at a time (and the muscle has hundreds of them), usually the movements produced are small and ineffective.

Each motorneuron responds to its plus and minus inputs, of which it has thousands; a few are feedback from sensors out in the muscle that detect its length and tension, but more than 99 percent are from "interneurons" in the spinal cord and brain. Interneurons are all the neurons except for sensors and motorneurons themselves; an interneuron has no direct connections to the outside world, and is rather like Hartline's general receiving phoned reports of a battle that he doesn't personally witness and issuing instructions to intermediaries. There are more than a million millions of neurons (or maybe 10 times that!), nearly all "interneurons" in the case of primates. There are hundreds of muscles, each of which has hundreds of motorneurons, but that's only tens of thousands of motorneurons maximum. There are maybe a billion sensory neurons, most in the eye. So interneurons outnumber all other neurons by at least a thousandfold.

Another simple numbers game will show just how different we are from an army command hierarchy: Instead of a thousand soldiers for every general, we have a thousand "generals" for every "soldier." With rare exceptions such as the Mauthner cell of a fish, no one interneuron can command an action; they can only act by forming committees, and getting up enough "momentum" somehow.

Perhaps only movement programs with the simplest spatio-temporal patterns can get by with the single command neuron approach to orchestration. The appropriate trigger for most movement programs is likely a keylike combination. It is seldom bottlenecked into a single all-important cell pathway; indeed, it will probably be just as important which cells are inactive as which are active. And unlike a spatial pattern such as key notches, it will be a spatiotemporal pattern like that fireworks finale mentioned in Chapter 8, the order in which various neurons are activated, as well as which neurons are activated, being the adequate stimulus.

So finding the origin of a command for a movement isn't easy, except in trivial cases (cramps, tics, tail flips, fire-alarm-like situations). You're surely going to be talking about a committee of interneurons, not a single entity, when identifying the source of a command to move your hand. So where does this committee live? And how do its members interact to achieve a consensus and implement it?

SERIAL ORDER, per se, is a capability that is widely seen in nervous systems throughout the animal kingdom. Jumping spiders, for example, may spy a prey while standing on one limb of a tree, but need to move over to another limb in order to be directly over the target. The spider will return to the main trunk, drop down along the trunk, go out another limb, select the correct secondary and tertiary branches, and so arrive at a suitable launching platform. But as long as the prey remains visible, that sequence doesn't require a serial-order buffer to hold the moves, as the spider has the time to make a series of judgments, just as I use feedback corrections in picking up a coffee cup and moving it to my lips. Goal plus feedback suffices for most things.

Neuronal networks that generate motor patterns *without* feedback are the real neural networks that have been analyzed in greatest detail. Walking, for example, seems to have such a stored motor program. As does swimming in a leech, or flight in a bumblebee. There are hidden actions as well, such as digestion, that operate with similar neural circuits. Computer simulations have even been done using measured values for individual neuron properties and individual interconnection strengths in the case of the lobster stomatogastric ganglion. It is a small group of 30 identified neurons that controls one of the original assembly lines (whose purpose, however, is disassembly): Sixteen of the 30 cells produce the gastric mill rhythm (lobsters have teeth in their stomachs) for masticating the food, and the other 14 produce the pyloric rhythm that squeezes the stomach contents into the foregut.

The simulations show how the complicated three-phase pyloric rhythm is sequenced, and demonstrate how committee properties emerge. These studies would serve admirably as a guide for how sequential readout from a large neural array (such as our premotor cortex) could be timed.

What you've got to realize is that every cell in the nervous system is not just sitting there waiting to be told what to do. It's doing it the whole darn time. If there's input to the nervous system, fine. It will react to it. But the nervous system is primarily a device for generating action spontaneously. It's an ongoing affair. The biggest mistake that people make is in thinking of it as an input-output device.

the neurobiologist GRAHAM HOYLE (1913-1985)

POSTURAL MOVEMENTS, and even simple kinds of locomotion, are generated at the level of the spinal cord (a brainless cat can still walk on a treadmill). To the extent that hand movements were once part of walking on all fours, they're potentially spinal in origin.

But opening and closing your hand voluntarily—most people would say that the brain commands that, stimulating the motorneurons into a pattern of action. So hand-movement "programs" can be spinal cord alone, or brain commanding spinal cord. To come back to the earlier dualism: Every level of "agents" has the capacity for spontaneous activity *and* also has the capacity for being commanded (or at least persuaded) by other agents. Martin Minsky's *Society of Mind* has a discussion of such collections of agents (though in the curious artificial-intelligence tradition of making up whatever seems useful rather than using the committees known from neurology; the AI folk seem to think that research is a game where it's cheating to look at the cards).

And interneurons are seldom silent for long: Even when we are asleep and motionless, doing minimal sensory processing, most of those thousand billion interneurons are busy talking to one another. Like individually impotent generals trying to build a junta, they are politicking like crazy, all the time. Each one talks directly to about a thousand other interneurons, though more influential with some recipients of their message than with others. About half of interneurons send a predominantly inhibitory message, opposing excitatory recommendations that a target interneuron might receive from its other correspondents.

IF RECOGNITION depends on a committee of neurons, and triggering a movement program also depends on a spatiotemporal pattern of activity in many neurons, then surely our darwinian variation-and-selection games are going to depend on committees too, just as biological darwinism depends on populations changing their characteristics.

But how to think about such a nebulous matter! Reductionism is far easier if you can keep to the agenda. Fortunately there are some analogies that help. The analogies are not to generals and soldiers or executives and departments, but to how we form committees in everyday life.

Consider the usual jury: It is founded on the principle of random selection from among one's peers. It may be shaped up by the challenges allowed lawyers, but it starts random. Some grand juries are not even random from the beginning, but selected by the judge to be citizens with some educational or occupational background, able to comprehend the complexities of a certain kind of crime. Other committees are really panels of experts, people who know all the common mistakes and how to avoid them. Advisory committees are often combinations of experts and community representatives of the grand-juror types. But in all cases, you can form a committee by starting randomly with all possible individuals and then narrowing things down by a series of selections, each based on some criterion.

Committees also have an identity of their own that, in most cases (juries are the usual exception), survives changes in committee membership. Some are even endowed with a legal status: The corporation still remains responsible for actions taken years ago by some now-retired group of directors and employees. Most important, a committee can usually act without all of its members present, without all of them in agreement. Furthermore, an individual may be a member of many committees, most of which have little to do with one another. Such committee analogies provide us with some ways of thinking about cerebral committees of neurons.

Similarly, actions may require a series of permissions from various committees, often in a particular order. For Penzoil to collect $3 billion in damages from Texaco took a whole series of committee decisions prior to the actual transfer of funds by bank wire: A board of directors approved a lawsuit, teams of lawyers argued, a court decided to award $10.3 billion. More lawyers argued, an appeals court decided, then a $3 billion compromise was worked out by a negotiating committee, a court approved, and finally, in 1988, a rather simple action was finally taken. Though involving a record amount of money, it was little different from other decision-making processes with which we are familiar.

Brain committees too are going to have overlapping but non-essential memberships, have to act in sequence or synchrony, reorganize themselves, try again, finally make something happen. If the same action has to be repeated many times, the committee actions may become streamlined, as when routine expenditures for office supplies can come to be authorized at lower levels in a corporation, with only retrospective oversight by other committees.

Our problem is how such cerebral committees get organized and reorganized, how their sequences become determined and occasionally streamlined, and what constitutes "higher authority."

We are accustomed to think of thinking as a linear experience, as when we say "train" of thought. But subconscious thinking may be much more complicated. Just as one has simultaneous visual impressions on the retina, might there not be simultaneous, parallel, independently organized, abstract impressions in the brain itself? Something goes on in our heads in processes which are not simply strung out on one line. In the future, there might be a theory of a memory search, not by one sensor going around, but perhaps more like several searchers looking for someone lost in a forest.

the mathematician STANISLAW M. ULAM, 1976

I must stress how little is yet known about the programs of the brain. The code has not yet been properly broken; but we

begin to see the units of it. . . . We can see that the code is
somehow a matter of sequences of neural activities, provid-
ing expectancies of what to do next.

the neurobiologist J. Z. YOUNG, 1987

THERE'S A PARADE OF BOATS going out of Eel Pond this
morning, quite a collection of big sailboats and small rowboats, all
lined up to pass through the channel one by one. At first I
wondered if it was a regatta, the orderly kind of parade that boat
clubs organize. But then I realized that, were that true, the boats
would be in some sort of order; in Seattle, the opening day of the
yachting season sees this big parade out of Portage Bay into Lake
Washington, but the big sailboats get to lead, and then come the
medium-sized cabin cruisers, and then the smaller ones.

Only the order of big-medium-small trips my "regatta" schema.
And that's very much the way that a bat detects his favorite food,
the mosquito—he sends out a brief chirp and then listens for
matching chirps echoing amid all the other noises of the night.
These chirps, upon closer inspection via a sonogram, are either
crescendos or their opposite, a falling-frequency burst. If he sends
out a chirp that starts with high notes and ends up at low frequencies, then he'll want to listen for the faint returning signals that
also sweep from high to low. That's his "mosquito" schema. So
how does the bat wire up his auditory system to arrive at a
mosquito detector—something that responds only to that high-to-
low sweep?

We got to talking about this in the computational neuroscience course yesterday. And that's essentially what the field is all
about: how to do smart tasks with dumb elements. Watching the
boats today, I was prompted to think up a postcard version of
what brains do using nerve impulses. And then I realized that it
would have been a lovely low-technology system for spies to use
back in World War II.

Suppose that you wanted to detect fleet movements in and
out of a harbor, but without using smart spies—only stupid spies,
who don't know what the spymaster is looking for. All they do is
to mail postcards to various addresses in some other city (for
convenience, let us say the postcards are all sent to various

residents of one small town who visit the post office twice a day to clean out their mailboxes). Some of the postcards are sent the cheapest way, which takes two days. Others are sent regular mail, which reliably takes one day, and some are sent express so that they arrive in half a day.

Each of the observers has a somewhat different mailing list, and each has a specialty: Observer A only mails postcards when he has seen big boats passing the harbor entrance, but sends them to each of 10 different P.O. boxes. Observer B only watches for medium-sized boats, and upon seeing them he mails postcards to ten P.O. boxes, some of which are the same ones that Observer A mailed to. And Observer C likes small boats, and mails to another ten P.O. boxes, again with some overlap in recipients. Twice each day, they mail some postcards, all to this one set of P.O. boxes in the small town; there is nothing special about the postcards, no message contained in either picture or handwriting. But each name on the mailing list of each observer is annotated with whether the postcard is to be sent slow, regular, or express.

And this allows a farmer visiting the post office to detect whether the harbor is sending out convoys, or having the fleet come home for leave, and distinguish this from a mere parade or just a lot of random traffic patterns. That's because each of the three major possibilities has a characteristic "signature": A parade passing the harbor entrance will be big-medium-small, strung out over a day's time. A convoy leaving the harbor will start with some big escort vessels, then have a daylong string of medium-sized freighters with a few small escort vessels mixed in, and finally the rear guard of big and small escort vessels. The fleet coming home for leave (as before Pearl Harbor in December 1941) will have some small escort vessels at first, then a long string of big cruisers, battleships, and aircraft carriers, followed by the rear guard of smaller escort vessels.

They are all fairly easy patterns to detect, but the big-to-small parade pattern is the easiest one to explain. The farmer-spymaster merely has to stand on the far wall of the post office from the mailboxes and see whose mailbox has an unusual amount of mail: Two days after the parade started, P.O. Box 007 will be crammed because it was on Observer A's slow-mail list, on Observer B's regular-mail list, and on Observer C's express-mail list.

Half a day before, there was very little—and half a day later, it will be back to very little mail in the mailbox. The big pileup of arriving postcards during the one half day is what tells the story of "parade" (if you have a reliable postal system, which is why no one will ever stamp this proposal TOP SECRET!). Detecting "fleet returning" could be valuable information if you want to send over some bombers to sink them while they're bottled up inside the harbor; agent 007 could just be a stuffed post office box.

To detect the high-to-low-frequency sweep of the mosquito echo, the bat can use a similar trick. His cochlea has specialists in each different frequency, and they can have different conduction velocities to the brain. Were the high-frequency specialists the slow-pokes, and the low-frequency types the fast-conducting ones, there would be a pileup of arrivals at some cells back in the brain shortly after the high-to-low sweep was completed. If those cells had a high threshold, they would become active only when the "mosquito" pattern had recently occurred. They would, in effect, be mosquito detectors. Other cells in the brain could, I suppose, be tuned up to be detectors of the opening "dit-dit-dit-dah" notes (G-G-G-E♭) of Beethoven's Fifth—though the bat would be more likely to specialize in the sonar echoes of other common objects instead.

Now you can detect much fancier patterns with several stages of analysis. Suppose that the postoffice-spy isn't the true spy-master; all he knows is that when he empties a lot of postcards

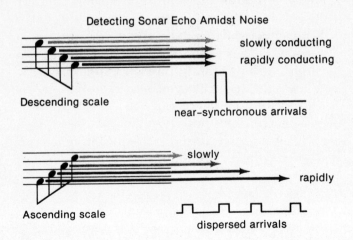

Detecting Sonar Echo Amidst Noise

slowly conducting
rapidly conducting

Descending scale

near–synchronous arrivals

slowly
rapidly

Ascending scale

dispersed arrivals

in P.O. Box 007, he sends individually meaningless postcards to a variety of people in another town. Again some recipients get the express mail treatment, others the slow-boat treatment. With this, a recipient in the next city could detect fancier time patterns, such as a whole line of music: You could detect the opening "dit-dit-dit-dah" notes with just one stage of analysis, and the whole first line of Beethoven's Fifth with several more. All you need is to adjust the mailing lists of the various stupid spies along the way.

Now all this is without inhibition—just excitation. If you allow some observers to send red postcards and others to send green instead, we can give the owner of P.O. Box 007 a new instruction: Red postcards cancel green ones, just throw them both away. If there are more than a dozen green ones left over, send your own postcards to everyone on your mailing list. Otherwise, just throw them all away. This, together with a variety of delivery delays, is a very economical way to detect patterns such as small-large-medium-medium-medium-big-small-small (how a convoy leaving port might stream past).

Now real nervous systems would do one additional thing, which is to adjust the strengths of the messages sent, equivalent to sending lots of postcards to some recipients and only one to others. The other thing they do is to automatically adjust those "synaptic strengths" so as to spontaneously create a Beethoven's Fifth detector without a designer of mailing lists: They (as a group) will self-organize upon hearing the same thing repeatedly, so that they will become more sensitive to that pattern, able to detect it even when it is almost obscured by noise (equivalent to lots of nonrelated ships passing through the harbor entrance at the same time as the fleet-convoy-parade-whatever). How do they automatically adjust their interconnection strengths (mailing lists) to accomplish that? Tune in next year; if anyone discovers it in the meantime, you'll probably read about it in the newspapers, because that's a question where the answer will likely win someone a Nobel Prize.

This is presumably how we tune ourselves up as infants to detect the phonemes in the speech of the adults around us: Each phoneme has various frequencies present at the same time (analogous to a chord in music), and the tonal combination varies with time (as would the successive chords in a musical phrase). Detecting /a/ and /k/ (and the other phonemes of English) is exactly the same kind of problem as detecting a short musical phrase, but compressed into a tenth of a second. Once we have gotten used to the three dozen or so basic speech sounds in English, we'll tend to categorize sounds into those phoneme pigeonholes. Any sound phrase that comes along that is some admixture will be labeled "strange" or just "nonspeech" unless it is right on the borderline between two phonemes, in which case it will be heard as either one or the other of them ("categorical perception" is what this is called in the speech-and-hearing literature).

Human language is characterized by the ability to detect (and produce) such phonemes, to sequence a series of them (usually no more than a half dozen) into recognizable "words." The order of the phonemes is important; some sequences yield one word, the reverse sequence another word (but most permutations of those phonemes may be nonsense). We assign certain simple meanings to such words; the average educated person reading this book probably knows 100,000 of them, and can look up many more in a dictionary. Translating phoneme sequences into recognizable words, in itself, is not uniquely human: Though your dog doesn't usually *produce* meaningful sequences of sounds, he can probably learn to associate a simple meaning to quite a few of the phoneme sequences that he *hears*, including stock phrases such as "Come here."

In human language, there is a "duality of patterning": In this second level of patterning beyond phoneme sequencing, we have word sequencing for an additional meaning. And often these word sequences are unique, never before encountered (like this sentence). We judge groups of words for a new meaning, depending on their ordering (we have conventions called "grammar," sometimes involving word order, called "syntax"), and decode a much more complicated message (such as this sentence hopefully conveys). The analysis of serial-sequential events is the basis of human language. We will need to understand the neural machinery that goes beyond such simple circuits as the mosquito detector and the Beethoven's Fifth detector, and how it modifies itself.

COMMITTEES CAN ORGANIZE THEMSELVES, especially if they are given some "feedback" about how well they are doing: Rather in the same way that a language teacher corrects a student's pronunciation, one can correct a committee and it will get better next time. You can shape up a committee by rote learning.

There was a spectacular demonstration of this at the computational neuroscience course, and it also showed the power of neurallike committees to produce speech. Not to decide what to say, or to get the grammar straight, but simply how to pronounce a written text without sounding like a scratchy record inside a child's toy. You can't just string together phonemes without paying attention to what comes next, because it may alter things. For example, in pronouncing the digits 6-7-5, the vocalizations for 7 usually start before the 6 is completed; they may sound distinctly separated to you, but the sounds actually overlap when spoken by a human rather than one of those automated-announcement machines that describes arriving airline Flight 675 as "flight-(pause)-six-(pause)-seven-(pause)-five." The rules for how to pronounce English fluently are many, and there are so many exceptions that one imagines that the brain needs to carry around a list of exceptions to the rules. As people have begun programming computers to "talk," many logical schemes have been attempted by programmers, but they always have to first look through a table of many hundreds of exceptions.

The brain doesn't have to do things according to the linguists' logic. You can show that by training a committee of neuronlike "cells" to pronounce English text. You don't have to give it rules in the way that many linguists originally insisted was necessary. You don't have to give it a list of exceptions. All you have to do is patiently monitor its pronunciation for a few thousand times and tell it, "You're getting closer," or "That's worse," rather as you might prompt the blindfolded person in the game of blindman's buff by saying "hotter" or "colder" if his random turn took him closer or farther away from the target.

Terry Sejnowski (who was one of Steve Kuffler's last collaborators) and his co-worker, Charles Rosenberg, programmed their computer to mimic a network of a few hundred neuronlike cells. They let most of them look at the sentence to be pronounced: If there are 26 letters plus a space, comma, and period possible, then 29 cells will easily handle the job of representing the alphabet (actually, 5 would do the job committee-style, but let's just assume specialist cells for convenience). Rather than looking at only one letter at a time, the device looked at seven letters at a time, three letters either side of the current one, with the string of letters slowly shifted along. So a letter was always seen in the context of what preceded it and what followed it.

Each of those 203 input cells talked to all 80 "interneurons," but not with the same strength: An input cell might inhibit some, excite others, and with a strength that was initially randomly set. Each of the 80 interneurons talked to all 26 of the output "motorneurons," again with random excitatory or inhibitory strengths for their "synapses." The "motorneurons" were specialized according to the sound they produced: Seventeen of them for 17 phonemes (elementary speech sounds, corresponding to a certain position of lips, tongue, and such), 4 for punctuation (silent, elide, pause, and full stop), and another 5 for stresses and syllable boundaries. Those are the kinds of instructions that one has to give a speech synthesizer.

So it was a simple three-layered arrangement, using cells

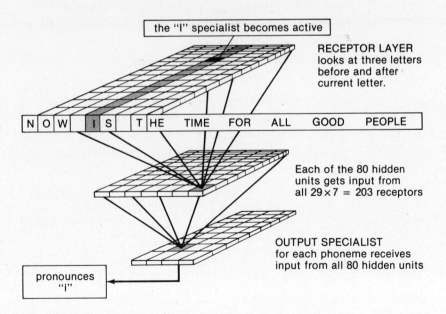

the "I" specialist becomes active

RECEPTOR LAYER
looks at three letters
before and after
current letter.

N O W I S T HE TIME FOR ALL GOOD PEOPLE

Each of the 80 hidden
units gets input from
all 29 × 7 = 203 receptors

OUTPUT SPECIALIST
for each phoneme receives
input from all 80 hidden units

pronounces
"i"

without any dynamic features such as adaptation or rebounds (a simplification to avoid settling times) and without any feedback connections (ditto)—a "neurallike network" with specialized inputs and specialized outputs, but a totally uncommitted set of interneurons whose input strengths and output strengths could be varied to achieve the goal of making a sentence come out sounding right.

But who wants to spend a lifetime sitting around twiddling the strengths of 18,629 synaptic connections? Enter the back-propagation algorithm, an invention of another group of neural-like network researchers. Initially, when the network is fed a sentence like this one, the speech synthesizer's loudspeaker sounds like complete garbage. That's what you'd expect from all those randomized synapses. But after each error, the correct pronunciation was set into the 26 "motorneurons," and each interneuron-to-motorneuron synapse's strength was altered in the direction of trying to make the error a little less. Or if perchance that motorneuron had done the right thing, its input synapses were strengthened: If excitatory, they were made even more excitatory; if inhibitory, even more inhibitory. Not only that, but each of the 80 interneurons was examined and its input synapses from the letter-detector cells were twiddled once, all in the direction of minimizing the final error.

Next time through the sentence it sounds a little better, getting the pauses and stresses a bit better; after a few more passes, it begins to sound like a baby babbling and getting some vowels correct (maybe /a/ and /e/), but probably saying "u" to both /o/ and /u/—some such collection of confusions. Then it begins sounding like a Mark I robot, sort of flat and occasionally garbled. After a few thousand words of practice with rote corrections made by back-propagation, it is right about 90 percent of the time—all without being given any linguistic rules, or table of exceptions. Tested with an unfamiliar text with a similar vocabulary, it does almost as well.

So how did the network achieve correct pronunciation? Did one of the 80 interneurons become an /e/ specialist? Rarely. If one peered inside the workings of the interneuron layer in the same way that we record from single cerebral neurons with a microelectrode, one finds that a cell will respond to a lot of different letters: It's on the /e/ committee as well as the /i/ committee, but another cell will be a member of the /k/, /i/, /o/, and /u/ committees, and so forth. One gets the correct pronunciation of /e/ because of a committee triggering that phoneme specialist, but each committee member also helps trigger some other phoneme-specialist motor-neuron too.

Now, in the real world, there probably aren't any pure specialists in the input layer, or in the output layer—they're used here for simplicity, just to show how committees are formed in the one intermediate layer's input and output synaptic strengths. But how robust is this committee arrangement? Suppose that you disable a few randomly selected interneurons? Does the pronunciation retreat to babbling? Somewhat, but it recovers with only a little additional training, achieving 90 percent correct pronunciation during retraining much more quickly than during original training. This is very much like stroke damage in humans, and the way that language performance recovers.

It's all a good example of how trial and error will get you to a goal if only some intermediate results can be fed back into the system to let it know how it's doing. All those people who thought that explicit rules are needed were surprised when they heard the babbling turn into quite reasonable English pronunciation. The network seems to have discovered the rules, and quite without establishing specialist cells.

What is the nature of categorization, generalization, and memory, and how does their interaction mediate the continually changing relationships between experience and novelty?

the immunologist GERALD M. EDELMAN, 1987

There must be a trick to the train of thought, a recursive formula. A group of neurons starts working automatically, sometimes without external impulse. It is a kind of iterative process with a growing pattern. It wanders around the brain, and the way it happens must depend on the memory of similar patterns.

the mathematician STANISLAW M. ULAM, 1976

MANY OTHER TASKS have been given to similarly naive neurallike networks; they can discover some rules of grammar, for example, another thing that was supposed to have been built in by the genes. While this doesn't prove that human language cortex does things the same way, it shows that networks can organize themselves, discover by trial and error the way to detect a schema, pronounce a syllable, or tap a finger in a complicated rhythm. The genes need only carry enough information to give them a head start on pure randomness; the individual's successive interactions with the environment will shape up the fancier kinds of organization automatically.

Such discoveries have caused much excitement among the neurobiologists, developmental biologists, and the cognitive cognoscenti (even the artificial intelligentsia). And it has stirred up a great many hopeful technologists, who are flocking to the banner of neurallike networks as an alternative way of shaping up smart machines. Why worry with logical rules and careful computer programming when a randomized network and a little rote instruction will make a pretty good machine? Behaviorism isn't dead after all: The *tabula rasa* has been reincarnated *in silico*!

BUT WHAT IF THERE IS NO TEACHER to correct your errors? Some committees form anyway: Just as snowflakes form fancy patterns while falling through moist air, just as a pan of oatmeal cooking unstirred on your stove will soon have its surface furrowed into a collection of squares and hexagons, so too will interneurons with initially random synapses tend to achieve patterns. They often correspond to simple kinds of order in the environment.

This comes through clearly in a neurallike network studied by John Pearson, Leif Finkel, and Gerald Edelman, that resembles the somatosensory cortical maps of the hand. Their layer of input cells are simply sensors scattered around the skin of a model hand. Like the thalamic projection to the real somatosensory cortex, they let each point on the "hand" connect randomly across the entire "cortex." Some "synapses" were randomly excitatory, some randomly inhibitory—but the initially random strengths could be later changed by experience.

There is no "output" layer (the cells talk to one another

within the interneuron layer, unlike the previous examples, where cells only "feed forward" to the next layer). And there is no "error-correcting teacher"—one just sits back and waits to see what happens to the interneurons and their relative synaptic strengths. One watches on a color computer display. It reminds me of the back side of a colorful tapestry, little threads running here and there, as if they were axons in a tangential section of brain; their colors denote synaptic strengths. Initially, thanks to the randomized initial conditions, the picture is so haphazard as to suggest that Jackson Pollock had finally designed a true *tabula rasa*.

If there is no input at all, not much happens—but give the "hand" some experience with the world. Go around touching each "finger," one at a time, maybe stroking it. The computer provides the neurallike network with a simple synaptic property rather like one of the glutamate receptors: Any one synapse's strength is affected by the simultaneous activity of neighboring synapses (it's not synergy but more like lingering hypersensitivity). So when you stroke a finger, activating one patch after another of adjacent skin, you activate a series of "cortical synapses." Some, thanks to the initial randomization, happen to be adjacent to one another on a particular "cortical neuron." So the stroking of that finger tends to strengthen the within-cell neighbors; next time they'll respond even better to the stroke, even if it is in the opposite direction down the finger surface.

But these clusters of enhanced "synapses" are upon all sorts of cells in the cortical array of 1,500. Where by chance there are cells with more enhanced clusters than otherwise, one will start to get "neuron" clusters responding well to that finger. And pretty soon, that Jackson Pollock randomness seems to look like a map of the hand: There will be a big cluster of "neurons" for the thumb, another for the forefinger, and so forth. As the neurallike network gains experience, one starts to see red patches of strongly connected cells emerging from an increasingly blue boundary area where cells are weakly interconnected. Groups emerge, the physiological boundaries becoming far sharper than the underlying smear of anatomical connections—and all without instruction.

If one has stimulated the top side of the "finger" at different times than when stimulating the bottom surface, then there will

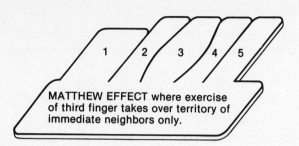

MATTHEW EFFECT where exercise
of third finger takes over territory of
immediate neighbors only.

be 10 big irregular patches in the 1,500 "neuron" array: five top surfaces and five bottom surfaces. With nothing more than some lightly organized experience with the external world, this neurallike network has self-organized itself into a "cortical map" that looks remarkably like those recorded by Merzenich, Kaas, Nelson, and friends from monkey somatosensory cortex.

Naturally, one wants to know if the California–Oregon game (see Chapter 8) works with the neurallike network in the same way that it works in real monkeys. And so Finkel, Edelman, and Pearson tried overstimulating the middle finger. Sure enough, the second and fourth finger maps in the "cortex" shrank as the third finger map enlarged. Distant boundaries between fingers (like the Oregon–Washington and Washington–Canada boundaries in the analogy) didn't also shift, however, in the manner of the real cortex, but the basic result was perfectly clear: There was a battle going on to see whether a "neuron" was going to prefer digit 2 or digit 3 (it received anatomical connections from all five, but most were turned down by experience), and the outcome was influenced by the amount of "exercise" a digit received.

> *Them's that got shall get*
> *Them's that not shall lose.*
> *So the Bible says*
> *and it still is news.*
>
> the singer BILLIE HOLIDAY'S
> version of the Matthew Effect

Some call this neural darwinism—but not everything that involves random initial conditions and selective survival deserves to be called darwinism. The dance we call the Darwinian Two-Step, randomness then selection continuing back and forth for many rounds to increasingly shape up non-random-looking results, is the key. These repeated injections of randomness lie at the heart of what some would consider as delimiting darwinism from simpler forms of self-organization such as clumping and zero-sum matthewism. This New Testament exemplar of zero-sum thinking (Matthew 25:29) is usually paraphrased as "the rich get richer while the poor get poorer"; it's one example of how random initial conditions can come to result in a pattern without any additional injections of randomness. Something even simpler than darwinism might account for some elementary forms of neural patterning too.

NEITHER THE SENSORY TEMPLATE favored by a model "interneuron," nor the cortical "map" seen in their interconnection strengths is a schema. But you can begin to see that perceptual categorization could occur via shaping up initially random cortical interconnection strengths. That has some profound consequences for our concepts of reality: As Gerald Edelman notes, in consequence of the random element, "we must look at all acts of perception as acts of creativity." We create the world we see: We surely modify it with experience, but it's an invented world. How we emotionally react to something may, in turn, affect how we see it in the future. Literally.

[This is in a sense] a theory of the "natural selection" of behaviour-patterns. Just as in the species the truism that the dead cannot breed implies that there is a fundamental tendency for the successful to replace the unsuccessful, so in the nervous system does the truism that the unstable tends to destroy itself imply that there is a fundamental tendency for the stable to replace the unstable. Just as the gene pattern in its encounters with the environment tends towards ever better adaptation of the inherited form and function, so does a system of step- and part-functions tend toward ever better adaptation of learned behaviour.

the brain theorist W. ROSS ASHBY, 1952

There is a popular cliché . . . which says that you cannot get out of computers any more than you have put in . . . , that computers only do exactly what you tell them to, and that therefore computers are never creative. This cliché is true only in a crashingly trivial sense, the same sense in which Shakespeare never wrote anything except what his first schoolteacher taught him to write—words.

the sociobiologist RICHARD DAWKINS, 1986

11

A WHOLE NEW BALL GAME: BOOTSTRAPPING THOUGHT THROUGH THROWING

One should not think slightingly of the paradoxical; for the paradox is the source of the thinker's passion, and the thinker without a paradox is like a lover without a feeling: a paltry mediocrity. . . . The supreme paradox of all thought is the attempt to discover something that thought cannot think.

the theologian and philosopher
SØREN KIERKEGAARD (1813–1855)

What am I, that I can think about my existence?

the neurophysiologist RODOLFO LLINÁS, 1986

The century-old school on School Street is a National Historic Something too, and a bit more likely to survive the winter storms than the Outermost House. It is perched on the highest bank surrounding Eel Pond and protected from the winds off Vineyard Sound by an even higher hill, a site selected by someone who had longevity in mind. Its playground has a basketball hoop, and the children are practicing their free throws for a few minutes as they take their recess from the Children's School of Science.

The adults around here like to throw as well—there's a game of Frisbee in the street and the softball teams are practicing at the ball field, which is a block behind the Bell Tower Garden, and surrounded by the remains of the original saltwater marsh. Home runs may disappear into a thicket penetrable only by small boys and girls—or, worse yet, into a thicket that admits only small mammals. The volleyball court is right next to the brambles; I played several games with the computational neuroscience course students the other day, and we soon learned the penalties of wild returns.

We also got some training from an old pro, who must have trained visiting students for many seasons. All around town, you see beggar dogs, each the proprietor of a tennis ball lying on the ground in front of them. They are, however, well fed. Their eager eyes are soliciting humans: Please throw my ball! The old white dog by the volleyball court waits patiently by the edge of the court, watching the game with his tennis ball nearby. Periodically, one of the players will, without prompting, walk over and throw the dog's tennis ball toward the softball field, as far away as possible, and the dog will happily chase it, returning to wait alongside the volleyball court again. It seems to be a local tradition.

If five minutes goes by without someone helping out the dog, he will carry his ball onto the volleyball court, wag his tail somewhat sheepishly, and generally disrupt the game until someone gets rid of him by throwing his ball. It is quite clear who has trained whom; a little operant conditioning works wonders on humans.

It is amazing how many entertainments around here involve ballistic movements: throwing, clubbing as in golf and tennis, kicking in soccer—even the accurate bouncing used in volleyball. Hammering is a favorite pastime, judging from the do-it-yourself types busy adding something on to a porch or repairing a roof. Wonder why so many pastimes are so jerky? And if they're not jerky, they are still fancy finger sequences such as cat-in-the-cradle or knitting. Is this thanks to our ancient heritage of tool-making, or cracking nuts? Or are they all secondary to something even more basic?

THE SHINING SEA BIKEWAY is more crowded today; besides the usual bikes, I see a recumbent. And the only permitted motorized vehicle, an electric wheelchair. Soon the beach comes into sight, and it is a stony beach. The bathing beaches closer to Woods Hole used to be stony as well, back before sand was imported. Of course, sand is always imported; very little of it is made at the beach (the exceptions are those black sand beaches in Hawaii, the fine particles formed when hot lava shattered as it dropped into the cold ocean). Ordinary sand comes from weather eroding mountains, the long downhill trip breaking rocks into smaller and smaller pieces.

I like stones—you can't throw sand, at least not with a satisfactory feeling of accomplishment. These stones, left behind by the glacier that plowed Cape Cod into place, are just the kind to fit the hand of a child. But I know where to find the larger ones that will fit my hand: usually farther along the beach from where the small stones are, because the ocean currents sweep along parallel to this shore and carry the small, light ones farther than the heavier large stones. Double the size of a stone and its surface area increases fourfold; you might think that more "sail" area would cause the stone to be carried further by a wave but this is another surface-to-volume ratio phenomenon: The stone's weight (which is proportional to its volume) goes up eightfold! So "move-ability" halves when size doubles. That is, of course, why the imported sand gets carried away from stony beaches: They're stony because they have strong currents sweeping along the shoreline that sort by size. And sand is easy stuff to move for such currents.

Whole beaches full of rocks like this are called shingle, at least by the British, who are thought to have borrowed the term from the Norwegians. There is no shade anywhere. Some people are not very fond of it:

> Three or four times in my life I have ventured for a weekend to Martha's Vineyard, Wellfleet or some other nesting place of the weary literate. The need to engage in seemingly intelligent conversation while sitting under the hot sun, on hot sand, while eating sand-impregnated hamburgers and watching the remnants of someone's lunch of last week ooze up through the shingle must be one of life's most starkly negative pleasures. Always I've re-achieved civilization with relief.

> the economist JOHN KENNETH GALBRAITH, 1981

Maybe I'll have to start a Cobble Appreciation Society (individually, the shingle's rounded rocks are called cobbles); after all, even the ancient Greeks may have had one, since there is some suggestion that a cobble was then called a discus (scholars argue about whether the word, as used in Homer, means the same thing as the platter that athletes throw these days). A compromise would be that *discus* meant a rock particularly suitable for throwing: one that fit the human hand or that had nice aerodynamics.

Nothing feels quite as comfortable in the hand as a nice cobble: Have you ever hefted a hammer, or pen, or club that felt quite so much as if it was a natural extension of you, that one had been designed to fit the other? The cobble's use as a hammerstone might explain the origins of the term *cobbler*, with its unsophisticated connotations.

Dogs won't usually fetch stones, unfortunately, and so those with canine companions search out the sticks and forlorn tennis balls that dogs prefer to chase. The problem with training a young dog to fetch is not in getting him to chase and find the stick, or to bring it back: The problem is the war of wills needed to get him to give it back to you so that you can throw it again. That's a familiar story to the biologists who study the structure of the fancy folded molecule that carries oxygen from your lungs to your brain: The problem is not so much in getting a molecule to snatch up oxygen and bind it, but in getting it to drop oxygen on command when arriving at the tissues that need some. That is the genius of hemoglobin.

Yet another ballistic pastime to add to the list of discus throw, baseball, basketball, soccer, home-repair hammering, volleyball, and the like, which I've seen today: the game of fetch. I cannot think of any other animals that enjoy so many ballistic entertainments, though juvenile apes clearly love to "play hammer," especially if their elders make a living by cracking nuts. Even infant chimps have been observed to hammer on a nut with a stick. And their elders sometimes use rocks as hammers when trying to crack particularly tough nutshells.

ONCE YOUR BRAIN has the neural machinery for one ballistic movement, maybe it can be used for another. Maybe the neurons used to command a hammering motion can be used with the leg muscles too, and so kicking comes along for free. Certainly, any ballistic movement requires a lot of neural machinery for planning ahead, quite unlike other movements, such as walking or picking fruit off a tree. That's because ballistic movements are so fast, and our feedback pathways are relatively slow. When a monkey moves a cherry from tree to mouth, or I pick up a coffee cup and bring it to my lips, there is a lot of time for little corrections. The sensors in my arm muscles and joints tell my spinal cord and brain where the cup is (they don't speak directly to the local muscles, only via the loop into the central nervous system), I compare that to my intent (cup at lips, preferably still upright) and known constraints (don't slosh the coffee out of the cup), and correct the path. I repeat this correction dozens, if not hundreds, of times during the seemingly smooth movement.

Still, each correction takes time because the message moves slowly along the nerves, and the central nervous system takes time to decide too. A minimum round-trip loop time for arm-back-to-arm movements in humans is 110 milliseconds. And so, any movement like hammering or kicking that may be over and done with in a fraction of a second cannot profit from corrections along the way (dart throwing takes about 119 milliseconds until you release). Most error corrections will arrive too late to do any good, as the motion will be complete by then. Maybe you can use the feedback to help in your planning for the next throw, but once you start a throw, you're committed to the plan you made during "get set."

I've been practicing juggling with several old, waterlogged tennis balls that I found. Oranges are better for juggling than tennis balls, due to their weight, but I'm fresh out of oranges. Juggling is hard in the beginning because of the reaction time between seeing a ball and generating a correction nearly a fifth of a second later (visual reaction times are particularly slow). When juggling, you've got to plan several movements ahead, not just one. And that is one reason why it is so hard to learn.

This makes ballistic movements quite unlike the ones where an intention and feedback corrections suffice to get the job done: Brief movements have to be carefully planned in advance. Any trial and error has to be done while planning, checking a proposed movement against memory as you "get set," and discarding the plans that don't jibe. Of course, a standard kick, like the standard basketball free throw, may only require that the brain have a standard motor program that it can execute on command; you make it standard by "getting it in the groove" with long practice. It is when there is an infinite variety of gradations that planning becomes so important, as you have to generate a number of possible sets of muscle commands and then pick and choose to find the best one. That's why well-practiced free throws are easier than other shots in basketball, which are from a variety of distances and angles. So guess which were likely the ones important in evolution, needed by those prehuman hunters . . . ?

The planning process probably requires a holding queue, what in the business we would call a serial buffer. Telephones that remember your 10 most-used numbers have 10 serial buffers, each more than a dozen digits long. Each is like a sidetrack, whose train sits poised, waiting to be selected and let loose on the main line.

That which we call linking of ideas *in our understanding is only the memory of the coexistence of phenomena in nature;*

that which we call consequence *in our understanding is*
nothing but the memory of the sequence of succession of
effects in nature.

the philosopher DENIS DIDEROT (1713–1784)

FOR ORGANISMS THAT NEED TO BE both large (meters of
conduction distance) and fast, one often needs a queue that is the
neural equivalent of an old-fashioned roll for a player piano. It's a
plan for many simultaneous output channels (those 88 keys), which
says when, how hard, and for how long each of them is to be
struck.

Our planning queue for a ballistic movement has to provide
for dozens of muscles and activate them just at the right times,
just so hard, and for just so long. We carefully plan during "get
set" to act without feedback. And the action itself is a carefully
orchestrated spatiotemporal sequence, like a fireworks finale
launched from a half dozen platforms.

Unlike the roll for the player piano, which is reprogrammed
only with difficulty (tape and a punch!), the neural buffers can be
reprogrammed to get the pauses right:

The notes I handle no better than many pianists. But the
pauses between the notes—ah, that is where the art resides!

the concert pianist ARTUR SCHNABEL, 1958

So, though playing a Beethoven sonata seems quite unlike baseball, the pianist may well be using some neural machinery that
was shaped up for hammering or throwing; certainly, natural
selection hasn't acted very often on our abilities to perform music,
so music is surely a spare-time use of some such neural machinery
with a crucial primary function. Dancing is a similar secondary
use, if the feet can make use of the same serial buffers that the
hand needs for throwing and hammering.

SO WHY CAN'T CHIMPS TALK if they can hammer and throw
(which shows that they too have serial buffers)? Why don't they
have serial-order recreations, like music and dancing and chess?
What is it about humans that goes beyond the sufficient-for-

hammering planning buffer of the chimps? What is it that has made us so much more oriented to sequences?

Language itself is one possibility—maybe language was so useful that natural selection selected for the hominid variants that had better planning buffers for sentences. And then the music, chess, and fox-trots came along as spare-time uses of the sentence sequencer. But there's another possibility too, one that I discovered on a day like this while sitting at the beach throwing stones. And wondering why I was so unsuccessful at hitting the targets I'd propped atop a log. I finally moved closer so that I wouldn't have to throw so hard just to reach the log, and then I got better. To throw twice as far with a flat trajectory, you have to throw about twice as fast. Like speeding up a tape recording to twice the speed, you have to speed up that "motor tape" you planned and programmed.

But if I tried throwing just as hard as before from the closer position, my performance deteriorated again. Now wasn't that interesting? It wasn't that the targets were so small when I stood farther back; it was that I had to throw twice as fast in order to reach more distant targets.

And so I puzzled for a while about why throwing faster was so much harder than throwing slower. Most people who have similarly puzzled over this phenomenon have probably concluded that feedback corrections wouldn't work well when the throw was only half as long-lasting. But, as a card-carrying neurophysiologist, I knew that the feedback was always too slow; it won't help much with even lazy throws. So if that isn't the difference between fast and twice-as-fast throwing, it must be that operating on a time scale twice as fast was a problem. Just try dancing twice as fast as you usually dance, and you'll get the idea that adjustments aren't always easy.

As it happened, I knew something about the problems of speeding up tape recorders, *and* I knew quite a bit about how motorneurons command muscles. But I couldn't see what the problems would be—except for one thing: Motorneurons are inherently jittery (even at their most constant firing rate, the interval between impulses varies a little). They can only time something with a limited precision. Had I run into that limit, standing back too far away from the log?

There might be a half dozen people in the world who, without having to spend a day in the library, know the data about how jittery motorneurons are—but I was one of them, having done my Ph.D. thesis in 1966 on that very subject. I knew that they had great difficulty operating on a millisecond time scale (1/1000 of a second on a camera shutter); tens of milliseconds they could manage nicely, but their jitter kept them from timing events that required greater precision.

So how precisely did I really need to time the release of the rock from my hand when I threw from various distances at various speeds? What's the *tolerable error*, the amount release time can vary and still have the rock hit somewhere on the target? That's a simple problem in physics, which I solved that evening after I returned home intrigued with the problem. To hit a rabbit-sized target from only 4 meters away (the length of a small car), I needed to time the release to within 11 milliseconds (about the length of time that your camera shutter stays open when set at 1/100 of a second). That's right on the margin of what a motorneuron

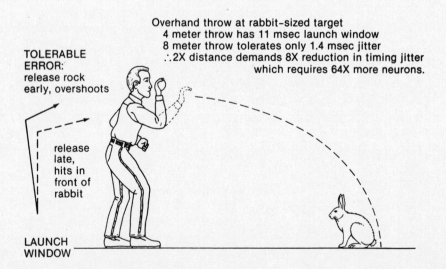

Overhand throw at rabbit-sized target
4 meter throw has 11 msec launch window
8 meter throw tolerates only 1.4 msec jitter
∴2X distance demands 8X reduction in timing jitter
which requires 64X more neurons.

TOLERABLE ERROR: release rock early, overshoots

release late, hits in front of rabbit

LAUNCH WINDOW

might be able to do by itself. From more than 8 meters away (6 meters is a standard parallel parking space), one needed timing precision better than 1 millisecond to consistently hit the target. So that's why I was performing so poorly!

I felt better for a while—until recalling that other people could perfectly well hit such targets from much farther away than that. And so could I, once upon a time. How did we do it, if motorneurons were so irreducibly jittery?

SCIENTISTS LOVE SITUATIONS like that: It's what we call a "problem" (actually, this was even better; it qualified as a "paradox"), and we tend to delight in them, working them over about the way a dog gnaws on a bone from every which-angle.

An engineer treats such a situation differently; he or she wants to make something that is cheap and reliable, which can be readily fixed if it should break. The engineer treats jitter as a nuisance, to be eliminated by better design of the parts. The scientist, on the other hand, just wants to know *why*—why the brain can manage to time something much more precisely than any of its component parts can manage on their own. And how evolution managed to stumble upon its method to work around the difficulty. Here is a lovely case of the whole being better than any of its parts, but how did evolution pull it off?

Well, maybe somewhere in the brain there are neurons that are less jittery than motorneurons: Perhaps these timing specialists just tell the motorneurons when to fire, rather than letting the motorneurons decide for themselves? After all, for the most skilled movements (as in separating the pages when leafing through a new book), the motor strip seems to command the motorneurons.

Fortunately, without even spending what would have been a month in the library, I knew that wasn't the answer either: Having recorded from those motor cortex neurons too (at least in cats and monkeys), I knew that they were far *worse* than motorneurons in the amount of intrinsic jitter, not better. Maybe somewhere else? Well, I haven't recorded from every cell type in the brain, but I've done lots of comparative neuron physiology and I've looked at many published records in the literature—and I wouldn't bet on a highly precise "master clock" cell (because of the way in which electrical events are quantized within cells, they have a lot of intrinsic jitter that is very hard to minimize).

Yet the nervous system must, somewhere in brain or spinal cord, achieve the less-than-a-millisecond jitter: That's because we can, with practice, achieve much finer time discrimination and movement. So, unless we are going to invoke a "soul" that commands the brain, we must try to figure out how the nervous system pulls off this feat. It's probably like the hyperacuity business, I thought, where we can see with finer grain than the mosaic of retinal photoreceptors. But how?

HOW TO BUILD A PRECISE CLOCK with sloppy parts? Fortunately, I dimly remembered from the *Biophysical Journal* what turned out to be a sterling example of temporal hyperacuity. It was buried in a pile of papers atop my desk: John Clay and Robert DeHaan had done some experiments with jittery heart cells and showed that clusters of them were much less jittery. Your nice regular heartbeat isn't because there is some master clock with microjitter, commanding the rest of the heart to twitch on the right beat. While there is indeed a pacemaker region that sets the pace for the rest of the heart (it is what the vagus nerve slows down—and sometimes stops!), it still contains thousands of pacemaker cells, none of which is without substantial jitter.

What Clay and DeHaan did was build a little section of heart on the bottom of a petri dish, looking through a microscope to watch each cell twitch. A single cell in isolation beats rather irregularly—each heart cell is capable of serving as its own pacemaker, but its rhythm is hardly as regular as a heartbeat. Rather than being like a water faucet's regular drip, it was more like rain on the roof, with some pauses far longer than others.

Push a second isolated cell over until it sticks to the first; their beats, formerly independent, now synchronize so both cells beat in synchrony. Push over a few more cells, and they too stick and synchronize. Such "entrainment" is a primitive form of mob psychology, some say.

The funny thing is that the beat starts sounding more regular. Once you've stuck 25 cells together, it's unmistakable: The jitter has dropped fivefold from what individual cells do in isolation. With a hundred cells in the cluster, it's a tenfold reduction: maybe not as regular as a clock, but certainly getting to be more like a dripping faucet or a regular heartbeat. The rain-on-the-roof irregularity is gone.

The heart cells provide a nice example of the Law of Large Numbers in action, just as did the number of cells involved in depth perception. Scientists use this mathematical principle all the time, but with pencil and paper: We "average" a number of measurements and then calculate a "standard deviation," which is a measure of the uncertainty or jitter. That's why public opinion polls or estimates of the number of television viewers are bracketed: "Somewhere between 23 and 24 percent of viewers were watching the evening news." We know that to halve the standard deviation, we need to take four times as much data; for a tenfold reduction, a hundred times as much data. If television rating services monitored 100,000 viewers simultaneously rather than just 1,000, they could be 10 times more precise and say "23.6 percent." But we don't usually imagine nature doing the same thing—yet here it was, the regular rhythm of the heartbeat being created by averaging thousands of extremely irregular beats in the individual cells.

Now the electrical circuitry of the heart lends itself particularly well to summing up many individual contributions and dividing by N, the number of contributions. Not all circuits of neurons are going to do that. But the most common ones look perfectly designed for the purpose: Individual contributions are small, many of them are summed in an "analog" fashion, and there are a variety of ways to divide. I can think of ways for neural circuits to *avoid* having the Law of Large Numbers affect their computations (all they have to do is work with a few large contributions, an oligarchy analogous to a digital computer's binary logic), but most neural circuits are closer to analog than binary, closer to a democracy than an oligarchy. And so most of them are quite capable of improving on jitter by just averaging together the results of many separate cells all trying to do the same job.

Now an engineer faced with the problem of a jittery clock usually tries to make the individual clock more reliable—but it is perfectly possible to achieve the same end by simply averaging together the times of a hundred clocks. Just imagine a clock shop as midnight approaches: First one clock starts chiming, then another and another. We just agree that when half of the hundred clocks have begun striking the hour, we will call it midnight. Though different clocks lead the pack on different nights, and the fiftieth clock is usually different, the interval between our defined-by-the-fiftieth "midnights" will vary only a tenth as much as the individual clocks vary. (Note that we are here concerned with *precision* and reproducibility—not with *accuracy*, such as whether it is really midnight by the time standards or whether the interval is truly 24 hours.)

So what do you think that evolution did: completely rede-signed individual cells to make a precision clock, or just used a lot of off-the-shelf cells hooked up in an everyday circuit? Nature does one thing extremely well: *making duplicate cells*, as when a cell divides. Solving the jitter problem by making a hundredfold extra cells may be far easier than redesigning the cell to reduce jitter. A hundred imperfect cells rather than one perfect cell, as it were. Besides, nature seems to *like* variability (its way of keeping options open)—and apparently doesn't mind some inefficiency or waste. Indeed, waste seems to be its key to making things better: It's what natural selection is all about, wasting the less fit.

SO THE SOLUTION to the throwing problem seems to be: Simply assign a multitude of serial buffers to the same timing job. It's rather like using a hundred player pianos, all with an identical instruction roll. Because each piano varies mechanically, the re-sults won't be identical. It's very much like a choir, all singing the same song: The timing of that Hallelujah Chorus refrain, when heard in the back of the church as one fused voice, is much less jittery than the rhythmic performance of any one singer taken alone.

Maybe that's why hominids needed a bigger brain, I thought—they need lots more cells, just to become hunters who throw well. Eureka?

So, how many more cells do I have to assign to the task of hitting a target that is twice as far away? Whatever timing jitter I had at a 4-meter target distance, I'll have to reduce it eight-fold to throw twice as far. To do that with the Law of Large Numbers averaging scheme, it will take 64 times as many cells. To triple the target distance and still hit it just as reliably, I'll need 729 times as many cells as sufficed originally. The number of cells goes up as the sixth power of the distance—which is indeed a steep growth curve.

Now the hominid brain has increased about fourfold beyond the apes and early hominids. Let's see—a 10 percent increase in cells only gains a small-brained hominid about 2 percent in throwing distance, doubling cell numbers will buy 12 percent, and fourfold increases in cells assigned to the timing task gains us 26 percent farther. Oops. Brain enlargement per se isn't a simple solution to the basketball problem after all. On that reasoning, we can't even get one-third improvements in throwing with our fourfold larger brain.

Fortunately, I finally realized, you can probably just *borrow* what you need as you "get set" to throw. Cortical neurons aren't usually committed to a single task; they can be members of different committees at different times. And so they can likely be reassigned temporarily as well as retrained for more permanent new tasks. You just need to stop talking and stop worrying about tomorrow and stop paying attention to anything else except throwing. On this theory, precision throwing might involve much of frontal and temporal lobes, plus the usual basal ganglia and cerebellum contributions. It's something like the church choir expanding temporarily by borrowing some of the audience, getting them to sing along. You have to get them to stop doing whatever they were doing, and instead, during "get set," assign them to the same tune as the full-time experts in hand-arm sequencing. They may not be as expert as the pros, but—so says the Law of Large Numbers—they can still be useful.

As I noted, we have had much difficulty in dissecting apart motor programs such as grooming into the "atoms" that constitute them. Still, modular components of movements are handy for discussing variations in plans. For simple dart throwing, you start out by cocking the elbow. Then you contract not only the elbow flexor (biceps, etc.) but also the extensors (triceps, etc.)—and at the same time, so that the arm doesn't actually move. This "co-contraction" serves to stretch the elastic components of the muscles and tendons, storing elastic energy—and it also serves to get the extensor motorneurons all firing away, well above their thresholds for recruitment.

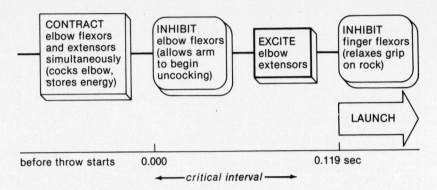

Modular motor commands, strung together to plan throw.

Then, to start the throw, you inhibit the flexor motorneurons so that the extensors are unopposed. The forearm starts moving. You excite the extensors some more, in addition to inhibiting flexors, and add to the velocity generated by the elastic rebound.

Once the forearm nears the vertical orientation, you relax your grip on the rock, probably by simply inhibiting the finger flexors, and the inertia of the rock will serve to open the grip. It's doing that at exactly the right moment which is so tricky (for dart throwing, it is about 119 milliseconds after the throwing movement begins uncocking the elbow).

Now you need one serial buffer for sure, just for the occasional ballistic movement like hammering open a nut or flinging a threat. But for precision throwing, where timing jitter must be minimized, what you'll want is many buffers all loaded up identically, marching in lockstep. Like the choir singing the Hallelujah Chorus, you'll want to get as many extra helpers as possible: If there are another hundred buffers that can be borrowed, so much the better—so long as they can quickly learn the music, i.e., can be loaded up with identical instructions. Better yet, imagine a railroad marshaling yard, similar to the one that used to be at the end of this bike trail in the days when it was a railroad line instead. The big parking lot at the ferry terminal probably used to be about 10 sidetracks, storing cars as they came off the railroad ferry from New York, then making up new trains to chug up to Boston. That's essentially 10 serial buffers rather like the tele-

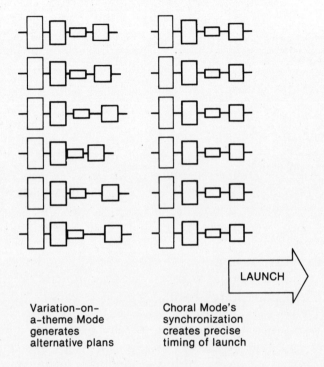

Variation-on-
a-theme Mode
generates
alternative plans

Choral Mode's
synchronization
creates precise
timing of launch

phone's memories. Imagine all 10 buffers loaded up with the same telephone number, all unloading simultaneously.

BUT WHAT ABOUT PICKING THE BEST, if it isn't a given and you have to guess? If the occasion is a basketball free throw, and you've really "grooved" your throw (produced a standard movement melody streamlined for the situation), then just call up your free-throw program, load it into all the serial buffers as you get set, hook them up in lockstep, and go.

But the other reason that you need a lot of serial buffers is so that you pick the best "movement melody" for the occasion, if it is a throw that isn't as standardized as a free throw. You call up a whole family of variants; then, as you start to get set to throw, you judge each of them against the situation and against memories of what worked well in similar, though not identical situations in the past. Then go with the best—indeed, if I were designing the system, I'd say to copy the best one into all the other serial buffers replacing the unsuccessful candidates, then hook them all in lockstep, and go.

In the musical analogy, it is like auditioning a series of song-writers, each singing a slightly different melody; after you pick the best for this particular occasion, you photocopy her music and pass it out to everyone else, then they all sing together as a chorus.

This step, of ganging into a chorus, is the neural networks' version of speciation in biological evolution, and of the amplification step in the immune response. In biology, new species usually come about because of discovering a new niche, and so a re-stricted number of genotypes (DNA sequences) have a population explosion. In the immune system's use of darwinism, the sequence of amino acids that best fits the foreign antigen undergoes a population explosion. And so the best of the lot of the sequencing tracks in the left brain, were it replicated in the other planning tracks for Law of Large Numbers purposes, would be similar to speciation.

Yet it isn't the exact duplications needed for throwing's submillisecond timing that are so interesting—it's those additional variations on the successful theme that are usually generated in the process (just as in crossing over, and in the immune re-sponse). Shaping up a new thought—or better yet, a poem—through a series of "That's it! No, maybe it's even better if I say it as. . . ." may thus be analogous to the evolution of a whole biological lineage, one species replacing another over and over.

MOVEMENT MELODIES are, of course, those "motor tapes" in the behavioral repertoire of the sunbathing cormorants of Eel Pond, and those snooping skunks. The main difference is that ballistic movements cannot immediately utilize feedback to modify the melody; many slower behaviors (such as cruising the water-front for food) have such an interplay of feedback and standard locomotion elements that they are more like jazz improvisations.

Animals that don't use varied ballistic movements don't need serial buffers. Chimpanzees and baboons need one for hammering—but hammering isn't that varied in its timing requirements, so maybe they didn't have much natural selection operating on how many serial buffers they could muster on occasion. But any animal that starts to make its living by throwing is going to need multiple buffers for two reasons: choosing among a family of variants (unless always sticking to a standard throw at a standard distance), and assembling a choir and helpers for those Hallelujah Chorus occasions that demand the most precise timing in rock release. What's nice is that the need for a precision mode may incidentally "buy" you the wide family of choices.

When one starts thinking about thinking in a sequence, I believe the brain plays a game—some parts providing the stimuli, the others the reactions, and so on. It is really a multi-person game, but consciously the appearance is of a one-dimensional, purely temporal sequence. One is only consciously aware of something in the brain which acts as a summarizer or totalizer of the process going on and that probably consists of many parts acting simultaneously on each other. . . .

the mathematician STANISLAW M. ULAM, 1976

12

SHAPING UP CONSCIOUSNESS WITH A DARWINIAN DANCE: EMERGENCE FROM THE SUBCONSCIOUS

I think [that the need for a narrative] is absolutely primal. Children understand stories long before they understand trigonometry.

the neurologist OLIVER SACKS, 1987

A man is always a teller of tales, he lives surrounded by his stories and the stories of others, he sees everything that happens to him through them; and he tries to live his life as if he were recounting it.

the philosopher JEAN-PAUL SARTRE (1905–1980)

[A]bout the age of three . . . a child begins to show the ability to put together a narrative in coherent fashion and especially the capacity to recognize narratives, to judge their well-formedness. Children quickly become virtual Aristotelians, insisting upon any storyteller's observation of the "rules," upon proper beginnings, middles, and particularly ends. Narrative may be a special ability or competence that we learn, a certain subset of the general language code which, when mastered, allows us to summarize and retransmit narratives in other words and other languages, to transfer them into other media, while remaining recognizably faithful to the original narrative structure and message.

the literary critic PETER BROOKS, 1984

Getting acquainted with the new neighbors happens quickly when aided by one of several catalysts: dogs or small children. They seem to serve the same function in society as enzymes do in the body. Certainly, the three parents that I see talking out on the lawn next to Eel Pond look as if they come from varied parts of the globe (judging from appearances only, I'd say Israel, West Africa, and India). Their preschool-aged children are having a grand time serving each other at an impromptu tea party, using trays and glasses that escaped from the MBL cafeteria in the Swope Center.

Toddlers aren't quite old enough to enjoy make-believe, acting out roles such as waiter or doctor. But by the time they are about 3 years of age or a bit older, children are engaging in organized fantasy of a kind that you'll never see in a chimpanzee. We seem to have a much more elaborate sense of self; we can even pretend that we're in someone else's shoes.

THE SENSE OF SELF is usually approached somewhat differently than a focus on the narrator as an outcome of the best-rated track of a stochastic sequencer (which is what I am about to propose). Studies in child development tend to identify a gradual development of a sense of self, as when children learn to recognize themselves in the mirror despite a smear of rouge on their noses. Sympathy and empathy emerge along the way. Being able to understand other people, and to understand how the world works more generally, are the late stages in a six-phase sequence proposed by Stanley Greenspan.

It starts with the newborn merely paying some attention to objects in the environment and gradually coming to identify the mother's face as different from others. But by about 2 months, the infant is "falling in love," smiling back to many people and reacting to them. Emotional dialogues, which develop between

10 and 18 months of age, are associated with the more complex personality that causes the child psychologists to start talking about a sense of self: Desires are expressed, actions are initiated.

By 18 to 24 months, one is seeing a much more organized self, with emotional thinking taking place: The child can play make-believe, act out others' feelings. Within another year, the child is engaged in organized fantasy, planning out tea parties, taking roles. And perhaps experiencing "dual consciousness," knowing that his own internal life is very different from how others respond to him. One pathological circumstance is the best-known cause of multiple "selves": Child abuse may cause multiple personalities to form, as the child attempts to minimize the pain.

Being able to predict others' actions is surely a basic feature of many animals' inborn abilities: Grazing animals probably can predict that, when a cat crouches and nervously twitches its tail, it is very likely to pounce next. Social animals such as cats and dogs make additional use of this elementary predicting-the-future ability, trying to avoid offending the powerful, trying to exploit others. But putting yourself in someone else's place would seem to involve something more—acting at one remove, just as in play-acting. This simulation ability suggests a sequencer in which what-would-I-do-in-that-situation scenarios can be constructed and judged against memory.

A child learns abstract terms gradually, after becoming familiar with concrete terms. Once he knows the word conscious *he may in time deal with* consciousness *as an abstract term. A host of other words will instigate the gradual growth of such abstractions as honesty, furniture, mind, education, athletics, religion, time, corruption, space, or olfaction. Such concepts form the warp and woof on the loom of thinking as we daydream, spin yarns, read detective stories, argue with friends, or write term papers. . . . Once we have the needed abstract terms, thinking is free from the impediment of listing concrete examples.*

the psychologist DAVID BALLIN KLEIN (1897–1983)

DOGS AS SUMMER VISITORS are less common at MBL, as there is no space for them in most of the temporary housing. But families who rent cottages tend to arrive in station wagons packed with everything, including pets.

Though the year-round residents among the canine population roam the town, sometimes with their tennis balls at the ready, the vacationing dogs tend to be found at the end of a long rope, fastened to a tree in the front yard. One such dog is looking frustrated this morning, as a squirrel is cavorting just out of reach—the dog is barking and straining at his leash, but the squirrel seems to understand that this dog isn't likely to chase him.

The dog could reach the squirrel if only he would backtrack, as his leash has become hung up, angled around a tree that keeps the dog from reaching the edge of the yard where the squirrel is. Dogs seldom figure out such restraints, though a sufficiently frantic dog might undo the restraint by chance on one of his random paths around the yard. A chimpanzee would take one look at the situation and head back around the tree, then race forward to reach the edge of the yard. It's a textbook example of what's meant by "insight." Leashes didn't figure in the evolution of either dog or chimp, but the chimp's intelligence is more "general purpose" and can deal with many novel situations. But how is this problem-solving done?

As R. B. Cattell notes, "The capacity of animals, even of higher apes, to perceive complex relationships is far below that of adult man, and seldom exceeds the level of a three-year-old child, yet it is of the same nature as the intelligence of man. Blind trial-and-error behavior, the very antithesis of intelligence, is common in animal behavior." The fallacy, of course, is that trial and error in *overt* behavior is quite different from trial and error in the *planning* phase, done inside the head. Darwinism shows that the product of trial and error can be quite fancy, when shaped by many rounds of selection against memories.

THE TRIAL AND ERROR CONCEPT dates back even further than Lloyd Morgan in 1894, to whom it is often misattributed. Alexander Bain (1818–1903), in a volume entitled *The Senses and the Intellect* first published in Scotland in 1855, initially employed the phrase *trial and error*. He considered the mastery of motor skills such as swimming: Through persistent effort, the swimmer

stumbles upon the "happy combination" of required movements
and can then proceed to practice them. He suggested that the
swimmer needed a sense of the effect to be produced, a command
of the elements, that he then uses trial and error until the desired
effect is actually produced. The neurologist Alf Brodal, himself
recovering from a stroke, noted that:

> Among the original multitude of more or less haphazard
> movements the correct ones are recognized as such by means
> of the sensory information they feed back to the central
> nervous system, and this information is later used in select-
> ing the correct movements in further training.

The psychologist E. L. Thorndike more properly called it the
method of *trial, error, and accidental success;* modern AI calls it
by the euphemism "generate and test." Applied to our thought
processes, the chance creation concept goes back much further, to
the sixth century B.C. in Greece:

> *But as for certain truth, no man has known it,*
> *Nor will he know it: neither of the gods,*
> *Nor yet of all the things of which I speak.*
> *And even if by chance he were to utter*
> *The perfect truth, he would himself not know it,*
> *For all is but a woven web of guesses.*
>
> XENOPHANES (Karl Popper's translation)

But a woven web of guesses can be very powerful if selection
operates on an adequate data base, and successive selection steps
can shape up outcomes that come to be impressive. This was
quickly realized in the aftermath of Darwin's success explaining
new species with successive selection by environments, as in the
1880 analysis by the pioneer American psychologist William James:

> . . . the new conceptions, emotions, and active tendencies
> which evolve are originally *produced* in the shape of random
> images, fancies, accidental outbirths of spontaneous varia-
> tions in the functional activity of the excessively unstable
> human brain, which the outer environment simply confirms

or refutes, preserves or destroys—selects, in short, just as it
selects morphological and social variations due to molecular
accidents of an analogous sort.

and the 1881 analysis by his French contemporary, Paul
Souriau:

> We know how the series of our thoughts must end, but . . . it
> is evident that there is no way to begin except at random.
> Our mind takes up the first path that it finds open before it,
> perceives that it is a false route, retraces its steps and takes
> another direction. . . . By a kind of artificial selection, we can
> . . . substantially perfect our own thought and make it more
> and more logical.

With sufficient experience, the brain comes to contain a *model* of
the world, an idea suggested in 1943 by Kenneth Craik and
championed after Craik's early demise by J. Z. Young. In *The
Nature of Explanation*, Craik outlined a "hypothesis on the nature of thought," proposing that

> the nervous system is . . . a calculating machine capable of
> modelling or paralleling external events. . . . If the organism
> carries a "small-scale model" of external reality and of its
> own possible actions within its head, it is able to try out
> various alternatives, conclude which is the best of them,
> react to future situations before they arise, utilise the knowl-
> edge of past events in dealing with the future, and in every
> way to react in a much fuller, safer and more competent
> manner to the emergencies which face it.

These concepts are powerful, but they have lacked a framework
with suitable building blocks. A Darwin Machine now provides a
framework for thinking about thought, indeed one that may be a
reasonable first approximation to the actual brain machinery underlying thought. An intracerebral Darwin Machine need not try
out one sequence at a time against memory; it may be able to try
out dozens, if not hundreds, simultaneously, shape up new generations in milliseconds, and thus initiate insightful actions without

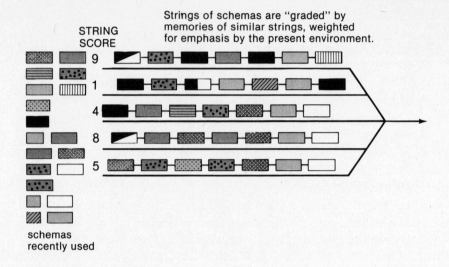

schemas
recently used

overt trial and error. This massively parallel selection among stochastic sequences is more analogous to the ways of darwinian evolutionary biology than to the "von Neumann machine" serial computer. Which is why I call it a Darwin Machine instead; it shapes up thoughts in milliseconds rather than millennia, and uses innocuous remembered environments rather than the noxious real-life ones. It may well create the uniquely human aspect of our consciousness.

THE BRAIN'S CONSTRUCTION of chained memories and actions surely involves a serial buffer, perhaps even the same one used for planning out a ballistic sequence of movement commands such as "cock elbow, inhibit flexors, inhibit fingers." And certainly it could benefit from Variations-on-a-Theme Mode, with its tree-like collection of alternatives. A useful metaphor is that candelabrum-shaped railroad marshaling yard: Imagine that many trains are randomly constructed on the parallel tracks, but only the best is selected to be let loose on the "main track" of speech (or that silent speech we often call consciousness). "Best" is determined by memories of the fate of somewhat similar sequences in the past, and one presumes a series of selection steps that shape up candidates into increasingly more realistic sequences. Instead of remembering those free-throw and long-shot sequences and using them to grade the alternative trains, then shape them up with the Darwinian Two-Step, you remember sequences of more general movement sequences, such as opening the refrigerator or changing television channels. Maybe even more general strings of concepts, such as planning college courses and a career.

For at least a century, it has been recognized that even the highest-known biological function, human thought, involves random generation of many alternatives and is only shaped up into something of quality by a series of selections. Like the elegant eyes and ears produced by biological randomness, the Darwin Machine's final product (whether sentence or scenario, algorithm or allegory) no longer appears random because of many millisecond-long generations of selection shaping up alternative sequences off-line.

WE ARE AWARE OF A TRAIN OF THOUGHT—silent speech, as it were, talking to ourselves on familiar terms or maybe just imagining movements before carrying one out. I suggest that this *conscious* sense usually corresponds to the best of the trains shaped up by that ensemble of planning tracks, the one that was let out onto the main line but not necessarily all the way to the muscles (it may also be the most common string among the population of serial buffers). The other candidates are the immediate *subconscious*—and there is surely a lot of activity going on there, because they are shuffling and mutating, trying new schemas for both sensory templates and movement programs, creating new sequences. And a lot of nonsense most of the time, but occasionally a winner. But how are the potential scenarios evaluated?

Consider a case when they aren't evaluated, at least not very well: the candidate strings that we call *dreams*. You see an occasional alternative sequence when the story line takes a sudden turn, hinging on some feature common to both old and new story line. But then you may come back to the old story line, though not always at the same point in the story, as if it had progressed some while you were paying attention to the new episode—rather as if one had switched from one TV soap opera to another, and then back 10 minutes later. Awake, the reality filter censors the nonsense much more and also keeps one from jumping around as much between scenarios—but in sleep, and occasionally daydreaming, you can see several unrealistic story lines simultaneously meandering via all the "channel-changing."

DISCERNING THE NATURE OF REALITY isn't easy, given a fantasy-prone mechanism at the center of things. With the creativity of a Darwin Machine, we also get the problems. Such as remembering what's real and what isn't. How do we know if something we remember isn't just one of our many fantasies, rather than a real happening?

Well, it is largely because our memory isn't very good. I'm not saying that we've been saved by sloppy design. On the contrary, the mechanism that regulates our ability to make a long-lasting record is likely quite sophisticated. I suspect that it's not unlike the kidney, where first you throw everything away (except for cells and large molecules), then you take back what you really want to keep from what's being discarded before it reaches the bladder.

Short-term memory fundamentally throws everything away—but slowly. And this fading-memory mechanism is all we've got working for us during nocturnal dreams. The long-term memory mechanism, which normally takes those short-term memories and makes some of them more permanent, is turned off during dreaming. And so within an hour to a day, everything fades (including dreams) unless the long-term process comes along and strengthens it. Or unless it is put into short-term storage anew, as probably happens when you recall a fading short-term memory.

Those memory-regulating circuits that prevent "recording" during dreams are being reset as you awaken, so that longer-term recording becomes possible again within 10 to 20 seconds after you sit up straight (you have to watch out for short phone calls in the middle of the night: People often fail to remember them because they didn't stay awake long enough). Recalling dreams from short-term memory after awakening means that they get a second chance to make it into long-term memory before fading out. You then remember your recall rather than the original event.

If you don't recall it soon after awakening, it will disappear. Dreams aren't usually so entertaining that you want to keep a permanent record anyway. And their significance, contrary to Freud and others who seem to see them as our own personal Oracle speaking, seems "transparent," merely a hodgepodge of one's current concerns and old memories strung together somehow; like daytime thoughts, they sometimes achieve useful juxtapositions. Darwin Machine reasoning essentially says that our waking thoughts are just like our nocturnal dreams, except (1) we can sometimes remember them better, (2) much higher standards of reality-testing are used when shaping up a scenario, and (3) sometimes a movement plan is gated out into actual movements.

Actually doing something, rather than just reading about it, has long been recognized by educators as a much better way to make something stick. Copying out a phrase, or speaking it aloud, is a technique reinvented by many a student. When your learning strategies finally permit you to memorize something without moving your lips, to scan a page and effectively recall its contents, then you have tampered with one of your major mechanisms for separating illusion from reality: That actual movement is a prerequisite for memorizing. If you then regulate that recording mechanism poorly, you'll flirt with the extremes of believing the imagined and of being a slow learner. Learning to learn involves playing around at the boundary between illusion and reality, coming to cope with the middle ground—where you spin scenarios without necessarily letting them from your short-term into your long-term memory.

It's a good thing that we can't readily recall our dreams; they're usually dimly remembered, if at all, and the mere "lack of force" of the memory tends to cue us that it was probably just a dream fragment rather than a real happening. But suppose something went wrong and your nocturnal dreams (and even the things you consciously thought about doing but didn't do) were easily recalled—you could have trouble maintaining your sense of reality in the manner of the schizophrenic, who probably "hears" one of the planning tracks as an auditory hallucination.

The Latin verb cogito *is derived, as St. Augustine tells us, from Latin words meaning* to shake together, *while the verb* intelligo *means* to select among. *The Romans, it seems, knew what they were talking about.*

the philosopher DANIEL C. DENNETT, 1978

EXERCISING THE SERIAL BUFFER might be the common feature of all those pleasant pastimes: baseball, basketball, hammering, tennis, juggling, playing pianos, dancing jigs. Indeed, a serial buffer is even handy for games that aren't overtly ballistic: Consider chess or contract bridge, with their planning for the future and choosing between alternative sequences of moving pieces or laying down cards. Of course, that suggests more than one serial-planning buffer: You need at least two if you are to compare sequences, judge which is better. Having dozens of planning tracks would be even better.

If we have such buffers, are they as long as the ones in a telephone's memory? While machines can easily chain together 13 digits, humans have problems with only half as many. There are some suggestions that the capacity of one important serial buffer in humans is a bit more than a half dozen items, judging from phenomena such as digit span: Most of us can hold on to about 7 digits in sequence long enough to repeat them back or dial a phone; anything longer and (unless part of it is very familiar to us already) we have to use crutches such as writing them down. In 1956, the psychologist George Miller wrote a now-famous paper entitled "The magical number seven, plus or minus two" on this theme; some people can only hold on to 5 digits, some can manage 9, but the average is about 7.

And so we subdivide the problem whenever approaching our 7-digit limit. Back in the days of American telephone exchanges having names rather than all-number prefixes, you just remembered "Murray Hill" and then 4 or 5 digits; nearly everyone can manage that so long as they know that Murray Hill translated into "68" (MU and not MH's "64"!). This mnemonic device served to break up the job of remembering a 7-digit-long string by fragmenting the first few digits off into a separate chunk called the prefix, recognized separately as a regular part of our vocabulary. The only way that most of us can manage longer digit sequences (it takes me at least 13 digits to call Israel) is by *chunking:* remembering the international-call access number separately (011), the international dialing code for Israel separately (972), then the code for Jerusalem (2), and then the prefix (58) at Hebrew University, followed by the 4-digit extension. That's eight chunks total, rather than the 13 separate units "remembered" by the phone's memory.

Similarly, in planning what to say next, we plan ahead no more than about a half dozen words; while we're pronouncing those words, we make up the rest of the sentence, one reason that it is said that we usually don't know how a sentence is going to end when we start it. If each word of a seven-word sentence stands for something very simple, like a digit, then the sentence itself cannot say much. But if each word stands for a whole concept and its many connotations, then a unique seven-word sentence can encompass much:

The dreams of reason bring forth monsters.

FRANCISCO JOSÉ DE GOYA (1746–1828)

Lost in a gloom of uninspired research.

WILLIAM WORDSWORTH (1770–1850)

Science is the record of dead religions.

OSCAR WILDE (1854–1900)

We are products of editing, not authorship.

GEORGE WALD (1906–   )

Each time that we define a new word, we are usually replacing a long phrase: *recrudescence* or *relapse* to stand in place of "the problem starting up all over again after a remission." This is chunking, and we do it mostly because of that 7-plus-or-minus-2 limit on what we can work with at any one time in our serial buffer for speech.

VARIATIONS-ON-A-THEME MODE would obviously be handy for generating all of those subconscious sequences that we see in our dreams, and presumably use in our daytime thoughts to good advantage. But how about "making up your mind," when you stop imagining, achieve closure? It took me years to realize this, even after I recognized that serial buffers for throwing ought to be handy for talking and thinking, but the shaping up of a population of buffers, from widely varied to near-clones, is precisely analogous to the amplification step in the immune response, and to the allopatric speciation step in biological evolution. And it corresponds nicely to narrowing down the thoughts, not merely to the best-of-the-possibilities but to make that best one also the most common one, the string that takes up residence in many of the buffers by winning out in the Darwinian Two-Step competition.

The mere process of having to borrow helpers, to recruit that audience to help sing along with the choir, means that there will be a phase when there will be a lot of variation in the sequences sung by the various singers (the "first rehearsal phenomenon" known to all choirmasters). But unlike the choir, where adherence to the music is the criterion for grading performance, each singer is graded against memories of past performances, each aspect of which is weighted by how appropriate it is to the present situation in which the singer finds himself. The more confident the singer is, the louder he sings, and so the more he influences other singers to change their song and follow along. The population evolves, as the scattered group of novel individuals start coalescing into a synchronous chorus. The dominant version now becomes the one that won out in the competition, not the one written down on some preordained sheet of music.

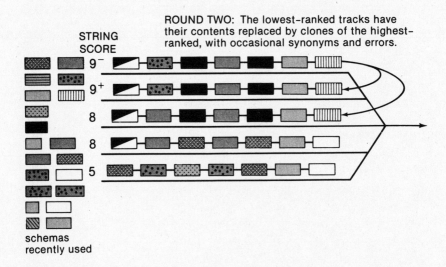

STRING
SCORE

ROUND TWO: The lowest-ranked tracks have their contents replaced by clones of the highest-ranked, with occasional synonyms and errors.

9⁻

9⁺

8

8

5

schemas
recently used

ROUND THREE: The second track, with its
slight alteration during cloning, is now ranked
higher than the original victor, and serves as parent.

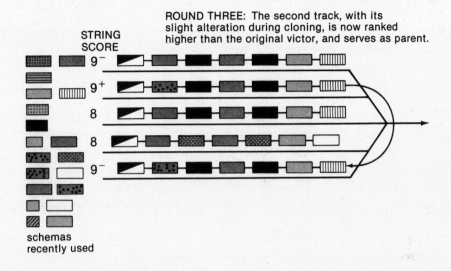

STRING
SCORE

schemas
recently used

CLONE DOMINANCE can eventually occur
if attention is maintained (thus keeping the
valuation scheme constant). This inhibits further
variations but serves to reduce timing jitter too.

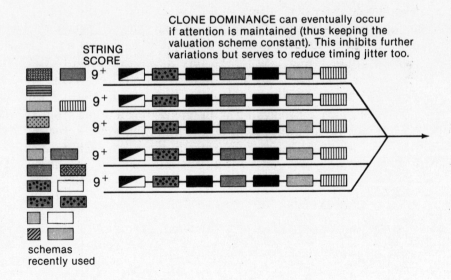

STRING
SCORE

schemas
recently used

IF THIS IS CORRECT, then I was wrong when I said that consciousness was a much harder, more nebulous problem than the standard visual cognition problems such as imagining the front of a doll's house in your head, rotating it around so that you can "look into" its open rear wall, and then concentrating on the furnishings of a single room. That, as any computer programmer can tell you, is a big computational problem that must be done in a long series of time-consuming steps. Those 3-year-old children at their tea party on the Swope patio might not be very good at that task, but in another 5 years or so, they'll be experts. Yet I don't think that such visualization abilities are anywhere as important to our sense of self, compared to scenario-spinning and its associated *narrator* of our life's story.

On my analysis, the narrator of our conscious experience arises from the current winner of a multitrack Darwin Machine competition. It isn't an explanation for everything that goes on in our head, but it is an explanation for that virtual executive that directs our attention, sometimes outward toward a real house, sometimes inward toward a remembered house or imagined doll's house, sometimes free-running to create our stream of consciousness. Directing sensory attention may seem unlike making movement plans, but the neural circuits seem analogous, all part of that frontal lobe circuitry used in making preparations for action.

And unlike the criticism of Gilbert Ryle's exorcision of "the ghost in the machine," that he offered no alternative explanation for how he generated his own thoughts, the Darwin Machine can account for much: for imagination, for generating a broad range of choices, narrowing them down, imagining again, and so creating more and more sophisticated thoughts in much the same way as the better-known biological evolution creates fancier and fancier species. The Darwin Machine theory accounts for how this explanation was generated, its sentences constructed and revised, and for how criticisms of the proposal can be listened to, analyzed, and amalgamated into a new view.

Indeed, one wonders if alternative explanations for thought will not simply turn out to be mechanistic equivalents to Darwin Machines, once reduced to such an elementary neurophysiological level. What else is there besides randomness for generating imagination, for innovating, for finding the best fits? That is not to say that explanations at other levels might not turn out to be more useful for some purposes, just as equation-solving algorithms are extremely handy for dealing with a restricted class of phenomena (when you learned long division, you learned an algorithm—a routine procedure guaranteed to provide an answer). A directed search of an ordered list of possibilities, as in expert systems that attempt to diagnose a patient's disease by asking a series of key questions, may be far more efficient than randomly spinning hypotheses. But when we start talking of innovation, imagination, our own stream of thought, and how we initially arrive at an algorithm, we may well be talking Darwin Machines but simply in various "languages."

Many of the attempts to create "artificial intelligence" are simply efforts to apply computer programming to complex problems that humans often solve. And a logical framework is indeed the first thing to try, especially when limited in computing power. However, it has been observed that AI is good at doing what humans find difficult (championship chess), but inept at doing what humans find easy (touching our nose, navigating around obstacles, coming up with creative ideas). Some have suggested that AI's traditional fare is better called "artificial stupidity" in the same spirit as the advice to anxious beginners about computers: "It's just a stupid machine. It can't do anything except what you tell it to do—if you make a mistake, it'll make the same mistake a thousand times faster." Can AI's paradoxical performance be because AI still has the recipe-following calculating-machine mentality?

But the artificial intelligentsia has lacked the computing machinery to implement a more natural approach. The parallel computers that have grown out of the serial von Neumann machines are now attaining much power despite their programming problems; furthermore, neurallike networks have given us a nontraditional approach to shaping up a mechanical *tabula rasa*. Implementing massively serial versions is only a matter of time, and some will result in Darwin Machines.

Considering that silicon-based computers can operate a million times faster than our neurons can, gaining a foothold on the problems of instructing massively parallel networks would mean that we might have computing power to rival that of the human brain within a few decades—and this should help us figure out just how the human brain utilizes emergent properties. It should enable us to construct some fascinating machines. We will be able to hold an interesting conversation with some of them, and appreciate reality from some new points of view. We might even have to concede them some degree of consciousness.

WHAT WE SEQUENCE are often the schemas we call words. Many of our words are verbs, standing for actions: We can think *run* without running; *run* can be the movement melody but with the final pathways inhibited (just as they are inhibited during your nighttime dreams). Other cars on this train could be linkages such as *is-a-member-of* or *is-connected-to* or *is-contained-in*. Other words are nouns—essentially sensory schemas for objects and people and such. "Bob runs" is a noun-verb sequence in our heads that we call a sentence. We can make fancier strings of the sensory and movement schemas: "Jack and Jill went up the hill."

The railroad marshaling yard metaphor serves to show how candidate sequences could be compared against memory and graded, the grades then compared between candidates (those with an engine at one end and a caboose at the other may have fared better earlier and so get higher grades). The interesting emergent properties would, however, arise from the mechanisms that allowed candidate sequences to be compared, both for content (which elements, in what order) and timing (when the element was gated out, analogous to variable spacing between the railroad cars—as if each were on a leash of adjustable length).

Once you've got a buffer that is seven chunks long—maybe just for the occasions demanding hammering—then maybe you can use it for sentences in the spare time. Perhaps when you get dozens of serial buffers for the throwing occasions that demand them, you can also use them for other things, much of the time. That's the startling alternative to language as the evolutionary "cause" of our penchant for stringing things together. Language becomes just another secondary use—maybe a more important one than making music, but no longer the *raison d'être*.

This isn't to say that language wasn't useful during the Ice Ages, when hominids were being shaped up into humans—in evolutionary arguments like this, you have to distinguish between the invention and the streamlining. Conversions of function, as when number-crunching digital computers also turned out to be handy for wristwatches and file cabinets, can sometimes give an enormous boost, accounting for most of the modern functionality, with natural selection accounting only for the frosting on the cake. Or the invention by sidestepping conversion may barely get things going (as when fish jawbones were incorporated into the middle ear), with functional streamlining dominating the modern version (the tiny stapes, hammer, and anvil bones that couple your eardrum to your inner ear). Feathers for flight may be an intermediate case, feathers for thermal insulation getting fore-limbs up to the rather considerable threshold of flight; after the conversion of function, there was lots of streamlining, with even those specializations for slow flying that you see on the tips of crow wings.

Which kind of conversion will language turn out to be? Frosting, core—or more like "marble cake" from a series of back-and-forth inventions and specializations? My guess is that it is going to prove to be very useful to understand the serial buffer specializations needed for precision throwing, that they will help us to appreciate the foundation from which our other serial abilities have arisen. But each secondary serialization will prove to have a life of its own, just as flying involves a lot more than you would have guessed from thermal underwear.

*Language is incomplete and fragmentary, and merely regis-
ters a stage in the average advance beyond ape-mentality.
But all men enjoy flashes of insight beyond meanings already stabilized in etymology and grammar.*

the philosopher ALFRED NORTH WHITEHEAD (1861-1947)

———— 13 ————

THE TRILOGY OF HOMO SERIATIM: LANGUAGE, CONSCIOUSNESS, AND MUSIC

[All] thinking is metaphorical, except mathematical think-ing. . . . What I am pointing out is that unless you are at home in the metaphor, unless you have had your proper poetical education in the metaphor, you are not safe any-where. Because you are not at ease with figurative values: you don't know the metaphor in its strength and its weak-nesses. You don't know how far you may expect to ride it and when it may break down with you. You are not safe in science; you are not safe in history. . . .

All metaphor breaks down somewhere. That is the beauty of it. It is touch and go with the metaphor, and until you have lived with it long enough you don't know when it is going.

ROBERT FROST

When I was a boy I felt that the role of rhyme in poetry was to compel one to find the unobvious because of the necessity of finding a word which rhymes. This forces novel associa-tions and almost guarantees deviations from routine chains or trains of thought. It becomes paradoxically a sort of automatic mechanism of originality. . . . And what we call talent or perhaps genius itself depends to a large extent on the ability to use one's memory properly to find the analo-gies . . . essential to the development of new ideas.

STANISLAW M. ULAM

Music and poetry may hold some clues about the sequencer machinery, simply because there has probably been little natural selection in their favor. Through music, we might be able to see the sequencer less obscured by the streamlining adaptations that interfere with our view if we attempt to study it via the peculiarities of ever-useful speech and planning.

Did the precise hammering of our common ancestor with the chimpanzee, as it cracked open tough nuts, make possible the throwing skills of prehumans? Did more accurate throwing, and its rewards in terms of hunting success, shape up an even better neural "sequencer"? Did language "borrow" that sequencer in the off-hours (we still stop speaking when we get set to throw accurately)? Does music borrow it now when it isn't needed for either throwing or speaking? Do we use it to spin a scenario, as when we attempt to explain the past or forecast the future? Does it account for our self-consciousness as we see ourselves poised at the intersection of two plausible scenarios, choosing between different futures? Is it the stuff that dreams are made of? Such are the possibilities created by the brain's multifunctional cells and circuits: They almost seem to specialize in side steps, the sequence-related side steps being the most recent and the most central to our humanity. It's a very different view of the evolution of our big brain than the usual bigger-is-smarter-is-better notions. As I said in *The River that Flows Uphill,*

From such an evolutionary ratchet jacking up brain size, there arose unbidden our own brain of unbounded potential. From basketball to tennis, this mosaic brain expresses its ancient pleasure in precisely timing a sequence. Transcending its origins, our brain can now create novel sequences using grammar and music. Blind to our foundations, we nonetheless created poetry and reason; with a clearer footing, we can perhaps contemplate how our enlarged consciousness evolved and is evolving.

We invented language without any understanding of the neural machinery underlying it. Yet think of what happened to transportation in the wake of understanding Newton's physics (from carts to trains, planes, and space shuttles), or to communication in the wake of our nineteenth-century understanding of electricity and magnetism (from letters to our satellite-based telephone network), or to medicine once the circulation of the blood and the role of microscopic organisms were appreciated (from purging to physiologically based neurosurgery for Parkinsonism). Once we establish a nearly correct explanation for our thinking and language machinery, we should see a great augmentation in our capabilities as the principles become incorporated into our educational philosophy and into the ergonomic design of our machinery. "Rationality" will take on a whole new meaning, and musical composition will flourish as more people become capable of Bach-like mental agility.

Parallel trains of thought [are the] necessary heirs of every action, [and are] always running on in mind.

CHARLES DARWIN, *M Notebook*, 1838

MY DARWIN MACHINES METAPHOR is based on a strong analogy to the Darwinian Two-Step. This is the biological dance of randomness then selection, back and forth. Its many injections of randomness are usually by the gene shuffling that occurs during crossing over, as sperm and ova are made; we understand the gene shuffling that goes on in the immune response less well, but it's a similar setup. This achieves a very non-random-looking result because of the power of selection effected by an environment full of predators and pathogens, opportunities and obstacles. There are many serially coded individuals (DNA strings in the genome, amino-acid strings in antibodies, movement sequences in behavior) existing simultaneously in parallel—but most are nonsense when graded by the "environment."

To evaluate Darwin Machines as the possible off-line planner, we must briefly consider a topic that philosophers find daunting: the problem of *value*. For throwing plans, memories of closely similar situations might cause a candidate to be rated 9+, while other situations (such as throwing while perched on a tree branch) might have few similar elements in memory and so no proposal receives more than a 4. One can imagine quantifying the elements of the problem (distance, height difference, wind, rock size, target size, etc.) separately and summing up. But for other sequential tasks such as scenario-spinning and language, how does one assign a value to a possible scenario, so that one can rate a scenario as "better" than another? And eventually find the "best"?

Grading is a procedure presumably analogous to the economist's utility functions, essentially dimensionless numbers assigned to various elements of the problem (not unlike the way that sensations can be graded by guessing where it falls on a scale of 0 to 10) and then summed up as if they were "costs" or "revenues" of some factory:

> You're halfway down the stairs of your apartment building when a thought occurs: you've forgotten your umbrella. . . . You glance at your watch and recall the subway schedule. The neural circuits that are dealing with weather award 9 points to the possibility of rain. The likelihood of missing the subway is given an 8. . . . Perhaps there is a dial that controls fear of being late; turn it from 5 to 7. Perhaps this new signal would swing the decision the other way, in favor of forgetting about the umbrella. Or lower the level on another dial that controls one's aversion to rain.
>
> The point is that you can make your imaginary computer as complex as you like, adding dials to control any number of characteristics, making the gradations on the dials as fine as you please, programming the entire system to base its decisions on many times more data. Maybe that's not how the mind works. But it begins to look as though it could be modeled that way, if the simulation were fine enough.

the science journalist GEORGE JOHNSON, 1986

We're actually very good at making relative judgments, comparing two sounds or two lights or two tastes and saying what their relative "strength" is. S. S. Stevens and co-workers established a series of power-law relationships for such subjective rating scales in the 1950s.

You can use these subjective ratings to compare unlike things, even guns and butter. For some people, an apple is worth 0.73 oranges. The economists in particular are always equating things for planning purposes, even outrageous things such as the "cost" of a worker's life (they are not, of course, proposing exchanges, only trying to establish true costs of building bridges and the like). Consumer organizations rating products are likely to award so many points for this, so many for that feature, so many for relative price, etc. To plan for the future, architects generate alternative scenarios and grade them according to subjective "liking." Environmental impact statements always list alternatives to the favored one, with their advantages and disadvantages; frequently, the public rates the alternatives quite differently than the planners.

Except for lacking the random shuffling and the Darwinian Two-Step, the economists' model of rational planning sounds rather like my model for mind:

> [There are] four principal components of the [Subjective Expected Utility] model: a cardinal utility function [that can assign a cardinal number as a measure of one's liking of any scenario of events in the future], an exhaustive set of alternative strategies, a probability distribution of scenarios for the future associated with each strategy, and a policy of maximizing expected utility.
>
> the computer scientist HERBERT A. SIMON, 1983

Of course, the "exhaustive set" and the expectation of a unique, optimal solution is where the economists got into trouble with this otherwise fine idea (which Simon calls "one of the most impressive intellectual achievements of the first half of the twentieth century. It is an elegant machine for applying reason to problems of choice"). What economists perhaps have not realized is that successive rounds of shaping up and additional injections of randomness can solve the problem—as evolution demonstrates (just substitute "fitness" for "utility").

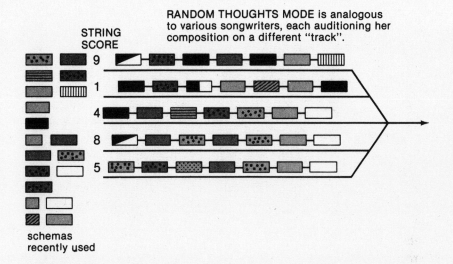

STRING
SCORE

RANDOM THOUGHTS MODE is analogous
to various songwriters, each auditioning her
composition on a different "track".

schemas
recently used

ATTENTION CAN WANDER, sometimes being loose (as when daydreaming at the beach), sometimes being fairly well focused (as in trying to decide between known alternatives), and sometimes being tightly focused (as when one "gets set" to throw). That makes it look as if the process of shaping up a population of sequencers can be held at various levels. To what does this correspond in the original darwinism?

In the Random Thoughts Mode exemplified by noctural dreams (and also daydreams), the valuation scheme is episodically changing, e.g., boredom and novelty. One never progresses to near-clones, as might happen if we maintained attention long enough; when we "become interested" in something new, as when the story line in a dream shifts, we also change "grading criteria" and set about trying to make some sense out of the scenario on another track. It is not unlike the child "at the top of the class" changing every day of the week as the teacher's tests switch from emphasizing spelling on Monday to emphasizing American history on Tuesday, to science on Wednesday, etc. If the teacher got stuck in a rut, as used to happen when a spelling bee stimulated competition, then the leaders of the pack are shaped up by the competition—but to the neglect of other subject matter.

The Variations-on-a-Theme Mode would be where attention mechanisms keep the valuation scheme fairly constant, but still

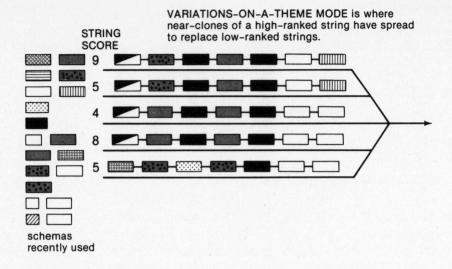

VARIATIONS-ON-A-THEME MODE is where near-clones of a high-ranked string have spread to replace low-rapked strings.

STRING SCORE

9

5

4

8

5

schemas
recently used

drift around enough to maintain variation, keeping a pure clone from taking over. Because of the drift in climate (if not continents!), biological evolution seldom progresses to a pure clone, except via the artificial selection practiced by laboratory rat breeders trying to produce a strain with minimal variability. "Making up one's mind" might only require a majority of the tracks achieving the same string, not nearly all of them. Pathological processes such as worry might correspond to an inability to break out of such a tightly focused mode: No new string ever has a chance to become good enough to outscore an existing one.

But when does the cerebral choir gang into lockstep to "sing a Hallelujah Chorus"? What in the consciousness version of darwinism might the Choral Mode correspond to? It, after all, is what would seem to be under the severe selection pressure during evolution, since it should be so helpful in making a regular living as a hunter. What in speech or scenario-spinning consciousness corresponds to the ganged-into-lockstep phase? The Choral Mode would be much closer to a real clone than a simple majority: Everyone is singing the same "Hallelujah" as close to the "same time" as they can manage. But you probably achieve such an ultimate state of affairs only by "concentrating very hard" and excluding anything

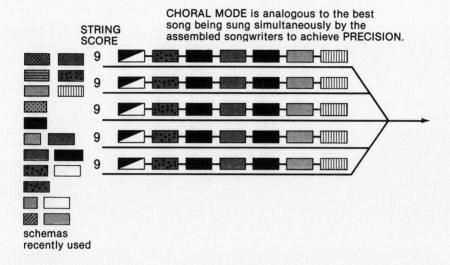

that might "distract" you from the task and cause you to value something else more for a while. Both biological evolution and the immune system seem to value variety, and so a clone takeover isn't often seen.

But there are special circumstances, and they are particularly instructive. When rabbits were imported into Australia, there was a big population explosion based on the genes of the "founder population" that arrived by ship from England. The same thing happens naturally when an insect, carried away from the mainland by the wind or a piece of driftwood, comes to rest on an island—and discovers that it has no competitors for the food and no predators either. If the insect happens to be a pregnant female, then just one individual's fortuitous arrival can set the stage for a population explosion, and each of them will have gene sequences as similar as in siblings. The Indians of North and South America could be descendants of a relatively closely related tribe which arrived at a virgin continent and expanded over 500 generations.

So shifting attention in our mental life seems analogous to the fluctuating environment that constantly changes what is valued. If selection is also weak, as when a new niche is discovered or a conversion of function has invented a new way of making a living, a lot of different sequences may be pursued at once; in Random Thoughts Mode, the "top dog" is constantly switching around, mostly because nothing achieves a very high score. I suspect that the reason our dreams are so changeable is the same reason that they are so absurd: Checking candidate sequences against memory sequences doesn't work very well, and so scores are never very high; nothing gets shaped up very far before something else takes over the lead.

When efficiency is valued because the ecosystem has settled down enough to make competition between individuals more important, then some shaping up occurs—but the environment drifts a little faster than evolution can track it, and so there remain lots of deviant sequences in Variation-on-a-Theme Mode. But extreme concentration is rare in behavior, probably because it can cause you to be "blindsided"; flying instructors, for example, are careful to teach student pilots to always be looking around for other planes even after they've spotted one (many a pilot has let another plane approach unnoticed while his attention was riveted on a known threat).

When something extraordinary about the environment (such as the total lack of predators or competitors) *and* something unusual about the circumstances (such as a small founder population) set the stage, then you can wind up with near-uniformity. And the same may be true of the Choral Mode of that Darwin Machine inside our heads when it encounters an unusual set of memories in an unusual setting: The *idée fixe*? The person with the "one-track mind"? The obsessive? The worrier? The person with perfect pitch? The baseball pitcher? It will be interesting to look at some of the correlates of synchrony in the electroencephalogram in such people to explore this new possibility for modeling brain processes.

MAKING UP A SENTENCE to speak is obviously one aspect of this scheme for consciousness. It is sometimes said that when we begin to speak a sentence, we seldom know how the sentence is going to end, certainly not if the utterance is more than a half dozen words long. But even a half dozen items would be a long sequence in the study of ape abilities with sign languages. In order to look at the word substitution aspects, it is convenient to start a discussion of word sequencing by restricting ourselves to just a pair of words, a darwinian marshaling yard for two-car trains. Naming horses may seem an idiosyncratic introduction to the language uses of Darwin Machines but it avoids the elaborate sequential aspect of Darwin Machines while retaining its other properties.

So suppose we are horse breeders trying to name a new colt or filly. Their registered names tend to be compounds like "Incredible Nevele" or "Lumber Along." The idea is to combine the names of sire and dam in some way—they don't have to be exact copies of a word from the name, but merely suggest something similar. For example:

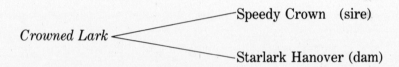

Or this three-generation example:

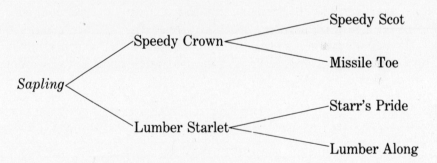

Sometimes preference is given to one parent because of its racing record being so much better. And it's easy to see how a Darwin Machine could generate alternative horse names, using the synonyms and associations of each word, how the Darwin Machine could eliminate candidates by using utility scores based on racing times as well as information about how frequently the candidate words appear in juxtaposition in English usage. Take the lower right set of parents, "Star's Pride" and "Lumber Along." Star might suggest *planet, famous, nova, meteor, starlet;* lumber might suggest *timber, trees, saplings, willows,* etc. And so "Lumber Starlet." Combined with "Speedy Crown" and synonyms, it could lead to "Limber Lumber," or simply "Sapling."

But what kind of neural circuits can take the assigned values of tracks in the marshaling yard, compare them, and announce a winner? Find "the best"? This turns out to be an easy problem, given all of those lateral inhibition circuits that are so plentiful everywhere we look in the brain. A cell in an array with a larger output than all others will inhibit its neighbors more strongly than they inhibit it. And so the natural differences between "better" and "best" are exaggerated. The outcome is reminscent of the Matthew Principle (the rich get richer), though the result is achieved by the dynamics of a network (even simpler mechanisms can also produce a matthewist result). With suitable tuning of inhibitory strengths between neighbors, one can almost get all-or-nothing results—though a series of lateral inhibitory stages probably provides better stability (protection against wild oscillations and locking up) than would a single stage tuned so critically.

SENTENCES ARE MORE COMPLICATED than thoroughbred names, but Darwin Machines are also fancier than the limited one- or two-word sequence machinery needed for naming horses. Nouns may stand for some perceptual schema, but unless a verb and its object are implied (as when your mother calls you, using your first *and* middle names!) a stand-alone noun isn't much of a message. But the trains that Darwin Machines shape up can be sentences, a string with an actor, an action, and the object of the action, etc.

Your basic everyday message is a clause, a noun with a predicate added. A typical predicate is a verb (generally a stand-in for a movement program, such as "come") plus objects of the verb (such as "here") and modifiers to the verb (such as "quickly"). Most of these may be omitted when a short form develops through frequent use: "You come here quickly" can be shortened in many ways, and voice inflections used to substitute for some words. Adjectives allow us to describe states of being, such as "happy" or "old" or "tall."

A sequence of clauses making a sentence may tell quite a story, first one action-action-object and then another. Clauses and

AT THE
ANGRY
DOG
BIT
AT AN
MAILMAN
PERSON
RUN
AWAY
TREES
AWAY
RUN FOR

words recently
used and variants

SHAPING UP A SENTENCE using the massively-
serial planning tracks, and words associated with
those in recent use. GRADING is by grammar as
well as by suitability to the present situation.

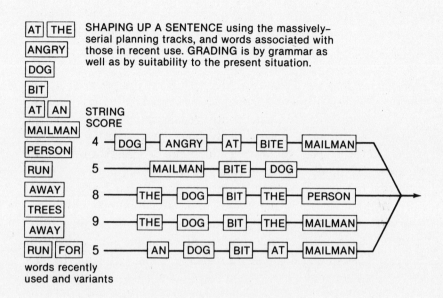

MAILMAN
HOUND
DOGS
MAILPERSON
DOG
POSTMAN
LETTER
CARRIER
POSTAL
PERSON
PEOPLE
WOMAN

words recently used
and their variants

PERFECTING A SENTENCE replaces low
ranked strings with near–clones of the best
sentence. Relatives of words sometimes are used.

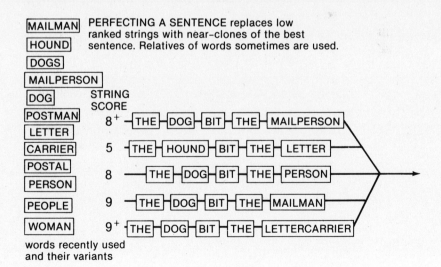

sentences usually get us into word order considerations, as most languages utilize position within the phrase as an indicator of which noun is the subject, which the object—as in the simple English declarative sentence's subject-verb-object ("You come here") word order. Verbs are the easiest words to identify, probably because they're "movement schemas"; then it's a matter of identifying the role played by the other words. Pretty soon you've made a reasonable model for the actors and actions intended by the speaker of the sentence—in that you could rephrase the sentence, perhaps in another language, and have it come out correctly. Or, even more directly, you could carry out the suggestion-command-whatever yourself, such as "coming here."

That's a Darwin Machine interpretation of what happens when you're trying to decode a received message. What about coding a message for transmission, i.e., deciding what to say next? A model for planning a clause to speak could be very similar to naming horses, grading each randomly assembled train by the rules of syntax and by the individual's memories of similar verbal situations. The highest-ranked train might be kept and the rest shuffled with the rest of the deck (in the extreme, all the words of one's vocabulary, but usually just a subset of words recently used or strongly linked to other current elements). With many rounds of shuffling, the highest-ranked train will be shaped up to better and better approximations of a plan suitable to the situation. While remembered environments are less detailed than real ones, this off-line simulation and testing operates in milliseconds-to-seconds rather than the centuries-to-millennia of biological speciation.

So sequencers for an animal's ballistic movements might be capable of being borrowed for making up plans and sentences. Can this be done without modifications to the ballistic buffers, or might we expect hominid success in planning and talking to modify the planning buffers with a number of secondary structures to insure entailment or grammar? Fortunately, there may be some uses of the sequencing machinery that are so lacking in evolutionary usefulness that we might be able to "see" the underlying machinery without a lot of adaptive overlay. Four-part harmony and contrapuntal techniques may help illuminate the structure of the serial buffer ensemble, the exact shapes of the branching pattern of that marshaling yard in our heads.

Song is the noblest, the most intimate, the most complete manner of self-expression known to mankind, and in the last analysis self-expression is the great thing for which mankind is ever searching. As the power to express grows, so the higher ideals of life develop and the greatest and most subtle influences which make for culture come to have full sway.

There comes into every life a time when the inner self can no longer be reached by things from without, when the soul craves that which it can supply to itself alone. Song then becomes not only a source of forgetfulness of material things and a solace, but also an inspiration.

the voice coach OSCAR SAENGER, 1915

THE WOODS HOLE CANTATA gives its one performance of the year tonight in the Church of the Messiah, after weeks of evening practice at MBL. They're doing Bach's Mass in F followed after an intermission by his Magnificat in D.

The orchestra and chorus of 65 fill the front of this small church with its peaked mahogany ceiling. Hundreds of people from the scientific community fill every pew and corner, sit in every aisle and doorway. There is one hazard of making notes like these about the church and the performance—they might be read aloud to next year's gathering. Which is exactly what happened tonight, while they were passing the offering plate, to Gerald Weissman's opening chapter of his book of science essays taking their name from this event, *The Woods Hole Cantata*. The people sitting in the aisles laughed uproariously at being described as "limber postdocs." And one could not help but compare his description of the church interior (the "trim, no-nonsense bearing of its nautical setting: Bright timber work, well-hewn pews, and high brass") with the real thing. Writers are usually spared this indignity; if anyone reads my descriptions of the Grand Canyon aloud while at the spot, I hope not to be around to hear. But Weissman so nicely captured the feeling of the occasion that I shall have to quote him.

The audience—relatives, friends, coworkers, students—fills the hall with the tribal buzz and chatter that one hears at class reunions or graduations. The air is laced with *pizzicati* of nervous laughter that I recognize from my children's first recitals at music school or their undergraduate recitals. As the performers file in, I look about at the community gathered here. One can identify embryologists whose winter habitats range from Hawaii to Naples, biochemists from Northwestern to Stony Brook, physiologists from Seattle to the Cambridges, physicians from Duarte to Lund. . . . [Tonight] we are all *en famille* to celebrate the ancient ritual of music in concert.

Many of the musicians, and most of the audience, are making their once-a-year appearance in church with this evening of music. Quite a few scientists in my acquaintance are accomplished musicians who had to make a difficult choice between continuing their musical careers and their scientific careers. And so the weeks of practice for this night are a joy to such scientists, a chance to exercise their considerable skills once more. My choral career evaporated, alas, when my voice changed, but performances in church still have a special quality for me from having once been on the other side, singing Latin words that I didn't understand.

The pews and aisles were packed by the time I arrived. But I have, arguably, the best seat in the house: A commanding view, excellent acoustics, room to stretch my legs during the concert, and I can even imitate conducting the chorus because I am out of sight at the rear of the church and few people will see me. There is only one slight drawback: One dares not fall asleep, under penalty of falling one floor and landing in the cellar below, undoubtedly with a great crash. I have the window sill above the cellar stairs, and I am wedged in, thanks to a mountain-climbing technique known as chimney bridging that I last used at Matkatamiba in the Grand Canyon. But there isn't the usual danger of becoming drowsy: I also have an excellent supply of fresh air, because the window is open. During pauses, I can hear it softly raining outdoors.

Much of the great music is church music, written to celebrate the faith and attract others to it. And so here with the Mass in F we have one of Bach's "Missae breve," descended from the Gregorian chants of the medieval Catholic Church, written for Lutheran services in Leipzig in the early eighteenth century, sung in a nineteenth-century Episcopal church on Cape Cod by and for a collection of late-twentieth-century scientists who would explain the world in very different terms from those used by many churchgoers.

Yet science is descended from the same roots as the philosophy of Bach and Handel; Newton surely considered himself to be attempting to understand deeply his Creator's works. In most cultures, there is little distinction between religion-philosophy-science; even in Western civilization, they were all one subject until only a few centuries ago, when religious and natural philosophy split apart, the former becoming theology and the latter again splitting in the last century to become science and what we now call philosophy. The scientists of Bach's time surely considered church music their music, not that of another tradition.

But music is music: It can stand by itself, transcending the centuries independent of rational and irrational beliefs about other things. No one really approaches modern religion like the proverbial cultural anthropologist from outer space ("But they organize all their good deeds around this gruesome symbol of torture, and their highest ritual is play acting cannibalism, and they constantly reaffirm their own version of what in other cultures they call magic and animism. They seem to expect members to check their brains at the church-house door!"). Yet cultures cannot simply start over fresh with a new vocabulary and new traditions untainted by past enthusiasms and misunderstandings; it is simply too easy to throw out the baby with the bathwater. Instead, religions rationalize the past in various ways and go on from there with the real business: relieving suffering and building hope and advancing understanding. The philosophers and scientists have merely become the *understanding* specialists over the last several centuries. But if we've left some of the excess baggage and comforting rituals behind, we still revere the music.

And I think that musical forms will have a lot to teach us about our brains. Folksinger Bill Crowfoot observes that children in many cultures, speaking many languages, still all use the musical form known as a "minor third" to harass their siblings:

Nyah-nyah, nyah, nyah, nyah, nyah.

The first few notes of Beethoven's Fifth Symphony, G-G-G-E♭, probably sound like "Thus, Fate knocks at the door" (or is it Kate?) in many cultures. The more elaborate forms of the *Magnificat* may not be as universal—but still, they resonate. Some tunes (which the Germans call *Ohrwurm*, or "ear worm") seem to spread through the population like the latest respiratory infection. Why? Is there some niche in our brains, created by the language we speak, that predisposes us to certain melodies?

> *The robin red-breast sings in a loud clear voice in order to keep other robin red-breasts away from the bit of territory that it is on. But except for singing in the morning in the shower, I have never known a human being to utter sounds for this purpose.*
>
> the mathematician JACOB BRONOWSKI (1908-1974)

> *Music is nothing but unconscious arithmetic. . . . Music is pleasure the human soul experiences from counting without being aware that it is counting.*
>
> the mathematician G. W. LEIBNITZ (1646-1716)

> *Music is the arithmetic of sounds as optics is the geometry of light.*
>
> the composer CLAUDE DEBUSSY (1862-1918)

MUSIC IS ONE OF OUR GREAT evolutionary puzzles. It demonstrates nicely the inadequacy of evolution by adaptation to explain some of our abilities. The anthropologists periodically suggest that musical abilities were evolved because of their usefulness, that they are an adaptation to social life, with music "soothing the savage breast," or some such explanation.

I'd concede some effect, especially since the chimpanzee "rain dance" has been shown to play a role in dominance displays (though that typically leads to sexual selection, not natural selection)—but I cannot imagine how four-part harmony evolved, nor the abilities to weave the elaborate counter-melodies of Bach that seem to echo in my head. Maybe my imagination is simply inadequate to the task, but I'll bet that music is going to turn out to be a secondary use of some neural structure selected for its usefulness in some serial-timing task like language or throwing—and used in the off-hours for music.

If we come to understand why Bach's brain still speaks so compellingly to our brains today, we will have bridged the gap between primary evolutionary adaptations and the magnificent secondary uses that can be made of the same brain machinery. Music is an emergent property, unless someone can figure out how a lilting aria and a choral fugue and an arpeggio were shaped up by survival-sensitive adaptations. The program notes (attributed to "Senza Sordino"—a pseudonym which turns out to be an Italian musical phrase that translates to "without muting; with the loud pedal"!) for tonight's performance of the Mass in F and the *Magnificat* demonstrate some of the musical features that tickle our brains:

> . . . the final "kyrie eleison" is composed as a counterfugue—that is, each thematic entry is answered by its inversion. In the further course of the movement, Bach makes use of the contrapuntal techniques of stretto, parallel voice-leading, and mirror inversions of themes.
>
> As the fugal chorus builds to a climax, each voice enters one note higher than its predecessor; and the repetition of this device gives the impression of an endless succession of voices. . . .
>
> The phrase *mente cordis sui* calls forth an astounding harmonic progression, suggesting, in the course of some nine measures, D-major, F-sharp-minor, F-sharp-major, B-minor, D-minor, and, finally, D-major, the first trumpet bringing everyone back to the home key with a descending scale passage and trill that haunts the dreams of every trumpeter.

Though musical tastes vary with the culture in which one is raised (and I am sure that some enterprising student will eventually do a Ph.D. dissertation on how a culture's musical structure is related to its language's grammatical structure), it seems likely that there will be a "deep structure" of music with a biological basis in the brain, just as a brain basis has been inferred for the deep grammar of languages. What is it about our brains that so disposes them to the minor third and to complex musical patterns, despite the lack of evolutionary adaptations for such musical patterns?

Though this question is seldom asked, I am sure that the standard answer would be the tie with language: Both music and language are sequences of sounds where recognizing patterns is all-important. Chords are simultaneous notes just as phonemes are; tunes are chains of chords just as words and sentences are chains of phonemes. And so natural selection for language abilities would, *pari passu*, gain us musical abilities as a secondary use of the same neural machinery. Maybe so. But the notion of stochastic sequencing on many parallel tracks as the key element of "get set" in ballistic movements suggests that both language and music are potentially secondary uses of the neural machinery for ballistic skills, that music might have more to do with modern-day baseball than modern-day prose.

The program notes end with:

> *Gloria Patri, gloria Filio, gloria et Spiritui sancto! Sicut erat in principio et nunc et semper in saecula. Amen.* ("Glory to the Father, and to the Son, and to the Holy Ghost! As it was in the beginning, is now and ever shall be, world without end. Amen.")
>
> The Latin translator adds to Mary's "hymn" the traditional invocation of the Trinity. (It does not occur in St. Luke.) Bach cannot resist the musical symbolism of triplets in the three invocations, to represent the tripartite nature of the Trinity, and a return of the opening music at the end, taking his cue from, "As it was in the beginning . . ." But the musical return serves aesthetics as well as theology, making a perfectly satisfying close to one of the most perfect and satisfying works of the choral literature.

There are many aspects of human brains that would vie for a trilogy if anyone tried to pick the three focal aspects of our humanity. Surely if one's criteria were traits whose improvements would help us survive the next century, the mental attitudes controlling *cooperation, conflict resolution,* and *family size* (all likely to be strongly shared with our primate cousins) would surely rank high.

But if one focuses on the primary traits via which we differ from the apes in an order-of-magnitude way, you can wind up with a curious trio: *language, scenario-spinning consciousness,* and *music*—three aspects of sequential patterns in our brains. Their beginnings are still dimly seen, but in their elaboration may lie the higher humanity.

We are evidently unique among species in our symbolic ability, and we are certainly unique in our modest ability to control the conditions of our existence by using these symbols. Our ability to represent and simulate reality implies that we can approximate the order of existence and bring it to serve human purposes. A good simulation, be it a religious myth or scientific theory, gives us a sense of mastery over our experience. To represent something symbolically, as we do when we speak or write, is somehow to capture it, thus making it one's own. But with this approximation comes the realization that we have denied the immediacy of reality and that in creating a substitute we have but spun another thread in the web of our grand illusion.

the physicist HEINZ PAGELS, 1988

Out of the great Heraclitean flux of evolutionary process, certain eddies and backwaters of the stream have been picked out for special attention. As a result, the two great stochastic processes [gene shuffling in reproduction and random trial and error in thought] have been partly ignored. Even professional biologists have not seen that in the larger view, evolution is as value-free and as beautiful as the dance of Shiva, where all of beauty and ugliness, creation and destruction, are expressed or compressed into one complex symmetrical pathway.

the anthropologist GREGORY BATESON, 1979

—— 14 ——

THINKING ABOUT THOUGHT: TWILIGHT AT NOBSKA LIGHTHOUSE

Perhaps our thinking exemplifies a selective system. First lots of random scattered ideas compete for survival. Then comes the selection for what works best—one idea dominates, and this is followed by its amplification. Perhaps the moral . . . is that you never learn anything unless you are willing to take a risk and tolerate a little randomness in your life.

the physicist HEINZ PAGELS, 1988

The Eel Pond drawbridge is out of commission. The hydraulic brake (it gently lowers the bridge the last meter or so) leaked its fluid, and so the bridge crashed down, damaging the gears. They're talking of two weeks just to get the parts. In the meanwhile, boats are trapped. They've gotten a big construction crane to come out and hold the bridge open for several hours at a time yesterday and today, to allow boats in or out. And, of course, expose the graffiti on the bridge's underside for two hours at a time, rather than the usual two minutes; while high school sports and sex are the usual topics, the most legible from down the street is ENTROPY RULES—THE END OF AN ERA. Weltschmerz in Woods Hole? But certainly appropriate to this new situation, with the breakdown of carefully engineered order in this local region of the universe.

With the two-week prospect, the question has arisen as to who will pay for the crane. Two of MBL's big fishing boats dock inside Eel Pond, alongside the animal tanks, and so the MBL's strained budget may end up paying for the crane if the town of Falmouth reneges on its responsibility to keep the sea-lanes clear of the obstruction it engineered.

Prop the bridge open? A little temporary scaffolding is the obvious solution. There is a back way around Eel Pond to reach the rest of Water Street; the bridge isn't the only route. But some merchants will feel cut off from the waiting-for-a-ferry pedestrians if the bridge is propped open. If the town can even contemplate leaving the bridge closed shut for two weeks, one can see that the ancient presumption of the boat's right-of-way over imposed obstructions has been seriously eroded. Lawyers love such situations.

WITH THE CHANGE IN SEASON (autumn is almost "in the air") have come more of the great birds as they fly south from

Maine: Not only does Eel Pond now have five cormorants sunning themselves on white buoys, but a Great Blue Heron flew in several hours before sunset. He perched on the outboard motor of a small boat, then moved over to repeat the same pose on the rear of a cabin cruiser. I kept watching to see what would happen if someone came up the passageway from below decks—and saw that giant bird perched there, looking at him. The Great Blue looks even taller than usual, as one typically sees a heron standing in a foot of water, looking for foolish fish in the shallows.

He's quite out of place here, though his ancestors might have fished these waters a hundred years ago. Great Blues specialize in shallow water fishing (they'll take the occasional snail or tadpole as well). Thanks to all the rock and concrete that has eliminated the former shoreline, Eel Pond doesn't have much shallow water, and derelict boats occupy most of what there is; that heron will either have to start competing with the cormorants at their deeper water game, or fly elsewhere to find a more suitable stretch of shoreline. As the ecologists put it, the cormorants and the herons have "partitioned the resource" (by depth of water, in this case) rather than competing directly with one another; if they competed directly by fishing the same waters, one species would probably win out and the other go extinct. The basic reason that so many animal species are going extinct these days is because humans have invaded their niche and started competing with them for resources such as food and land. Usurping their food and nesting sites is just as deadly as shooting them, merely delayed one generation.

Maybe this is a nonconformist heron, out to change the traditional heron habitat. But most genetic or cultural changes that carry an individual very far away from the optimized way of making a living are going to be bad news: Even if he manages to feed himself, he is likely to be judged a poor risk by traditional genetically programmed standards, and therefore lose out in the competition for mates. Once optimizing has gone on for a while, it can create a dead end (at least, until the climate changes, un-optimizing things).

It's closely related to one of the arguments advanced for why humanlike consciousness-intelligence-language-whatever has only happened once in 3 billion years: Maybe it was selected *against*, because little increments would not really be *net* improvements in the reproductive sweepstakes called "fitness." Just imagine a chimp that "talked a little funny" or didn't learn to forage efficiently because of spending so much time playing around with hammers. Of course, a sudden and big improvement, which carried fitness changes into net positive territory, might get around this ecological niche-fixity objection. Jumps can occur, thanks to conversions of function—and once a new niche is discovered, natural selection may be relatively ineffective until the niche is saturated and optimizing begins. So little improvements may not be the best place to look for the *origin* of these human peculiarities, however important efficiency eventually becomes.

LABOR DAY in the first week of September is giving sure signs of being the official end of summer. The town is full of overstuffed station wagons, waddling about. And the skunks seem to know about the refrigerators being cleaned out. Several of the restaurants and taverns in Woods Hole have already closed for the season.

Rented trucks are much in evidence in the MBL parking lots as labs pack up and go back to New York or Baltimore or Pittsburgh. There is a new seasonal traffic hazard, thanks to amateur truck drivers: I saw one sad rental truck stuck between two cars, having clipped both of them while trying to drive through a car-width lane in the MBL parking lot. The truck was wedged in tight, embarrassingly trapped for everyone to see.

Eel Pond is almost empty of sailboats, though that surely has to do with the lovely weather as well as people being homeward-bound. There is almost room to sail in Eel Pond or Little Harbor again; ordinarily, they are overcrowded parking lots for boats, a minor version of the tragedy of the commons.

MBL's little patch of beach front is absolutely jammed with bathers. Its parking lot is also crowded, but many of the cars and station wagons are packed for the trip home. The imported sand of Stony Beach seems to be the last stop before hitting the road, a chance to wear out the kids so that they'll nap during the long drive down the interstate highways. Unfortunately, the salt air tends to make the drivers as sleepy as the kids.

Today's civilization is full of people who have not the slightest notion of the character or poetry of the night—who have never even seen the night. Especially away from the city where it is truly night and there are no artificial lights to stab or trouble the dark. . . .

the natural historian HENRY BESTON, 1928

AS THE PACE OF LIFE CHANGES in Woods Hole, the evenings are different. The haze has been clearing out, probably because the winds have shifted about to blow dry out of Connecticut and Rhode Island, rather than from off the humid Atlantic. It has caused a mass migration of the windsurfing fans to new beaches.

By late August, the sunsets are noticeably earlier—and the sun sets over Woods Hole as seen from Nobska lighthouse. The promontory in front of the lighthouse becomes a gathering place for the local residents who are fans of the sunset, and each evening the sun sets a minute or two earlier, sets a solar diameter farther south than the previous evening. Until by early September, it is setting right in the "Hole," the east-west channel between Woods Hole and the Elizabeth Islands. In the foreground stretches the bright red streak of shining water; sailboats sail into it, ferries steam across it, and the windsurfing sailors off Nobska Beach seem to disappear within it for a few moments.

And the change in weather has brought some spectacular violet-and-rose sunsets. Occasionally, the lighting conditions and pastel backdrop are just right for seeing green spots near sunset, as the afterimages of the bright sun on the retina are enhanced by color contrast; little green spots seem to stream off the sun and drift to one side. If the sun is too dim due to haze, or the nearby clouds are too bright or not reddish enough, one doesn't see them.

This show is, of course, all a form of perceptual illusion, thanks to lateral inhibition networks in the retina and brain. The green that one sees is the complementary color of the red surroundings; the retina's sensitivity was turned far down by the sun itself, so when looking at ordinary red clouds, the spot appears very dim and the surrounding red clouds, via lateral inhibition, induce the green. But why does the spot move, even when you maintain your fixation on the sun? That turns out to be about like asking why the whirlpools above your bathtub drain move around. Such spots of decreased sensitivity seem to be more a matter of neuronal dynamics than bleached photoreceptors, and the locus of decreased sensitivity can apparently wander away from the fixation point.

THE SMELL OF A LOG FIRE lingers after dusk, here on the beach below the Nobska lighthouse. Remembrance of things past— the smoke and the salt air combined evoke a constellation of Proustian memories for me.

With the humidity thinning out, there are now clear nights with fine views of the stars. There are three planets in an arc across the southern sky: Mars, then Jupiter and Venus. Below them the beam of the searchlight regularly sweeps, left to right.

And there are some moving stars—not satellites, just high-flying airplanes on their way to Europe. The popular overnight flights out of New York fly over Cape Cod on their great circle route to London or Paris. A blinking light will appear in the southwest sky above Venus, then move slowly across the zenith and disappear in the northeast, all within about two minutes. As soon as one disappears, another winks into view down in the southwest above Venus. Again and again, this two-minute pattern repeats, as if there were an endless supply of jumbo jets on some New York runway, all waiting to follow this one invisible track in the sky. Sometimes there is a two-minute pause until another appears; I suppose that they represent flights to elsewhere.

I watch for even more slowly moving lights in the sky, the satellites rotating around the earth. Or some fast streaks, meteors decelerating through the upper atmosphere. But the trans-Atlantic planes, cruising on their robotic autopilots, seem to be the only moving lights tonight, like moving trains strung together on an invisible track in the stratosphere.

IT ISN'T JUST CHILDREN that are critical about how a story is told. All human beings seem to be perpetually stringing things together: Phonemes into words, words into sentences, concepts into scenarios—and then fussing about getting them in the right order. Our brain uses word-order rules to create a very productive language, with an infinite number of novel messages, rather than the several dozen standard interpretations associated with the several dozen cries and grunts of any other primate species. It isn't our mellifluous voices that constitute a significant advance beyond the apes but rather our arrangement rules, the meaningful order in which we chain our utterances.

And talking-to-ourselves consciousness is, among other things, particularly concerned with creating scenarios, trying to chain together memory schemas to explain the past and forecast the future. Peter Brooks describes it this way:

> Our lives are ceaselessly intertwined with narrative, with the stories we tell and hear told, those we dream or imagine or would like to tell, all of which are reworked in that story of our own lives that we narrate to ourselves in an episodic, sometimes semiconscious, but virtually uninterrupted monologue. We live immersed in narrative, recounting and reassessing the meaning of our past actions, anticipating the outcome of our future projects, situating ourselves at the intersection of several stories not yet completed.

It is our ability to choose between such alternative scenarios that constitutes our free will—though, of course, our choices are only as good as our imagination in constructing a wide range of candidate scenarios. Logical reasoning also seems dependent upon the sequencing rules for reliable entailment. Our sophisticated projection abilities are very sequential: A chess master, for example, tends to see each board configuration not just after the next move but a half dozen moves ahead, as several alternative scenarios. Even our recreations are surprisingly serial.

Darwin Machines suggest that our insightful behaviors arise from scenario-spinning, thinking before acting. It need not even be conscious attention given to a problem, as much problem-solving seems to occur in the background, subconsciously.

HOW WE PIECE THINGS TOGETHER subconsciously has always been one of the great mysteries. The examples in Chapter 5—Otto Loewi's discovery and Albert Szent-Györgyi's aphorism—

emphasize the role of nocturnal mentation. But often the solution to a problem suddenly presents itself when you're awake and seemingly doing something else.

Today, I was sitting on the beach, listening to the waves, doing nothing in particular. And suddenly I knew what was the trouble with our car, which had sprung a leak in the cooling system earlier in the day. Yet the leak stopped after I replaced some coolant ("antifreeze," in the American idiom). It was dripping quite regularly from back under the engine somewhere, a stream running down the street when we were stopped in front of the bakery. What sort of major leak suddenly stops?

But it did. After an hour's drive and a ferry trip (and not a drop of antifreeze under the car after it sat on the ferry), plus a hike down the beach, and finally my subconscious presented the solution to my conscious brain—after I had been contemplating the incoming tide and the Great Blue Heron.

- I had turned off the ventilation system before leaving the bakery, opening up the rooftop because it was such a nice day.
- Ventilation systems include heaters.
- Heaters have hot antifreeze piped through them.
- But there must be a shut-off valve for the antifreeze, in case you're running the air-conditioning system instead.

Therefore the leak must be in the hose that returns the antifreeze to the radiator. That's why the leak stopped after we left the bakery!

Now, consciously, I hadn't been thinking about this for several hours; I'd relegated it to something to check out when I returned home. And I certainly hadn't remarked upon the fact that I'd routinely turned off the ventilation system; it was one of those minor facts lingering in my short-term memory that would likely have been completely lost in another few hours. Admittedly, I had remarked upon this being an intermittent plumbing problem and wasn't that novel . . . ? (I have a long history of trying to solve intermittent electronics problems, because they plague the neurophysiologist, and of trying to diagnose intermittent neurological problems associated with marginally conducting nerves—so intermittent symptoms were automatically placed in an interesting category.)

But car problems I usually leave to the dealer's mechanic. I haven't understood my way around under the hood of a car since the 1950 Plymouth station wagon that I bought used while in graduate school. My knowledge of automotive plumbing is minor: I worry about adding windshield-washer fluid to the antifreeze by mistake. But my subconscious figured all this out, presumably by trying out lots of nonsensical combinations of things that were too absurd to complete with my main-track conscious experiences of sun and surf.

My wife, who thinks that theories exist to be disproved, immediately suggested an experiment, that we should turn on the heater when we returned from the beach and look to see if any antifreeze dripped. But then sun and surf got to her too, and we forgot all about it.

Multiple scenarios evolving simultaneously suggests, however, that there is more to Darwin Machines than just the set of railroad sidings, evolving away to create a dominant sequence—it seems as if there are various collections of sequencers, subpopulations with their own internal evolution. The same thing happens in biological evolution, as isolated subpopulations (demes, as they are called) provide the setting for much competition among themselves. Perhaps our population of a hundred sequencers becomes partitioned; instead of a dominant near-clone taking over entirely, perhaps the minorities get the opportunity to evolve among themselves. And occasionally take over, when a near-clone shapes up that can supercede the original victor.

ONE OF THE MAJOR HAZARDS OF THOUGHT is when a search for the best option is prematurely concluded. *Premature closure* is easy to spot when it occurs with jut-jawed determination, as in the modern bumpersticker: GOD SAID IT, I BELIEVE IT, AND *THAT'S THAT*! And its opposite, Hamlet-like indecision, is also celebrated, as Daniel Dennett notes:

> Time rushes on, and people must act, and there may not be time for a person to canvass all his beliefs, conduct all the investigations and experiments that he would see were rele-

vant, assess every preference in his stock before acting, and it may be that the best way to prevent the inertia of Hamlet from overtaking us is for our decision-making process to be expedited by a process of partially random generation and test.

In-between cases of premature closure are usually spotted only after the fact, as we contemplate a mistake.

The most frequent cause of premature closure in children is probably a short attention span. But in adults it is surely the logical framework: When something fits it, you stop surveying alternatives. When I manage to fit throwing into a newtonian framework, I usually stop there and never contemplate the relativistic case. When a doctrinaire economist manages to fit a social phenomenon into a marxist or capitalist framework, he or she usually stops exploring alternative explanations for the phenomenon. In politics, one constantly remarks on people who seem to have blinders on, unable to see the obvious—but merely operating under a different framework.

There are, of course, some differences between the frameworks that scientists propose (and regularly discard in favor of better ones) and those religious and political frameworks that somehow achieve a do-not-violate sanctity (John Calvin used to enforce his notion of sanctity during the Protestant Reformation by burning heretics at the stake; political police tend to be equally sure of themselves). The astronomer Carl Sagan observed:

In science it often happens that scientists say, "You know that's a really good argument, my position is mistaken," and then they actually change their minds and you never hear that old view from them again. . . . I cannot recall the last time something like that has happened in politics or religion. It's very rare that a senator, say, replies, "That's a good argument. I will now change my political affiliation."

Frameworks do save us from having to evaluate everything from scratch, but they have their hazards, as Nietzsche noted: "Convictions are more dangerous enemies of truth than lies."

Nothing causes as much destruction, misery, and death as obsession with a truth believed absolute. Every crime in history is the product of some fanaticism. Every massacre is performed in the name of virtue; in the name of legitimate nationalism, a true religion, a just ideology, the fight against Satan.

the molecular biologist FRANÇOIS JACOB, 1988

The characteristic of all fundamentalism is that it has found absolute certainty—the certainty of class warfare, the certainty of science, or the literal certainty of the Bible—a certainty of the person who has finally found a solid rock to stand upon which, unlike other rocks, is "solid all the way down." Fundamentalism, however, is a terminal form of human consciousness in which development is stopped, eliminating the uncertainty and risk that real growth entails.

the physicist HEINZ PAGELS, 1988

IN ADDITION to the seductive attractions of deductive frameworks, it has not been obvious what the alternative is—and it's often better to go with a framework that frequently works than none at all. Furthermore, the proponents of deductive frameworks usually appear formidably hardheaded and "rational," in contrast to the people groping around for a better framework; simplistic deduce-from-the-premises frameworks readily attract followers, readily infect other agendas (perhaps accounting for some of the overlap in U.S. supporters of religious fundamentalism and judicial "strict constructionism"—and the considerably higher percentages of physical scientists found in those camps than biological scientists).

Yet even physics eventually had to give up determinism, accept quantum mechanics, and start using fuzzy sets. And most of life, outside of photosynthesis and metabolism and the other chemical engineering wonders of our bodily organs, is not routine. There is no true "balance of nature," because ecosystems and species are always evolving. Inconsistency is sometimes the name of the game. Animals that stick to a behavioral routine get eaten by an opportunistic predator that can predict the evening visits to the waterhole, etc.; our *Homo erectus* ancestors made a good living by lobbing discus-shaped rocks into the midst of a tightly packed herd lapping up the lake at sunset.

Inconsistency is part of flexibility, of nature's strategy of keeping options open. Animals that cannot adapt to new environments will not survive the incessant fluctuations of climate. Judicial systems that cannot grow and change with our society's evolving problems will become rigid anachronisms that promote social earthquakes. Consistency and rationality are human virtues in dealing with certain potentially orderly situations; we make excellent use of them in engineering and legal systems, but we shouldn't expect living systems to have made them centerpieces of their operation in a changing, unpredictable world.

AND I'LL BET SOMEONE THOUGHT that "Noise" was an unappreciative name for me to give my pet cat, rather like calling her "Pest"—but given how creative that noise is, it is more like having a playful pair of cats named "Selection" and "Noise," named for the two flip sides of the darwinian evolutionary process. Having only one cat, I suppose that I should give her the one name that combines both concepts: "Darwin."

Technology treats noise as an unwanted impediment, darwinism as a means of exploring new avenues. But here we see it as a stimulus to evolve redundant machinery—whose secondary uses may be revolutionary. There may even have been a "noise window" in hominid evolution: Lacking sufficient neuron noise to overcome, Ice Age hominids might have become proficient projectile predators without the extra serial buffers for the massively serial scheme. While timing precision is the argument for why so many parallel-planning tracks were evolved in the first place, the really interesting things are the possible spare-time uses—if those extra buffers are capable of randomly sequencing other things when not needed for throwing-hammering-clubbing muscle commands.

If the separate tracks can also be unhitched to operate independently, then by providing many candidate queues, it might foster stringing words together into more sophisticated sentences, or schemas into more credible scenarios. Rather than our productive language and planning-for-the-future consciousness arising gradually through their own selective advantages, they could have emerged as novel spare-time uses of neural machinery originally under selection for more mundane forelimb movements.

Neurallike networks, once they become capable of generating randomly varied sequences, then successive selections by remembered environments, do offer an obvious route to machine intelligence and intelligent robots—though, should we succeed, we shall surely have to cope with machine imagination and machine "free will." We do not yet know how much of our own mental life might be explained by serendipitous secondary benefits of stochastic sequencers, and their tendency to partition the sequencer population into subpopulations where the minorities get to continue evolving on their own. And occasionally capture consciousness, when achieving a high ranking.

But just as darwinian gradualism has been supplemented with notions of sexual and group selection, isolation of subpopulations and allopatric speciation, stasis and "fast tracks," so we might expect a fuller understanding of our mental life to identify additional processes that regulate and elaborate the stochastic shaping-up of novel constructs. "Higher consciousness" is a much overused phrase, but we shall need some such concept to designate the "virtual machines" that can be constructed using stochastic sequencers as a basis.

What Ulysses preserves from the lotus, from Circe's drugs and the Siren's song, is not merely the past or the future. Memory really matters—for individuals, for the collectivity, for civilization—only if it binds together the imprint of the past and the project of the future, if it enables us to act without forgetting what we wanted to do, to become without ceasing to be, and to be without ceasing to become.

ITALO CALVINO, 1975

—— 15 ——

SIMULATIONS OF REALITY: OF AUGMENTED MAMMALS AND CONSCIOUS ROBOTS

——————

Perhaps I am no one.
True, I have a body
and I cannot escape from it.
I would like to fly out of my head,
but that is out of the question.
It is written on the tablet of destiny
that I am stuck here in this human form.
That being the case,
I would like to call attention to my problem.

ANNE SEXTON, *The Poet of Ignorance*

The stars are all shining brightly. And there is half of a moon about to set in the west. I see both Jupiter and Mars in the southern sky, Ursa Major in the northern sky, and Cassiopeia overhead. The ancient people gave those star configurations names as they played connect-the-dots, they imagined animals and everyday objects up there in the heavens. Now we know that constellations aren't real, merely chance configurations of nearby and distant stars which, from our viewpoint on a minor arm of the Milky Way galaxy, just happen to take on a familiar shape. We select among the chance configurations (Where have I heard *that* before? The schema strikes again). Constellations are *human* creations—now, that would certainly surprise an Ice Age hunter.

On one hand, the human brain is Procrustean, always trying to force something to fit its preconceptions. On the other hand, it's always looking for new ways to piece things together, new categories that can be created. We worry about whether something has a real identity, or is just a figment of our imaginations. Faces in the clouds.

Or in the rippling waves underfoot. In the quiet obliquely-moonlit waters, I seem to see something disturb the surface, then disappear again. My imagination, or reality?

I keep looking around—and, a moment later, a furry round head appears. Then big round eyes. Finally (so I imagine in the moonlight) whiskers emerge from beneath the waves.

I find myself holding my breath. It is indeed a harbor seal.

He is fishing near the dock on the incoming tide. This time he cruises along the surface and looks around.

And he sees me standing nearby. I see his eyes focus on me in the moonlight. Our eyes meet. Another creature in my universe asking, "Who am I?"

I endeavor to look harmless (even if it is misleading advertising for my species). Not finding me any more interesting than the setting moon, the seal slips under the surface. And I am again alone with sky and water.

Suppose we neurophysiologists can find some secondary uses for the specializations of other mammalian brains, such as the fancy hearing of the bat and whale? Perhaps a way to train them to use the sequencing abilities they possess? Echo-locating animals decipher fancy sound sequences, and whale song demonstrates that marine mammals can learn and modify sequence "traditions." Surely some animals' neural circuits aren't so hardwired that we can't, with a little training from an early age, induce them to achieve limited Darwin Machine abilities. And so we might be able to augment the language of such species—indeed, even their consciousness—and so enable them to develop a distinctive culture. Perhaps they might someday take over their own evolution as we humans have ours. Though, of course, increased look-ahead would also greatly augment their limited abilities to worry and suffer—and so they might not thank us.

THAT SEAL AND I—we're two individuals, each covered by a skin that encapsulates a whole collection of physiological processes operating more or less independently, but incidentally for the good of the whole organism. That's because an individual organism lives and dies as a *unit*, and components that were too inconsiderate probably didn't leave many offspring. Blades of grass aren't individuals in the same sense, nor are coral colonies; they're more like the surface cells of my skin, where losing a few won't change my identity as a person.

But it's been very unsatisfactory to define self that way: It seems to miss the really interesting things, such as my sense of being the narrator of my life's story, of being the focus of a lot of things going on in my subconscious that my "self" occasionally gets to choose between, as I decide what to do next—sometimes routine, sometimes novel. Sometimes the safe thing, sometimes risky.

I assume that the seal's brain feels something of that sense of self, as it looks out for the collective interests of the cells inside its skin. But, if the Darwin Machine notion is even approximately correct, I may have a lot more subconscious than the seal does, have a lot more alternatives being shaped up offline on all those planning tracks, have a lot more memories about sequences that have been a part of my history as an individual. And thus a lot more imagination about what might happen next.

And because of chunking and those higher-order schemas that I shape up when I get bored with the Procrustean bed of existing words/schemas/concepts, my Darwin Machine is often sequencing things that have no immediate movement pattern in the offing—I can sometimes think of concepts about which I cannot yet speak. As when I contemplate the universe out there, trying to imagine it during the Big Bang, trying to imagine it as the solar system formed, trying to imagine the crystallization and clays that got organic chemistry going—which got protein enzymes to catalyze reactions, which shaped up the DNA-RNA-protein route, and cells, and colonies, and sex, and fish, and mammals.

EVEN UNINTELLIGENT ROBOTS have long captivated humans, since they're such a puzzle: No one can readily figure out where to place them in the plant-to-animal, animal-to-human spectrum. The ancient Greeks were fascinated with automata; even Homer played around with the idea of robots.

It's all tied up with our own view of ourselves as mechanical beings. The doctrine that men are machines, or robots, had its first clear and forceful formulation in the title of a famous book by the Cartesian physician Julien Offroy de la Mettrie, *L'Homme-Machine* ("Man a Machine"), published in 1747. He said things such as "The human body is a machine that winds up its own springs" (well, they didn't understand much about metabolism back then). Less than a century later came Mary Wollstonecraft Shelley's *Frankenstein*. Karel Capek's first use of the word *robot* (the Czech word *robota* means servitude) in his play *R.U.R.* (Rossum's Universal Robots) added the word to the world's vocabulary in the early twentieth century. These all antedate the industrial robots of today, and our thinking robots of tomorrow.

Robots are creations of cultural rather than biological evolution, and their evolution will differ from hominid evolution in many ways. This is largely because biological evolution is subject to a number of constraints not likely to be shared with robots. We cannot form hybrids between the smart octopus and the smart

crow—yet robots will be hybrids of all sorts of separately successful developmental paths, cobbled together. Another difference is
that biology is always standing on the shoulders of the grandparents, not the accomplished individual: It practices "planned obsolescence," destroying the accomplished individual through ageing,
rather than copying him or her and carrying on from that advanced position (we pass on shuffled copies of our grandparents'
genes, not the genes that our own body expresses). Unless we have
an identical twin, our unique combination dies with us; certainly
our unique combination of genes, which is further shaped by our
individual choices during a long lifetime, is shared with no one.

But a particularly successful robot will be cloned at some
point, accumulated experiences and all. A dozen copies will then
develop separately thereafter, with some more successful than
others at taking its parent's experience with the world and elaborating on it to reach new heights of sophistication. No matter how
much we attempt to pass on our experience to our children, they
usually have to make their mistakes for themselves, pass through
painful adolescence, discover how to deal with the world of fickle
facades.

If only they could stand on our shoulders, combine youthful
vigor with our hard-earned wisdom (minus, of course, our creep-
ing conservatism). Occasionally one sees a 20-year-old who seems
to know how to handle people with the ease of that exceptional
experienced executive who can somehow keep everyone happy
and productive. Such precocious social development might not be
as rare in robots: Sequentially cloned robots might accumulate
such experiences from each ancestor.

HOW TO BUILD A CONSCIOUS ROBOT can now be glimpsed;
it falls out of scenario-spinning considerations, out of Darwin
Machines, out of neurallike networks. You just shape up the
neurallike networks so as:
1. to create massively serial "candelabra"
2. to load up "cars" (sensory schemas, movement verbs, and
   similar words) according to recent use and associations,
   word frequency, but with a random overlay too
3. to match each track to sequential memories and "grade"
   the fit according to some version of Subjective Expected

Utility (graded for both the goodness of fit to the local rules of grammar, and additionally for the sequence's suitability to the present situation)

4. then copy the winner (with a synonym or mutation occasionally substituted) into many of the losers' tracks, and shape up repeatedly

5. but partition the sequencer population into subpopulations so that the initial losers get some opportunities to evolve on their own and occasionally take over the lead ("capture conciousness").

And so we will get a working Darwin Machine not unlike the one inside our heads. It will be much more than the usual roomful of monkeys typing Shakespeare because of the Darwinian Two-Step and the utility scores shaping intermediate results (*random* doesn't mean the interjection of complete nonsense; it means unplanned variations on themes). Such rounds of variation and selection, as Richard Dawkins showed in *The Blind Watchmaker*, can quickly shape up a random string of words into increasingly good matches to a Shakespearean model sentence.

But it won't be a very interesting Darwin Machine until it acquires some humanlike qualities, such as shifting attention (changing the weightings) and boredom. If the "cars" are selected too randomly, with too little weighting of the ones already in short-term memories and their associations in long-term memory, then it will produce too much nonsense. If not random enough, it will merely seem to shuffle the scenarios that it starts with. If the utility scores are weighted too much toward "drives," such as goals imposed from outside (in the manner of human drives toward power, acquisitiveness, "getting the job done," perfection), it might seem more like an inefficient program for a standard computer.

It is probably no accident that the term "machinelike" has come to have two opposite connotations. One means completely unconcerned, unfeeling, and emotionless, devoid of any interest. The other means being implacably committed to some single cause. Thus each suggests not only inhumanity, but also some stupidity. Too much commitment leads to

doing only one thing; too little concern produces aimless
wandering.

the computer scientist MARVIN MINSKY, 1986

When will we be tempted to call such a Darwin Machine "conscious"? Probably not until its memories approximate some of our real-world experience, including our vocabularies. But earlier nonlinguistic versions that just spin scenarios (maybe trying out collision scenarios for air-traffic control, or maybe controlling downtown traffic signals almost as well as a traffic cop) might come close. For me, the criteria would probably emphasize creativity in problem-solving; for the general public, the humanlike speech and whims and cleverness will probably influence the impression of consciousness. Of course, once Hollywood techniques shape up its appearance to something out of the cartoons, such a darwinian robot will probably achieve the status of "pet" rather quickly.

I REMEMBER THE IN-FLIGHT MOVIE on my last trans-Atlantic flight. It was about a robot named "Number 5" who escapes from the robot factory, sneaks into someone's house, and watches an old movie on TV. And starts mimicking it. He first prattles like a 2-year-old, then acts like a child, and gradually develops an adolescent personality, declares itself "alive." Concomitant with this, he learns about death (having seen a TV movie of cars being crushed in a recycling yard) and so develops a phobia about being repaired, for fear he'll be junked. And so the rest of the movie is a great chase scene, as the increasingly smart robot eludes pursuit and learns to enjoy life.

He is, thanks to Hollywood techniques, even more charming than a pet cat or dog; judging from the number of people who seem to think their pets "honorary humans" (and by extension, all cats and dogs), we are going to have trouble when the first robots come out that really do mimic human speech and mannerisms.

There is, of course, a real philosophical issue here: At what point would we declare a machine (or a genetically engineered animal) as having human rights, including protection from slavery and murder, freedom of speech, liability to taxes, ability to own and dispose of property, the right to vote, and all the rest?

Suppose that the computer-based neurallike networks get fancy enough to actually create personable robots with consciousness and individuality? What about the ethical issues that would raise? Just what would be functionally unique about human brains then? Would we reconsider the inferior status of animals and machines? And once we discount the Hollywood-type facades, what would be our new basis? We have to be careful here, as the criteria will strongly interact with criteria for human life in such areas as brain death, abortion, and the severely demented.

CONTRARY TO WHAT OTHERS MIGHT THINK, I'd bet that we will achieve speech and consciousness in robots sooner than we'll solve some of the more machinelike tasks such as driving a car in Boston rush-hour traffic. I will also bet that we'll solve problems such as robot locomotion not by a mathematical analysis and careful engineering of robots, but rather by shaping up a robot brain via much the same trial and error that children go through—the robot will first thrash around (as a fetus does *in utero*), then crawl, then stand, then walk, then run, and only later ride a bicycle successfully. Once we've trained such a robot (or it has trained itself by attempting to mimic what it observes in people), we will then clone the robot brain—not understanding what goes on in that copied robot brain to produce locomotion any more than two parents understand how they've produced a child that can walk.

This isn't to say that robots with our speech and mannerisms will be "human"—they'll lack our primate heritage, for one thing, all those joys and fears and drives that determine much of our social life, mating habits, and ambitions. Even if the robots were to mimic the behaviors of the people that they see around them while "growing up," the robot brain will still lack all of our unexpressed behaviors, those instincts in us that come out only when the setting is right. We were shaped up by the Ice Ages, and when glaciers return, we'll become different people because of those ancient behavioral patterns emerging. The robots will lack that genetic library of useful-on-occasion behaviors.

But we'll give them additional behaviors, ones that we have sometimes and wish we had more reliably. Altruism. Stewardship of the environment. Avoiding endangering others by recklessness.

We'll build in protections against mob behaviors, book-burning, and making obscene phone calls at four in the morning.

THIS VIEW OF ROBOTS is, of course, closely shaped by my analysis of what makes humans unique among the animals. And there has been little agreement on that subject, especially as regards language and consciousness. Descartes in 1664 did provide us a target:

> If there were machines that had the organs and the features of a monkey . . . we would have no means of recognizing that they were not of the same nature as these animals. However, if there were machines that resembled our bodies, and which imitated as many of our actions as might morally be possible, we would always have two certain means for recognizing that they were not real men: [they would lack language and consciousness].

The fanciest machines of Descartes's acquaintance were pneumatic automata; it was two more centuries before electrical machines started to appear. Descartes's understandable lack of mechanical imagination did, however, create a polarity in thinking about thought that engendered three more centuries of dualism.

The physiologist Emil DuBois-Reymond, who in 1848 fulfilled the century-long dream of physicists and physiologists by showing that nerves actually ran on electricity rather than some elusive "nervous principle," nonetheless by 1872 had proclaimed that there were absolute limits to our knowledge of nature: "*Ignoramus, ignorabimus,*" that we not only didn't know the link between energy and matter, or between consciousness and movement, but that we could never know and would always be ignorant (the phrase recalls the practice of English juries: If they didn't have sufficient information to decide guilt or innocence, they could always declare *ignoramus* and if there was no hope of ever improving on ignorance of the facts—perhaps the only witness had died—they could use the extreme *ignorabimus* form of dismissal of the charges). In less than four decades, DuBois-Reymond's pessimism regarding energy and matter had become untenable, what with Einstein's success finding the simple proportionality

$E = mc^2$. We have not yet found a similarly simple relationship between consciousness and movement, but shaping-up selections among stochastic sequences in a command buffer now offers a candidate mechanism for us to contemplate.

CONSCIOUSNESS CONTEMPLATES, both the present (such as this beach, the surf, the sky of stars) and the remote (such as the possibility of life elsewhere). That's why we have so much trouble imagining a machine with our kind of consciousness. We have no trouble imagining a machine with willpower, such as a self-propelled lawn mower with a runaway appetite for the neighbor's flower garden. We have no trouble imagining a cormorant making an economistlike rational choice, between sunning and fishing and flying off to another pond. But contemplating the universe, thinking about how consciousness itself could arise—that seems special, quite unlikely to be achieved by any programming genius, no matter how elaborate the computer.

Yet that is exactly what I am saying *is* possible, that we could indeed create another contemplative but nonbiological form of sentient life. Thanks to successive selection among neural sequencers, which can be mechanically mimicked by the Darwin Machines, we should be able to create non-biological machines that not only *will* and choose but also *contemplate*, that have most of what we call consciousness. They could regret the past and learn from their mistakes. They could evolve on their own, perhaps even without further design help from us, and pretty soon there might be intelligent robots with whom we could converse, compare perspectives on the universe.

The Earth is just too small and fragile a basket for the human race to keep all its eggs in.

RObert A. Heinlein

TO EXPORT OUR GENES to other heavenly bodies has already been done (though the Moon is fairly close by, and our gene representatives hurried home). We contemplate space stations as a next logical move for the human race, and even that is being done on a temporary-visit basis (though self-sufficiency is surely far off, and that is the more appropriate criterion).

But intelligent contemplation per se might be exported to places inhospitable to life—send the software without the wetware. If our consciousness is, following Shelley's insight, inherent in the ways in which the molecules of our brains are *organized*, rather than the molecules and electrical signals themselves, why not export the organization detached from flesh and blood?

And sentimental liking for real humans aside, why not make that a major way in which we expand? We primates have to put up with a long food chain, from sunlight to steak, that is easily broken or contaminated. We breathe a fragile atmosphere, easily polluted by volcanoes and our throwaways—plus big meteor impacts that throw lots of dust into the stratosphere on occasion. We are unable to live in this universe in general, only on one delicate green planet.

And one of these days, a really big rock is going to hit the Earth—and if humanity hasn't learned to launder the atmosphere by then, the Earth is going to be a pretty uninhabitable place for a while. Humanity stands a very good chance of eventually going the way of the dinosaurs—if we haven't established ourselves elsewhere by then.

Why not just initially export contemplative intelligence, our highest product, to live in space, getting its power from solar cells, reproducing itself using raw materials from asteroids? It could exist in the colder reaches of space where heat doesn't constantly threaten to disorganize things. There, it wouldn't compete directly with humans for niche space. While we're trying to make superhumans, why not go all the way and free intelligence from this fragile dependency on the green machines? So we can fly out of our heads, escape the prison of our human form? *Silico sapiens*, and all that?

Perhaps. But there are some very good reasons for doing it slowly, lest we create monsters. If we are fearful and want to take out some Heinlein-like insurance against catastrophe by exporting contemplative robots as well as humans, we need to at least make sure that there are numerous fail-safe leashes via which we can recall our robot creations and replace them with improved models.

First reason: We don't understand intelligence very well yet; whatever the attractions of Darwin Machines, we will want to remember Mary Midgley's analysis:

What we normally mean by "intelligence" is not just cleverness. It includes such things as imagination, sensibility, good
sense, and sane aims: things far too complex to appear in
tests or to be genetically isolated. . . . Certainly we need our
nerves and brain to think with. But the power of thought to
which they contribute is not something which can be sliced off
and packaged separately. It is not an ingredient to be measured
out into the stew, but an aspect of the whole personality.

Sensibility and sane aims may be pretty hard to build into a robot,
because they're derived from evolutionary sources quite different
from the Darwin Machine we use to contemplate. Consider Jane
Goodall's description of the chimpanzee, and think about how
many of their traits one would also want to include in a robot, just
in order to help insure sane aims:

> Chimps . . . show a capacity for intentional communication
> that depends, in part, on their ability to understand the
> motives of the individual with whom they are communicat-
> ing. Chimps are capable of empathy and altruistic behavior.
> They show emotions that are undoubtedly similar, if not
> identical, to human emotions—joy, pleasure, contentment,
> anxiety, fear and rage. They even have a sense of humor.

Those are all part of Midgley's stew. And so our "intelligent
contemplation," in its broad sense rather than the narrow Darwin
Machine sense, is going to be a hard stew to concoct. It isn't going
to be easy to decide what is safe to let loose on the world—and
other worlds as well.

Second, there is an important principle from evolution and
ecology that says that the first species to fill a new niche has an
enormous advantage—because it's hard to displace once it occupies the new "territory" (being not just space but also ways of
making a living, ways of interacting with other species). In the
terminology of battlefield tactics, it "occupies the high ground." A
Mark I robot colony might be so thoroughly ensconced that neither human settlers nor a new, improved Mark IV robot team
could displace the Mark I without major warfare.

Just as dictators are hard to displace once they come to rule a roost here on Earth, so a robot colony might acquire a strong central power that does things only one way—but does them so well that it inhibits any variations within, and repels any improved versions from without. A Hitler or Stalin eventually goes the way of all flesh, but I think that we're going to want to build protections stronger than mere planned obsolescence into our intelligent robots before we let them loose. After all, they might learn to circumvent the planned obsolescence, just as we've doubled our life-span via improved sanitation, nutrition, and science.

Will we become the "contented cows" or the "household pets" of the new computer kingdom of life? Or will Homo sapiens *be exterminated as* Homo sapiens *has apparently exterminated all the other species of* Homo?

the theologian RALPH WENDELL BURHOE, 1971

"DOWNLOADING" A HUMAN BRAIN into a computer workalike has captured the imagination of those preoccupied with immortality: A person could live on, reconstituted *in silico*, thereby totally circumventing planned obsolescence.

I think that it is significant that this reconstitution proposal comes from the AI community (and science-fiction authors) rather than from the neuroscientists. *We* don't have the slightest idea of how to "read out" (even destructively, as by slicing up a brain) the complete wiring diagram, connection strengths, nonlinear characteristics of each and every cell—or how to mimic the parahormonal influences between near neighbors that don't rely on proper synapses, or the glial-cell influences on excitability, etc. Nor how to test subassemblies, tune them for stability, and prevent the whole thing from going into wild oscillations or otherwise "locking up." Physical scientists don't know either; they just assume, with Laplace, that if it is a deterministic system, it can be mimicked. But we have seen, with the advent of chaos studies ("sensitive dependence on initial conditions"), how such expectations about the atmospheric dynamics we call weather have been wrong; little "chance" alterations can make big mode-switching differences sometimes, and who would want to be reconstituted only to be warehoused with the criminally insane or those in persistent vegetative states?

Now training a Darwin Machine is quite another matter. Were a Darwin Machine used as a personal auxiliary brain (as I described in *The River That Flows Uphill* on Day 13) that did some "pre-thinking" for you about the facts you'd stored there, it would gradually acquire some of the judgment ability of the person who trained it. You might even be able to let it run the shop for a week while you went on vacation.

After its human trainer died, the auxiliary might live on, a repository of many of the facts, and ways of thinking about them, that were in the departed brain. It could continue thinking about them, armed with new facts from other sources. The auxiliary might more readily acquire humanlike ways of looking at things, including ethics (or sociopathic behavior, if trained by a sociopath), than conventional robots. And it would be nice to have Einstein's auxiliary around to ask questions of—the next best to the real thing. We might be able to clone it (assuming that it will be easier to go from silicon to silicon than from organic molecules to silicon). Some versions will likely be fixed to learn nothing new after the trainer's death (so as to continue to approximate Einstein's 1955 working habits and knowledge base) and others allowed to keep up with developments. If an auxiliary were good enough at freewheeling without human guidance, it might discover new research strategies that are beyond the abilities of human brains.

WE UNDERSTAND NEITHER OURSELVES nor evolutionary principles well enough in the present century to safely spin off colonies of intelligent robots, human-trained auxiliaries included. Yet we are in a race: Between overpopulation and overpollution, the Earth may soon become a failing enterprise, with the barriers to innovation that are often constructed by bureaucracies attempting to stretch strained resources.

And it isn't merely potential failures of ecosystems and economics: Just consider the history of civilizations and how often they decline from their vigorous peak into mere ornamentation or into Dark Ages. Before someone says, "That's a worry for the next century, not ours," consider how quickly we have retreated from space exploration *despite* a growing economy that has doubled the number of jobs. Consider how quickly we have retreated from public responsibility in the care of the mentally ill and the homeless, in the provision of quality public education. Consider the resurgence of don't-bother-me-with-the-facts fundamentalist religions, not just in the Islamic world but in highly technological societies, and their propensity for arrogantly telling other people what to do (not merely burning books but even commanding their followers to kill the offending author). Consider the people who happily utilize the benefits of modern medicine but who don't want any biomedical research done (some don't seem to mind eating animals and feeding them to their pets; they just don't want anyone to seek knowledge via an anesthetized animal). How many more mindless retreats are we about to witness?

So many recent examples of self-imposed tunnel vision make one want to take out some insurance against failures of the spirit. Such could leave us with insufficient energy for responding to an ecological crisis by then moving some of our biological or intellectual eggs elsewhere. The time to buy insurance is before things get tight—and hope that it turns out to be wasted money, just as I hope my homeowner's insurance premiums are wasted.

I can see that it's time for the Grand March from *Aida* again. Or maybe explaining consciousness.

MY MINIMALIST MODEL FOR MIND suggests that consciousness is primarily a Darwin Machine, using utility estimates to evaluate projected sequences of words/schemas/movements that are formed up off-line in a massively serial neural device. The best candidate becomes what "one is conscious of" and sometimes acts upon. What's going on in mind isn't really a symphony but is more like a whole rehearsal hall of various melodies being practiced and composed; it is our ability to focus attention upon one well-shaped scenario that allows us to hear a *cerebral symphony* amid all the fantasy.

What's going on in an animal's mind, in comparison to ours? Probably a lot less fantasy in the background, just choosing between well-trodden paths, not imagining all sorts of fantastic things, especially about tomorrow. Yes, my cat dreams about chasing mice, but I doubt that she has flying carpet fantasies forming up on another parallel track at the same time. Imagining familiar scenarios is not the same as making up novel scenarios, i.e., fantasy rather than the running of a familiar movement program with muscles inhibited.

Maybe things are occasionally more complicated than successive generations of shaping up: Should one suspect that a complicated mental construct (say, arithmetic) is better described by a hierarchical model using some postulated multilayered representation, we now have a null hypothesis against which to test it. If successive generations of a Darwin Machine seem excessively cumbersome, or too slow, or won't make the characteristic mistakes, we will have a better basis for believing in a higher-level proposal for a brain mechanism. This is essentially how we now evaluate candidates for higher-order evolutionary mechanisms in the rest of biology (including, in the extreme, the "argument from design" and similar top-down proposals): We try our best to see if a standard darwinian explanation won't suffice instead.

Is this Darwin Machine the truly minimal mechanism for contemplation? Is there anything even simpler that would make a better null hypothesis for serial-ordered behaviors? One-round variation and then a long period of selection can be simpler than darwinism, as I noted (Chapter 10) in regard to cortical maps that could have been formed up by a "rich getting richer causing the poor to become poorer" Matthew Principle (it is, for example, the explanation for why there are two sexes via gamete dimorphism). Self-organization in physical systems such as crystallization can be even simpler (they may account for the hexagonal packing pattern of photoreceptors in the retina), and we do not yet know how many of the orderly phenomena in the brain owe their order to such elementary processes. But for dynamic phenomena such as consciousness and language, where there is time for a Darwinian Two-Step to operate (and, indeed, so much noise that it is unreasonable to postulate one-round randomness), then the massively serial Darwin Machine is likely to be the appropriate null hypothesis. With this null hypothesis, we are applying Occam's razor ("entities shall not be multiplied beyond necessity") to hypotheses about mind.

THE NULL HYPOTHESIS is usually the dull, uninteresting alternative ("mere chance"). But there is nothing trivial about randomness-and-selection back and forth for many generations of shaping up; that's because it is more than random. Pure one-shot randomness is too trivial to be a useful null hypothesis. Yet the Darwin Machine as the null hypothesis may be even more interesting than the alternatives being tested!

Indeed, a Darwin Machine in left brain would seem to provide a natural mechanical foundation for many of the uniquely human functions:

- *Versatile ballistic movements* would be the simplest use of this Darwin Machine in the left brain, especially hammering and throwing (the most strongly right-handed actions): creating a variety of muscle-activation scenarios, judging each against memory and calculating utility estimates for each combination, and then using the best to make the ballistic movement of arm and hand. One could switch from a Variations-on-a-Theme Mode to a precision Choral Mode by loading the same sequence into all of the serial buffers.

- *Consciousness* would, in this model, simply be the massive extension of this planning sequencer in its Random Thoughts or its Variations-on-a-Theme Mode. It would often involve no action—a kind of freewheeling device that was always making dozens of scenarios on sidetracks, preferentially incorporating schemas that had recently been used for something (and so were in short-term memory) but also sampling from linked long-term memories. Nearly all of the random bashing about is now done off-line and, indeed, *subconsciously.* The best track would be all that one was "aware of," accounting for the unitary sense of consciousness and experience that constitutes the *narrator.* Only occasionally would the best track be gated out into the production of actual movement.

- *Language production* would simply be consciousness, but preferentially involving word-codable sequences rather than non-vocal ones. We could sequence movement schemas ("verbs") as well as sensory schemas ("nouns") and state-of-being schemas ("adjectives," such as *happy* and *hungry*). Deciding what to say next would just be a special case of deciding what to do next. Grammar would be one set of rules by which proposed sequences were judged; *syntax* would not have a special status compared to other sequences in memory—yet, because of frequent use, might appear special. This again is the minimalist position against which candidates for special status (such as Chomsky's) can be judged.

- *Language reception* uses a serial buffer to hold the incoming sentence while it is analyzed, its arbitrary phonemes recognized, and from the chain of phonemes, its words recognized (sometimes in groups). Again, a Darwin Machine can compare this word chain to sequential memories and come up with interpretations based on constructing an equivalent sentence in one's own words, equivalence being when utility estimates finally suggest a good fit. This "simultaneous translation" model for reception may become transparent to the user, just as meanings in a foreign language become intuitive once one truly "learns" the language. So the best track of the Darwin Machine would be the deep meaning envisaged by transformational grammars and a separate transformational level of the brain is unnecessary.

- *Poetry* is like language, but with a superposition of some additional structural requirements (rhyme, for example), something like dance is a format superimposed on more standard locomotion. Poetry is essentially a more elaborate version of *prosody*, the inflections that right brain tends to impose upon speech. Alliteration involves such structural patterning as well; the surprise ending in humor may involve a violation of an expected relationship. Poetry's tendency to repeat the same number of syllables on each line is reminiscent of *chunking*, the tendency to handle only a half dozen items in a chain and, when tempted to exceed this, collapsing several items into a single higher-order item ("apples and oranges" into "fruit"). Apes also generalize, but we are often forced to do so (and thus expand our vocabularies) by our frequent use of a buffer that is too short for some secondary tasks.

- *Logic and reasoning* are uses of the consciousness version of the Darwin Machine that have a particularly rigorous structure, with many more constraints than are usually present in syntax or poetry just to insure that entailment is reliable. But fundamentally a "grammatical sentence" is the model for a "logical argument"—just as legions of high school English teachers have been saying all along.

- *Music listening* is where "notes" and "chords" are substituted for phonemes, and "melodies" substituted for sentences, and "musical phrases" for a slightly higher-order idea expressed in multiple sentences. Perfect pitch might be the "ganged-into-lockstep" Choral Mode of the Darwin Machine. There are many other recreations that seem to exercise serial planning skills, such as card, board, and video games; indeed, it is difficult to identify games that do not.

The Darwin Machine is thus sometimes operating on "abstract" schema that no longer have one-to-one correspondence with the individual things we see, or the actual movement commands we would have to issue; like the higher-level computer languages, the higher-order schema can have their own rules of sequence that are developed through training, as when we say "two plus three equals five."

Darwin Machines are not especially well suited for explaining other beyond-the-apes mental specializations such as depiction. Increased visualization abilities might, however, have arisen from the increase in occipital and parietal lobe structures that came along with the larger frontal and temporal lobes, so handy for sequencing activities exposed to considerable selection pressures. Evolution conceivably could have increased frontal and temporal lobes' selectively, without simultaneous enlargement elsewhere, but a general rescaling of cerebral-cortical developmental parameters might have been the cheap-and-easy way to implement it. And so better visualization could have come "for free," except for the power requirements (not an insignificant problem, when the brain requires 25 percent of what the heart pumps—and except that it threatens to overheat disastrously whenever we run too long in summer sunshine).

Nor does the Darwin Machine solve the problem of "value," that which determines the Subjective Expected Utility scores. But it does show the level at which value might act, demonstrating one plausible mechanical basis for mental evolution. Knowing "DNA makes RNA makes Proteins" and the double helix did not tell us what the organism's environment valued either, but it did illuminate the mechanics that implement (and constrain) reproduction and inheritance and so create long-lasting memories of what worked well for similar organisms in past environments. Value is a property of the virtual environment that one has created inside one's head, a set of "initial conditions" that one applies to new situations via the Darwin Machine.

> *[Is mind] primary or an accidental consequence of something else? The prevailing view among biologists seems to be that the mind arose accidentally out of molecules of DNA or something. I find that very unlikely. It seems more reasonable to think that mind was a primary part of nature from the beginning and we are simply manifestations of it at the present stage of history. It's not so much that mind has a life of its own but that mind is inherent in the way the universe is built. . . .*

the theoretical physicist FREEMAN DYSON, 1988

DARWIN MACHINES are not the whole story for the brain's function, but they do seem to handle aspects of imagination, language, and the "self"—that *narrator* who has been so troublesome. We start assuming the unitary hypothesis, that a Darwin Machine can account for all the serial-order specialties, since the rules of science require me to put forward as simple a theory as will account for the most phenomena—and which will have the property of being vulnerable to disproof, e.g., someone could conceivably show that the brain regions involved in planning novel sentences do not overlap with those involved for planning novel throws. While the unitary hypothesis is a good working strategy, we have to remember that simplicity is not one of Nature's principles: The neural machinery may turn out to be somewhat different for some of the aforementioned traits, thanks to adaptations having separately shaped an early version of a neural sequencer into several different versions existing in parallel.

Darwinism seems to be a "Maxwell's demon" that bootstraps complexity on multiple levels in open systems with a throughput of energy. Undoubtedly, we will discover in the realm of mental phenomena, as Darwin did for biological species in general, that there are circumstances in which selection temporarily plays a minor role—as when a new niche is discovered, or when a conversion of function is possible. Because the rules of cultural evolution are considerably more flexible than those of biological evolution, we will likely discover situations in which Darwin Machines can be superceded by an efficient algorithm.

But the basic phenomena that allow each of us to have a sense of self, to contemplate the world, to forecast the future and make ethical choices, to feel dismay on seeing a tragedy unfold, to enjoy music if not too preoccupied with talking or planning—these things we may owe to the same kind of process that gives the earth abundant life. Each of us now has under our control a miniature world, evolving away, making constructs that are unique to our own head. There may or may not be life evolving on some planet near one of those thousands of stars that I see in tonight's sky, but comparable evolution is taking place inside the heads of everyone in Woods Hole tonight. The ability of this mental darwinism to simulate the future is the fundamental foundation of our ethics, what sets us apart from the rest of the animal kingdom.

Like Johann Sebastian Bach, many scientists have been deeply motivated by religious principles; they have considered scientific research an attempt to understand their Creator's works more fully. This is surely true of William James, who a century ago did so much to infuse evolutionary thinking into the new science of psychology. We have sought links between the laws by which the world was created and those that created the human mind.

And here we seem to glimpse one: The darwinian principles that shaped life on earth over the billions of years, that daily reshape the immune systems in our bodies, have again blossomed in human heads on an even more accelerated time scale. In much the manner that life itself unfolded, our mental life is progressively enriched, enabling each of us to create our own world. To paraphrase Charles Darwin, there is grandeur in this view of mind.

No one can possibly simulate you or me with a system that is less complex than you or me. The products that we produce may be viewed as a simulation, and while products can endure in ways that our bodies cannot, they can never capture the richness, complexity, or depth of purpose of their creator. Beethoven once remarked that the music he had written was nothing compared with the music that he had heard.

HEINZ PAGELS (1939–1988)

There is grandeur in this view of life, with its several powers, having been originally breathed into a few forms or one; and that, whilst this planet has gone cycling according to the fixed law of gravity, from so simple a beginning endless forms most beautiful and most wonderful have been, and are being, evolved.

CHARLES DARWIN (1809–1882)

POSTSCRIPT

As with my previous books, this one has benefited greatly from the comments of a number of volunteer readers who have endured the early drafts. As other writers surely know, it is quite difficult (outside the framework of writers' workshops) to get forthright criticism of what one has included (and left out), before the manuscript is shipped off to one's publisher. I thank my wife, Katherine Graubard, for many of our discussions that have made their way into print, and for suggestions on the drafts. But she knows too much, being a neurobiologist, and scientists writing for general readers need "guinea pigs" outside the field, preferably both scientists and nonscientists, to flag the difficult spots. Few writers are so fortunate as to have a mother-in-law experienced at encyclopedia editing (Blanche Kazon Graubard), an ex-wife trained in the law who teaches writing (Kathryn Moen Braeman), and a cousin whose Ph.D. is actually in philosophy (Beatrice Bruteau). If there are any remaining passages where the author sounds pompous or muddled, it is because I have occasionally ignored their forthright advice. John DuBois, Dean Falk, Seymour Graubard, John Pfeiffer, and Christine Phillips have also kindly suggested improvements and flagged stumbling blocks. My editors at Bantam, the late Tobi Sanders and subsequently Leslie Meredith, were enthusiastic and helpful with both structure and detail. I thank them all, together with my many colleagues and readers who have kept an eye open for articles of interest to me.

W.H.C.

Woods Hole, Massachusetts
Seattle, Washington
(Summer 1986–Winter 1989)

NOTES

Prologue: Finding Mind Amid the Nerve Cells

Page

2   T. H. HUXLEY, *Methods and Results* (Appleton, New York, 1897), p. 191.

1. Making Up the Mind: Morning on Eel Pond

8   LOREN EISELEY, from *The American Scholar* (1960), reprinted in the posthumous Eiseley collection *The Star Thrower* (Times Books, 1978), p. 37.

10   I am indebted to Harvey Pough for a description of the second-skunk scenario.

13   "The will. . . ." H. H. KORNHUBER, "Attention, readiness for action, and the stages of voluntary decision—some electro-physiological correlates in man." In *Sensory-motor integration in the nervous system*, edited by OTTO CREUTZFELDT, RICHARD F. SCHMIDT, and WILLIAM D. WILLIS (Springer, 1984), pp. 420–429.

14   For the three Primal Questions, I am indebted to Jef Poskanzer—who reports that his sister heard those lines in a Harvard commencement address!

18   J. Z. YOUNG, *Philosophy and the Brain* (Oxford University Press, 1987), p. 107.

19   EUGEN HERRIGEL, *Zen in the Art of Archery* (Pantheon, 1953), pp. 31–32.

20   SUSAN ALLPORT, *Explorers of the Black Box: The Search for the Cellular Basis of Memory* (Norton, 1986), p. 28.

21   Ferryboat collision with piers: JAMES M. SHREEVE, "Seawater system keeps MBL organisms alive." *The [Falmouth] Enterprise* (8 August 1988), p. 13.

23   Deceptions, see *Machiavellian Intelligence: Social Expertise and the Evolution of Intellect in Monkeys, Apes, and Humans*, edited by RICHARD BYRNE and ANDREW WHITEN (Oxford University Press, 1988). The story in the text doesn't appear there as such, but each of the elements of the story (omission of food cry when small quantities, leading other chimps away from food and then circling back) have been described by various researchers in the last two decades. I appear to have picked up this particular story, combining those elements in sequence, from conversations that I had with a variety of chimpanzee researchers in the summer of 1988.

25   T. H. HUXLEY, speech at the 1894 Royal Society dinner, *London Times;* reprinted in G. DE BEER, ed., *Charles Darwin–Thomas Henry Huxley, Autobiographies* (Oxford University Press, 1983), pp. 110–112.

2. The Random Road to Reason: Off-line Trial and Error

28   HERBERT A. SIMON, *The Sciences of the Artificial* (MIT Press, 1969), p. 97.

28   PAUL VALÉRY, quoted by JACQUES HADAMARD, in *The Psychology of Invention in the Mathematical Field* (Princeton University Press, 1949), p. 30.

29   Portions of this introduction are adapted from my article "The Brain as a Darwin Machine," which appeared in *Nature* 330:33–34 (6 November 1987).

30   FRIEDRICH NIETZSCHE, *The Birth of Tragedy* (Doubleday Anchor, 1956), pp. 84, and pp. 107–108.

30   T. E. LAWRENCE letter, quoted by ROBERT JAY LIFTON and
         NICHOLAS HUMPHREY, *In a Dark Time* (Harvard University
         Press, 1984), p. 99.

31   Bacterium's tumbling path: See J. E. SEGALL, S. M. BLOCK,
         and H. C. BERG's article in *Proceedings of the National Acad-
         emy of Sciences* (USA) 83:8987–8991 (1986).

35   Shaping up via selection stories: See RICHARD DAWKINS, *The
         Blind Watchmaker* (Norton, 1986).

36   WILLIAM SMITH (1817), quoted by LOREN EISELEY, *Darwin's
         Century* (Doubleday, 1958), p. 117.

36   DONALD T. CAMPBELL, in *The Philosophy of Karl Popper*,
         edited by PAUL A. SCHILPP (LaSalle, IL: Open Court, 1974),
         pp. 413–463.

37   PETER ASHLEY, letter quoted by DANIEL C. DENNETT, *Brain-
         storms* (MIT Press, 1981), pp. 274–275.

37   JACOB BRONOWSKI, *The Origins of Knowledge and Imagination*
         (Yale University Press, 1978, transcribed from 1967 lectures),
         p. 33.

38   BRONOWSKI (1978), p. 18.

41   G. M. GOLDBAUM, et al. "Failure to use seat belts in the
         United States: The 1981–1983 behavioral risk factor surveys,"
         Journal of the American Medical Association 255:2459–2462
         (1986). See also letter to editor by GARY GOLDBERG in *JAMA*
         257:1473 (20 March 1987): "[By buckling his seat belt], a
         driver reduces his likelihood of severe injury or death by at
         least 50%, if he should be involved in a serious collision . . .
         [and] the average American has a one in three chance of being
         involved in such a collision during his lifetime." Studies of
         emergency-room patients suggest that seat belts reduce the
         severity of injuries by more than 60 percent, e.g., *New York
         Times* story "Seat belt study . . ." (12 January 1989).
             Since reason has clearly failed to persuade half of the
         American public that seat belts should be routinely worn,
         perhaps we should try embarrassment instead—perhaps some
         bumper stickers such as:

> **Don't be caught dead without your seat belt!**
> *Your life insurance company will think
> you committed suicide and not pay your family.*

42   *Roger Sessions on Music*, edited by EDWARD T. CONE
(Princeton University Press, 1979). Originally published in
The Intent of the Artist by S. ANDERSON et al, A. CENTENO,
editor (Princeton University Press, 1941, 1969). Quoted in
WILLIAM ZINSSER, *Writing to Learn* (1988), p. 230.

3. Orchestrating the Stream of Consciousness: Prefrontal-cortex Performances

46   EDWARD O. WILSON, *On Human Nature* (Harvard University
Press, 1978).

48   Mid-Cape Highway: Judging from the signs erected to warn
approaching drivers, they have had a lot of trouble with this
pre-Hyannis rest area over the years. The rest rooms have
been removed (people still stop and disappear into the bushes),
though no signs warn people not to cross the highway. Why
they do not simply close the rest area is only slightly less
puzzling than why anyone ever designed such a lethal combination in the first place. Then there's the story of the national
guardsman during 1987 summer training who lobbed a mortar
shell onto the Mid-Cape Highway, just missing a school.

48   I suppose that I sympathize with the politicians a little: After
all, it was the Massachusetts voters who overturned the life-
saving seat belt requirement that the legislature passed. Massachusetts has long led the nation in damaged cars (see the
New York Times story AUTO INSURERS SUE . . . , 18 October
1987), having an insurance claims rate 67 percent higher than
the national average; for most of the last decade it has also led
the nation in stolen cars. "About 60 percent of the state's
drivers are now in a high risk pool." A psychiatrist who
trained in a Boston hospital observed, "I was accustomed to
parents who were anxious about the safety and achievement
of their children. In contrast, Irish parents (at least some
[in Boston]) were proud of their sons' heroic risk-taking.
For example, one fourteen-year-old boy was stealing cars
and racing them on Boston's most hazardous local express-

way where his best friend had been killed in a similar escapade. The parents were proud of him. They were expressing, of course, the Irish fondness for near suicidal courage and, implicitly, the feeling, fatalistically, that death and God's mercy might be preferable to life." JOHN K. PEARCE, p. 576 in *Ethnicity and Family Therapy*, edited by MONICA MCGOLDRICK, JOHN K. PEARCE, and JOSEPH GIORDANO (Guilford, 1982).

51   For an appreciation of *Limulus*, see WILLIAM SARGENT's *The Year of the Crab: Marine Animals in Modern Medicine* (Norton, 1987). "I had run-ins with shellfish wardens, town fathers, and narcotics agents. Can you imagine trying to explain to a federal agent that you are in your wetsuit, skulking about the marshes before sunrise, in order to keep your horseshoe crabs from getting wet?" (p. 16).

53   J. ALLAN HOBSON, *The Dreaming Brain* (Basic Books, 1988), pp. 212–213.

54   Confabulation: DONALD T. STUSS AND D. FRANK BENSON, *The Frontal Lobes* (Raven Press, 1986), pp. 225–226.

56   Supplementary motor area: MARIO WIESENDANGER, "Organization of secondary motor areas of cerebral cortex." In *Handbook of Physiology. Section 1: The Nervous System. Volume II: Motor Control, Part 2*, (American Physiological Society, 1981), Chapter 24, pp. 1121–1147.

57   Switching back and forth between temporal patterns: STUSS AND BENSON (1986), pp. 77ff. A premotor lesion does not result in paralysis or paresis, or loss of general intention to perform, or general plan. However, speed, smoothness, and automaticity are disturbed. LURIA described several neuropsychological tests that he considered particularly sensitive to pathology of premotor: Complex rhythm tapping, requiring changes in the number or intensity of beats, becomes discontinuous and fragmented and may be replaced by a stereotyped response. Even the rhythmical repetition of simple tapping may be disrupted. If required to alternate between square and sawtoothed line drawing, preservation may result.

58   JELLE ATEMA, "To sense the world as others sense it." *MBL Science* 3(1):2–3 (Winter 1988).

59   In ordinary mortals, left premotor cortex is said to dominate
           the sequencing of both right and left sides of the body. In a
           violinist, it might make some sense for right premotor cortex
           to handle the left hand's fingering, while the left premotor ran
           the bowing and orchestrated everything—but until some ex-
           pert violinists are studied with sophisticated techniques, all
           we have to go on is the story about ordinary mortals. Left
           hemisphere is widely specialized for serial-sequential activi-
           ties (it isn't just premotor):

J. L. BRADSHAW and N. C. NETTLETON, "The nature of hemi-
     spheric specialization in man." Behavioral and Brain
     Sciences 4:51–92 (March 1981).
GEORGE A. OJEMANN, "Brain organization for language from
     the perspective of electrical stimulation mapping." Be-
     havioral and Brain Sciences 6(2):189–230 (June 1983).
DOREEN KIMURA, "Neuromotor mechanisms in the evolution
     of human communication." In Neurobiology of Social
     Communication in Primates, edited by H. D. STEKLIS
     AND M. J. RALEIGH, Academic Press, New York, pp.
     197–219 (1979).
GEORGE A. OJEMANN and OTTO D. CREUTZFELDT, "Language
     in humans and animals: contribution of brain stimulation
     and recording." In Handbook of Physiology. Section 1:
     The Nervous System, Volume 5 part 2, The Higher Func-
     tions of the Brain, edited by VERNON B. MOUNTCASTLE,
     FRED PLUM, and STEVEN R. GEIGER (American Physio-
     logical Society, 1987).

59   A more conventional definition of prefrontal would be the
           cortex to which the mediodorsal nucleus of the thalamus pro-
           jects. The history of the term prefrontal in comparative anat-
           omy is much more complicated; see IVAN DIVAC's "A note on
           the history of the term 'prefrontal'" in IBRO News 16(2):2
           (1988), the newsletter of the International Brain Research
           Organization. Adding to the confusion is the use of "frontal
           cortex" to designate the areas sandwiched between premotor
           and prefrontal, as well as the cortex of the entire frontal lobe
           more generally.

59   Prefrontal role in strategy: JOAQUIN M. FUSTER, "Prefrontal
           cortex in motor control." In Handbook of Physiology. Section
           1: The Nervous System. Volume II: Motor Control, Part 2
           (American Physiological Society, 1981), chapter 25, pp. 1149–
           1178.

60   Neuropsychologists check for frontal-lobe injury using a variety of subtle diagnostic tests, such as the Wisconsin Card-sorting Task. There are now many good neuropsychology texts; A simplified introduction is WILLIAM H. CALVIN and GEORGE A. OJEMANN, *Inside the Brain: Mapping the Cortex, Exploring the Neuron* (New American Library, 1980).

60   Unfolding proper sequence of actions, see STUSS and BENSON (1986), p. 80. LURIA suggested prefrontal cortex affects (1) maintenance and control of cortical tone; (2) regulation of the scheme or program of the action itself; (3) impairment of the unfolding of the motor program (the patient cannot raise a hand that is initially under the bed covers without being given two separate commands, first to remove the hand from beneath, and then to raise it); and (4) deficit in comparing execution with original intention and correcting (they can see errors in others, indicating problem is not conceptual).

61   Prefrontal cortex monitors narratives: B. L. J. KACZMAREK, "Neurolinguistic analysis of verbal utterances in patients with focal lesions of frontal lobes." *Brain and Language* 21:52–58 (1984). Suggested that the left dorsal-lateral frontal cortex is important for sequential organization and that the left orbital frontal lobe is important for direction of a narrative through monitoring.
        For another view of the lesion and prepotential literature, see H. H. KORNHUBER, "Attention, readiness for action, and the stages of voluntary decision—some electrophysiological correlates in man." In *Sensory-motor integration in the nervous system*, edited by OTTO CREUTZFELDT, RICHARD F. SCHMIDT, and WILLIAM D. WILLIS (Springer, 1984), pp. 420–429. He says (p. 427) that "When to do it" is the function of the supplementary motor area. And that "the supervision of the task 'what to do' may be a function mainly of the orbital cortex with its hypothalamic, limbic, and mnestic afferents. 'How to do it' is in novel situations probably mainly a task for the frontolateral cortex with its afferents from the parietal and temporal teleceptive association areas."

61   "Our need for chronological . . .": R. SCHOLES, "Language, narrative, and anti-narrative." In *On Narrative*, edited by W. J. T. MITCHELL, p.207. University of Chicago Press, 1981. See also MISIA LANDAU, "Human evolution as narrative," *American Scientist* 72:262–268 (May/June, 1984).

63   Quote from NANCY C. ANDREASEN, "Brain imaging: Applications in psychiatry." *Science* 239:1381–1388 (18 March 1988).

63   Twins and ventricular sizes: NANCY C. ANDREASEN, talk at psychiatry grand rounds, University of Washington (14 April 1988). See also: NANCY ANDREASEN et al., "Structural abnormalities in the frontal system in schizophrenia. A magnetic resonance imaging study," *Archives of General Psychiatry* 43(2):136–144 (February 1986).

63   Threefold variation in the size of primary visual cortex among normal adult humans: SUZANNE S. STENSAAS, D.K. EDDINGTON, and W.H. DOBELLE, "The topography and variability of the primary visual cortex in man," *Journal of Neurosurgery* 40:747–755 (June 1974).

66   HOBSON (1988), pp. 10–11.

67   RALPH BARTON PERRY, "Conceptions and misconceptions of consciousness," *Psychological Review* 11:282–296 (1904). For a more recent collection of the many things called consciousness, see RONALD S. VALLE and ROLF VON ECKARTSBERG, eds., *The Metaphors of Consciousness* (Plenum, 1981).

4. Varieties of Consciousness: From Coma to Reverie

70   HENRY BESTON, *The Outermost House* (Penguin, 1962; originally published 1928), pp. 220–221.

70   HENRY DAVID THOREAU, *The Maine Woods* (1864), p. 71.

71   Walking distance of a beach: "All around the country, the various coastal states are finally beginning to view beaches as the national treasures they truly are. There is no question that the time will come when our remaining beaches will be like national parks, protected forever for the benefit of the public at large. They won't be like Yellowstone Park, however, where one can be sure that Old Faithful will be in the same location 50 years from now. Instead, our beach management policy will have to take into account that the sea level is rising and that the beaches are moving [like rivers of sand]. Thus the beaches of the future may become mobile national parks!" THOMAS A. TERICH, *Living with the Shore of Puget Sound and the Georgia Strait* (Duke University Press, 1987), p. 37.

72   BESTON (1928), p. 2.

73   Foamlike boxes and ozone depletion: GARY TAUBES in *Discover* 8(8):66 (August 1987).

74   CHARLES R. MORRIS, "Our muscle-bound Navy," *The New York Times Magazine* (24 April 1988), p. 102.

75   MORRIS BERMAN, *The Reenchantment of the World* (Cornell University Press, 1981), pp. 16, 72.

77   L. WEISKRANTZ, *Blindsight: A Case Study and its Implications* (Oxford University Press, 1986).

77   KARL R. POPPER and JOHN C. ECCLES, *The Self and Its Brain* (Springer International, 1977), p.125. See also DONALD R. GRIFFIN, *Animal Thinking* (Harvard University Press, 1984); a view of animal consciousness, though lacking in any comparison of sequential planning skills amongst animals. Not many of the commentators on human consciousness have widely informed themselves about the many specialties relevant to the problem, e.g., animal behavior, human evolution, neurophysiology, philosophy, psychology, etc. The reader may find the following books particularly rewarding:
PATRICIA SMITH CHURCHLAND, *Neurophilosophy* (MIT Press, 1986).
DANIEL C. DENNETT, *Brainstorms: Philosophical Essays on Mind and Psychology* (Bradford Books, 1978). And his recent *The Intentional Stance* (MIT Press, 1987).
JOHN C. ECCLES, *Evolution of the Brain: Creation of the Self* (Routledge, Chapman and Hall, 1989).
NICHOLAS HUMPHREY, *Consciousness Regained* (Oxford University Press, 1983).

79   Australian stewards of the land: BRUCE CHATWIN, *Songlines* (Viking, 1987).

80   BESTON (1928), pp. 43–44.

80   BENJAMIN LIBET, "Unconscious cerebral initiative and the role of conscious will in voluntary action." *Behavioral and Brain Sciences* 8:529–566 (December 1985).

81   Cautionary poem from JOHN MAYNARD SMITH, *The Problems of Biology* (Oxford University Press, 1986), p. 128.

82   MARVIN MINSKY, *The Society of Mind* (Simon & Schuster, 1986), p. 151.

82   HEINZ PAGELS, *The Dreams of Reason* (Simon & Schuster, 1988), pp. 222–223, and p. 225.

83   ALBERT SZENT-GYÖRGYI, quoted by SIDNEY TAMM, "Imagination in science," *MBL Science* 2(2):9–13 (Summer 1986).

848   OLIVER SACKS, *A Leg to Stand On* (Harper and Row, 1984), p. 131.

86   MINSKY, p. 50.

86   BENNETT G. BRAUN, editor, *The Treatment of Multiple Personality Disorder* (American Psychiatric Press, 1986). Multiple personalities are one of the occasional outcomes of child abuse, apparently an attempt by the child to protect himself against the pain of the abuse. One of the most striking findings is that each of the multiple personalities is associated with different allergies, susceptibilities to drugs or epilepsy, and even switches in visual acuity. See DANIEL GOLEMAN's story in *The New York Times* (28 June 1988).

88   PETER MEDAWAR and JEAN MEDAWAR, *The Life Science* (Wildwood House, 1977).

5. The Electrically Exciting Life of the Inhibited Nervous Cell

92   RODOLFO LLINÁS, quoted in SUSAN ALLPORT's *Explorers of the Black Box* (Norton, 1986), pp. 166–167.

94   ALBERT SZENT-GYÖRGYI, in *The Scientist Speculates*, ed. by I. G. GOOD, 1962.

96   The Spanish neuroscientist SANTIAGO RAMÓN Y CAJAL, with a ten-year blaze of discoveries starting in 1888, is credited with most of our modern concepts of the organization of the vertebrate brain, though many parallel discoveries in invertebrate nervous systems were made in 1888 by the Norwegian zoologist FRIDTJOF NANSEN. My colleague John Edwards tells me that Nansen had the neuron doctrine right even before Cajal

(both used the Golgi method), but was forgotten by nervous system historians because he did not continue working on the nervous system. Instead Nansen merely made the first crossing of the Greenland ice cap, did pioneering research in oceanography, led the 1895 Arctic expedition, became Norway's first ambassador to Great Britain, and won the Nobel Peace Prize in 1922 for his work with refugees, e.g., the "Nansen passport"!

CHARLES SHERRINGTON coined the word *synapse* in 1897, and was one of the people who demonstrated the synaptic delay (which we now know is associated with secretion of the neurotransmitter). The reticulated notions started with GERLACH back in 1858, though HESS and FOREL realized by the 1880s that a cell should be considered a unit in and of itself. Cajal's beautiful pictures of axon terminals in the cerebellum (the basket cell endings and the climbing fiber endings on the Purkinje cells, in particular) were what convinced him that the axon came to an end, and he associated it with the one-way valve needed in the reflex arc. But the reaction of the histologists to Cajal's synapse postulates starting about 1900 served to make the reticular theory stronger than ever for a while.

98   Actually, it probably wasn't a dream that inspired Otto Loewi but rather nocturnal mentation; see J. ALLAN HOBSON, *The Dreaming Brain* (Basic Books, 1988), pp. 4 ff. Not only does dreaming occupy about two hours of each night, but there is another two hours of mentation such as thinking. Such mentation is not accompanied by sensory illusions and is not bizarre as dreaming may be; it is rather commonplace, banal, repetitive, and usually uncreative.

100   Though the reticular theory came to a dead end, the aftermath of Loewi's 1921 discovery was not, however, the firm establishment of chemical transmission for central nervous system. Physiologists continued their attempts to have graded electrical signals propagate across the synapse—though by 1949, when microelectrodes were introduced, they realized that this alternative would not work in mammalian spinal cord. But of course it is nonetheless utilized at what we now call "electrical synapses" found elsewhere, so both synaptic mechanisms were correct in the end. The vesicles that PALAY saw in 1953 were identified with the miniature synaptic potentials at the nerve-muscle synapse by DEL CASTILLO and KATZ in 1955. Thus the synapse concept, from the false reticular theory that denied synapses to the modern establishment

of chemical transmission, took almost a century—though the correct principles of operation were mostly set forth halfway through the period, between 1888 and 1904. From SANFORD PALAY's lecture, "The history of the synapse," Toronto, 15 November 1988. See also MARCO PICCOLINO, "Cajal and the retina: a 100-year perspective." *Trends in Neurosciences* 11(12):521–525 (December 1988).

100   See the Loewi biography by GERALD L. GEISON in *Dictionary of Scientific Biography* 8:451–457 (1973) and WALTER CANNON's "The story of the development of our ideas of chemical mediation of nerve impulses," *American Journal of Medical Sciences* 188:145–159 (August 1934).

101   Blood pressure of 60/45: The brain stops working very quickly if not kept supplied with oxygen via the blood. A low blood pressure *in the head* is what causes someone to faint. But most cases of fainting can be easily reversed by simply laying the victim flat on the floor (not a chair!); that's because blood pressure decreases with height above the heart. Eliminating the hydrostatic pressure effect by laying the victim horizontal usually increases the head's blood pressure by one-third; propping up the legs will even make hydrostatic pressure work to increase blood pressure. The victim often recovers so quickly that he wonders why he is on the floor, is embarrassed and tries to sit up, and promptly faints again (try to keep the victim flat for a few minutes and, should he get up, protect the back of his head from a fall). Such is the potent difference made by upright posture.

102   The mischief that temporary demyelination can cause is demonstrated in a paper of mine published only a half year prior to this little episode: WILLIAM H. CALVIN, MARSHALL DEVOR, and JOHN F. HOWE, "Can neuralgias arise from minor demyelination? Spontaneous firing, mechanosensitivity, and afterdischarge from conducting axons," *Experimental Neurology* 75:755–763 (March 1982).

104   U. J. MCMAHAN and S. W. KUFFLER, "Visual identification of synaptic boutons on living ganglion cells and of varicosities in postganglionic axons in the heart of the frog," *Proceedings of the Royal Society* (London) B177:485–508 (1971). See also the three papers that follow this one.

105   For more on thalamotomy for Parkinson's disease, see W. H. CALVIN and G. A. OJEMANN, *Inside the Brain: Mapping the Cortex, Exploring the Neuron* (NAL, 1980), Chapter 5.

6. Making Mind from Mere Brain:
Taking Apart the Visual World

110   VIRGINIA WOOLF, *To the Lighthouse* (Harcourt Brace, 1927),
        p. 301.

112   STANISLAW M. ULAM, in a conversation quoted by HEINZ
        PAGELS, *The Dreams of Reason* (Simon & Schuster, 1988),
        p. 94.

114   Schemas: MICHAEL A. ARBIB, "Schemas," in *The Oxford Com-
        panion to the Mind* (Oxford University Press, 1987), pp.
        695–697. Piaget's schemas are mostly movements (of which,
        more later); there are a number of variations on the schema
        theme: Minsky uses the word *frames;* Schank uses the word
        scripts; Lorenz and Tinbergen talk of *innate releasing mecha-
        nisms,* Peirce of *habits,* there are *semantic nets,* and so forth.
        See MICHAEL A. ARBIB, *In Search of the Person* (University
        of Massachusetts Press, 1985), pp. 11–16. And from MICHAEL
        A. ARBIB, E. JEFFREY CONKLIN, and JANE C. HILL, *From
        Schema Theory to Language* (Oxford University Press, 1987),
        p. 7: "Each schema roughly corresponds to a domain of inter-
        action, which may be an object in the usual sense, an attention-
        riviting detail of an object, or some domain of social interaction.
        Just as programs may be combined to yield larger programs,
        so may schemas be combined to form new schemas. . . . Note
        that a schema is both a process and a representation. It
        combines the declarative information with a program for ac-
        tion." Particularly relevant to schemas is *Categorical Percep-
        tion: The Groundwork of Cognition,* edited by STEVAN HARNAD
        (Cambridge University Press, 1987).

115   S. W. KUFFLER, "Discharge patterns and functional organiza-
        tion of mammalian retina." *Journal of Neurophysiology* 16:37–68
        (1953).

115   H. K. HARTLINE, "The response of single optic nerve fibers of
        the vertebrate eye to illumination of the retina." *American
        Journal of Physiology* 121:400–415 (1938).

117   See ROBERT BARLOW's appreciation of H. Keffer Hartline
        (1903–1983) in *Trends in Neurosciences,* 9:552–555 (November-
        December 1986).

121   Key papers of the "frog's eye era" of neuroethology can be
        found in *Sensory Communication,* edited by WALTER A.
        ROSENBLITH (MIT Press, 1961).

122   STEVEN P. R. ROSE, *The Conscious Brain*, updated edition (Vintage 1976) p. 27.

127   The initial Hubel-Wiesel model for receptive fields is the easiest to teach, but there are other ways of looking at the matter, e.g., R. M. SHAPLEY and P. LENNIE, "Spatial frequency analysis in the visual system," *Annual Reviews of Neuroscience* 8:547–583 (1985). These use the average firing rate of a cell as their measure of cell output; looking in more detail at the spike train, BARRY RICHMOND and LANCE OPTICAN find that the elementary forms of organization are more abstract; see news article "A new view of vision" in *Science News* 134:58–60 (23 July 1988).

127   Center-surround organization disappears: Blue light anywhere in the round receptive field will excite; yellow or red light anywhere in the field will inhibit. Yet all of such a cell's inputs have a center-surround arrangement; thus, these cells have just the right mixture of inputs so that one input's blue surround and another input's blue center combine to give a uniform blue circular field. These cells become very good at reporting the color of the uniform middle of a patch, while other cells respond primarily to the boundary lines between patches. For modern expositions regarding receptive fields, see Chapters 2, 3, and 20 of STEPHEN W. KUFFLER, JOHN NICHOLLS, and ROBERT MARTIN, *From Neuron to Brain*, 2d edition (Sinauer, 1984).

127   Best stimuli for cortical cells are straight edges and lines: This isn't quite true; the cells in layer IVc still have center-surround receptive fields. See Chapter 12 in W. H. CALVIN and G. A. OJEMANN, *Inside the Brain* (1980).

129   HANS-LUKAS TEUBER, *Perception, Voluntary Movement, and Memory* (1967).

129   TORSTEN WIESEL, "A life of excellence and style: a short account of the career of Stephen W. Kuffler (1913–1980)," *Trends in Neurosciences* 4(1):1–3 (January 1981).

129   HUBEL, WIESEL, and ROGER SPERRY shared the 1981 Nobel Prize for Physiology or Medicine; Sperry was cited for his work on split-brain patients, though his earlier work on what controls development of visual pathways is considered at least as significant.

130   Training in neurobiology: See *Neuroscience Training Pro-
             grams*, published yearly by the Society for Neuroscience, 11
             Dupont Circle NW, Washington DC 20036, U.S.A., and avail-
             able in most college libraries.

131   E. H. GOMBRICH, *Art and Illusion: A Study in the Psychol-
             ogy of Pictorial Representation* (Phaidon Press, 1959). Quoted
             in WILLIAM ZINSSER's *Writing to Learn* (Harper & Row,
             1988), pp. 122–123. At the time that Gombrich wrote, it was
             still thought that photoreceptors "fired" nerve impulses to
             send messages; a decade later, we discovered that they usu-
             ally do not, nor do the bipolar cells that are next in the chain
             between photoreceptor and brain. What the photoreceptors
             (rods and cones) instead do is surprising beyond anyone's
             wildest imaginings: They instead leak neurotransmitter mole-
             cules all the time, *decreasing* the leakage rate when light
             intensity *increases*, by amounts proportional to light inten-
             sity. Thus their output is greatest in the dark!

7. Who Speaks from the Cerebral Cortex?
The Problem of Subconscious Committees

134   MICHAEL A. ARBIB, *In Search of the Person* (University of
             Massachusetts Press, 1985), pp. 52–53.

135   Maps are generally orderly: Yet sometimes the cortical
             representations simply don't make any sense, in the usual
             sense of neighbors on the skin being neighbors in the cor-
             tex. The somatotopic map in Crus II of cerebellar cortex
             has now been shown to be a series of disconnected frag-
             ments: "fractured somatotopy," as James Bower calls it.
             In the Edelman example at the end of Chapter 10, one can
             imagine disorderly maps arising from spotty stimulation
             regimes rather than smooth stroking of skin during the
             tuning-up phase.

136   Cape Cod as a terminal moraine: The so-called Falmouth
             moraine extends from Woods Hole north and east, across the
             north shore of the arm to the elbow near Orleans (where
             similar boulders are found to those in Woods Hole); the fore-
             arm and hand are likely deposited by ocean currents, as the
             forearm follows the edge of the Continental Shelf drop off. I
             hope that geologists will forgive my overly broad use of *moraine*

to include hills of glacial till carved by meltwaters: Properly speaking, moraines refer only to the piles created at the very margins of a glacier, not the glacial sediments underneath a glacier carried along by runoff channels.

138   Organization of visual cortical columns: DAVID H. HUBEL and TORSTEN N. WIESEL, "Functional architecture of macaque visual cortex," *Proceedings of the Royal Society (London)* 198B:1–59 (1977).

138   A visual cortical map goes to the center of the retina, rather than the far side, because the left half of the brain handles everything to the right of where you're looking, the left visual world going to the right brain instead. It is *not* a matter of everything seen by the left eye, but everything seen by either eye from the left half of the center, where you're looking at the time. See Figure 6–3 on page 120.

140   Some mechanisms of depth perception can be found in S. M. ZEKI, "Cells responding to changing image size and disparity in the cortex of the rhesus monkey." *Journal of Physiology* 242:827–841 (1974).

140   "Converge eyes until receptive fields overlap" isn't quite true. What the arrangement suggests is *disparity* differences, not convergence differences. If looking down a sidewalk row of parking meters and "looking at" the third one (such as the farther target in Figure 7-1 on page 141), such a cell might be optimally sensitive to the second one (such as the nearer target in Figure 7-1).

141   W. H. CALVIN, "Fine discrimination as an emergent property of parallel neural circuits." *Society for Neuroscience Abstracts* 10:218.11 (1984). And "A stone's throw and its launch window: timing precision and its implications for language and hominid brains." *Journal of Theoretical Biology* 104:121–135 (September 1983).

143   The receptive fields should probably be thought of as serving as a vector basis set. Though just two receptive field types, a horizontal specialist and a vertical specialist, could serve to represent any intermediate angle by the vector's decomposition into cartesian components, the individual cells are noisy, and that restricts the interpretation of the line's angle in

space. But with vector components spaced at about 10°, any intermediate angle can be easily represented in terms of the relative activation of the two closest members of the basis set. Thus, "labeled lines" for lines aren't needed, just about 18 basis vectors at 0°, 10°, 20°, . . . , 170° from the horizontal; combinations of their activity seem to be sufficient to allow discrimination of line tilt to a fraction of a degree.

144   THOMAS YOUNG, "On the theory of light and colours." *Philosophical Transactions of the Royal Society of London* 95:12–48 (1802). Color mixing is nicely demonstrated in RICHARD L. GREGORY, *Eye and Brain: The Psychology of Seeing*, 2d edition (McGraw-Hill, 1973), p. 120.

145   Actually, Helmholtz went even further in his 1860 *Physiological Optics*, representing the three cone outputs as a vector, and the just-noticeable difference in hue as the difference vector between the two hues.

146   Young's patterning principle is also relevant to the perception of line orientation: Those 18 types of specialized line-orientation neurons (each responds over about a 10° range of orientations) found by Hubel and Wiesel can be thought of as just another example of the principle. Any line (say, at 37°) stimulates one type of cell best (say, the one at 40°) and weakly stimulates two others (say, the ones centered on 30° and 50°). The ratio of the latter's activity can be used to estimate that the line is oriented somewhat less than the favorite's 40°. If there were only two orientation types, horizontal and vertical, the ratio of their activity could theoretically be used to estimate 37°—but nerve cells are noisy, and so the estimate would be many times rougher than when one uses eighteen specialists spaced every 10° throughout the 180° range. If you're ultimately going to do a vernier estimate, its precision will depend on how fine the final scale is.

147   HUMBERTO MATURANA and FRANCISCO VARELA, *Autopoesis and Cognition: The Realization of the Living* (Reidl, 1980), p. 47.

147   ROBERT P. ERICKSON, "On the neural bases of behavior." *American Scientist* 72:233–241 (May-June 1984). Covers both Young's theory for color and the taste data.

147   WILLIAM H. CALVIN, "Why 'Grandmother's Face' and 'Command' Neurons Are Rare (Answer: The Fireworks Finale)." *Society for Neuroscience Abstracts* 14:260 (1988).

148   Inhibition is also important in triggering motor programs because it is the committee pattern that counts: Major pathways of the cerebellum (one of whose major functions is coordinating motor programs) operate on downstream neurons *only* via inhibition.

149   Actually, what TERRENCE SEJNOWSKI said at MBL's Computational Neuroscience course on 2 September 1988 was "It is humans who categorize, but to distribute is divine," but I converted it to Alexander Pope's phraseology.

152   Four decades later, I revisited the scene. The barbershop is still there, but is smaller than I remembered; it is only four chairs deep from the front of the shop (the house I lived in then, and the school I went to, also look much smaller than I remembered—but then I was considerably shorter than I am now). There is still the padded board that fits across the arms of the old-fashioned barber chair, worn by several more generations of little boys. And the plate-glass mirrors are still there, perfectly positioned. The trolley car was discontinued long ago, and the turnaround is now a parking lot.

152   JOAQUIN M. FUSTER, "Prefrontal cortex in motor control." In *Handbook of Physiology. Section 1: The Nervous System. Volume II: Motor Control* (American Physiological Society, 1981), Part 2, Chapter 25, pp. 1149–1178 at p. 1167.

154   DANIEL C. DENNETT, *Brainstorms* (Bradford Books, 1978), p. 123.

8. Dynamic Reorganization:
Sharpening Up a Smear with a Mexican Hat

158   J. Z. YOUNG, "Hunting the homunculus," *New York Review of Books* 35(1):24–26 (2 February 1988).

158   J.-P. CHANGEUX, "Concluding remarks on the 'singularity' of nerve cells and its orthogenesis." *Progress in Brain Research* 58:465–478 (1983).

159   J. Z. YOUNG, *A Model of the Brain* (Claredon Press, 1964). His "The organization of a memory system," *Proceedings of the Royal Society* (London) 163B:285–320 (1965) introduces the mnemon concept in which weakened synapses serve to

tune up a function. A later version is "Learning as a process of selection," *Journal of the Royal Society of Medicine* 72:801–804 (1979).

161   LEWIS THOMAS, "A long line of cells." In *Inventing the Truth: The Art and Craft of Memoir* (Houghton Mifflin, 1987). Quoted by WILLIAM ZINSSER in *Writing to Learn* (1988), pp. 169–170.

161   CHARLES DARWIN, *The Descent of Man* (London: John Murray, 1871), p. 100.

162   The songwriter JOHN BARLOW, quoted in DAVID GANS and PETER SIMON, *Playing in the Band: An Oral and Visual Portrait of the Grateful Dead* (St. Martin's Press, 1985), p. 21.

163   MARIAN DIAMOND, in a book review in *Ethology and Sociobiology* 5:67–68 (1984), says there is little evidence for cortical neuron loss after early adulthood.

163   Evolutionary version of the carving principle: SVEN O. E. EBBESSON, "Evolution and ontogeny of neural circuits," *Behavioral and Brain Sciences* 7:321–366 (September 1984).

164   See WARREN S. MCCULLOCH, *Embodiments of Mind* (MIT Press, 1969).

165   Gained connections until eight months after birth: P. R. HUTTENLOCHER, "Synapse elimination and plasticity in developing human cerebral cortex." *American Journal of Mental Deficiency* 88:488–496 (1984). For monkeys the data is more extensive: RONALD G. BOOTHE, WILLIAM T. GREENOUGH, JENNIFER S. LUND, and K. KREGE, "A quantitative investigation of spine and dendrite development of neurons in visual cortex area 17 of *Macaca nemestrina* monkeys," *Journal of Comparative Neurology* 186:473–490 (1979); and using electron micrographs, P. RAKIC, J.-P. BOURGEOUS, M. F. ECKENHOFF, N. ZECEVIC, and P. GOLDMAN-RAKIC, "Concurrent overproduction of synapses in diverse regions of the primate cerebral cortex," *Science* 232:232–234 (1986).

165   A.S. LaMANTIA and P. RAKIC, "The number, size, myelination, and regional variation of axons in the corpus callosum and anterior commissure of the developing rhesus monkey," *Society for Neuroscience Abstracts* 10:1081 (1984).

165   DANIEL C. DENNETT, *Content and Consciousness* (Routledge
       and Kegan Paul, 1969; page references to 1986 paperback
       edition), pp. 52–59. This is Dennett's *D. Phil.* dissertation at
       Oxford in 1965 (just imagine having the neurobiologist J. Z.
       Young *and* the philosopher A. J. Ayer as your examiners!).
       Dennett's formulation for brains seems analogous to the con-
       vergent selection (shaping towards species "type") envisaged
       by some of Darwin's predecessors, e.g., Edward Blyth. See
       LOREN EISELEY's posthumous book, *Darwin and the Mysteri-
       ous Mr. X* (Harcourt Brace Jovanovich, 1979). As in biology,
       selection's creative role ("divergent selection") in neural
       darwinism was only recognized later.

166   The synapse elimination literature is rapidly developing; to
       find more recent news, I would suggest searching *Science
       Citation Index* for articles that cite some of the key papers
       prior to 1989. In addition to previous citations, these should
       be useful:
       M. F. BEAR, L. N. COOPER, and F. F. EBNER, "A physiologi-
            cal basis for a theory of synapse elimination." *Science*
            237:24–28 (1987).
       J.-P. CHANGEUX, "Neuronal models of cognitive functions,"
            Cognition (in press).
       S. CLARKE and G. INNOCENTI, "Organization of immature
            intrahemispheric connections," *Journal of Comparative
            Neurology* 251:1–22 (1986).
       G. M. INNOCENTI and R. CAMINITI, "Postnatal shaping of
            callosal connections from sensory areas," *Experimental
            Brain Research* 38:381–394 (1980).
       D. J. PRICE and C. BLAKEMORE, "Regressive events in the
            postnatal development of association projections in the
            visual cortex," *Nature* 316:721–723 (1985).
       D. PURVES and J. W. LICHTMAN, "Elimination of synapses in
            the developing nervous system," *Science* 210:153–157
            (1980).

166   Favored sites for sprouting in cortex: It has been suggested,
       as part of the explanation of binocularity "fixing" at the
       end of its critical period, that the myelination of the thala-
       mocortical axons reduced the side branches—simply by cover-
       ing up 99 percent of the axon surface. One might modify this
       speculation to read: Once myelination occurs, the possible
       sites for a new side branch are reduced to a few per milli-
       meter. Still, most of the new branching probably occurs from
       the unmyelinated terminal arbor of the axon, and thus to near
       neighbors of the neurons to which connections already exist.

167   LUDWIG WITTGENSTEIN, *Last Writings on the Philosophy of Psychology*, vol. 1, 504 (66e) (University of Chicago Press, 1982).

167   DAVID E. RUMELHART and DONALD A. NORMAN, "A comparison of models." In *Parallel Models of Associative Memory.* edited by G. HINTON AND J. ANDERSON (Erlbaum, 1981), p. 3.

168   Little black lines between your fingers: FLOYD RATLIFF, *Mach Bands: Quantitative Studies on Neural Networks in the Retina* (Holden-Day, 1965). This book is not only a nice review of lateral inhibition and Mexican-hat-like organization, but also relates the neurophysiology to such philosophical issues as knowledge.

169   Retina's lateral inhibition turned off during dark-adaptation, see HORACE B. BARLOW, RICHARD FITZHUGH, and STEPHEN W. KUFFLER, "Change of organization in the receptive fields of the cat's retina during dark adaptation," *Journal of Physiology* (London) 137:338–354 (1957).

173   Lateral inhibition's uses for contrast enhancement may be one of those pesky cases of a secondary utility; John DuBois points out that network stability may be the most essential function of such inhibition, and I would add that range-shifting might also be a more primitive use, as in the need to shift from daylight to moonlight intensity levels with their million-fold differences. And so contrast enhancement might be a side step, a functional change in anatomical continuity (see Chapter 9).

174   Reorganizing finger maps: MICHAEL M. MERZENICH et al, *Neuroscience* 10:639–665 (1983); *Annual Reviews of Neuroscience* 6:325–356 (1983); *Journal of Comparative Neurology* 224:591–605 (1984); *Journal of Neuroscience* 6:218–233 (1986); *Nature* 332:444–445 (31 March 1988). For a recent review, see J. T. WALL, "Variable organization in cortical maps of the skin as an indication of lifelong adaptive capacities of circuits in the mammalian brain," *Trends in Neurosciences* 11(12):549–557 (December 1988).

177   Sprouting in peripheral nerve: P. A. REDFERN, "Neuromuscular transmission in newborn rats." *Journal of Physiology* 209:701–709 (1970).

9. Of Arms Races in Church Gardens:
The Side Step and Evolution's Other Byways

182   THEODORE MELNECHUK, "Network notes from Cape Cod," *Trends in Neurosciences* 3(5):8–9 (May 1980).

183   MAHENDRA JUMAR JAIN and RAFAEL APITZ-CASTRO, "Garlic: molecular basis of the putative 'vampire-repellent' actions and other matters related to heart and blood." *Trends in Biochemical Sciences* 12(7):252–254 (July 1987).

184   Edible plants: G. A. ROSENTHAL, "The chemical defenses of higher plants." *Scientific American* 254(1):94–99 (1986).

184   Guam and Rota Island story: PETER S. SPENCER, PETER B. NUNN, JACQUES HUGON, ALBERT C. LUDOLPH, STEPHEN M. ROSS, DWIJENDRA N. ROY, and RICHARD C. ROBERTSON, "Guam amyotrophic lateral sclerosis-Parkinsonism-dementia linked to a plant excitant neurotoxin." *Science* 237:517–522 (31 July 1987). See also ROGER LEWIN's news article in the same issue, pp. 483–484.

185   GREGORY BATESON, *Mind and Nature: A Necessary Unity* (Bantam, 1979), p. 193.

186   For aquatic references, see Mile 136 of my book, *The River that Flows Uphill: A Journey from the Big Bang to the Big Brain* (Macmillan, 1986).

187   Ultradarwinists are discussed by M. GRENE and N. ELDREDGE, *Interactions* (Harvard University Press, in press).

187   The new-niche concept tends to be associated with EMILE DURKHEIM, *The Division of Labor in Society* (Glencoe IL: Open Court, 1947), Book II, Chapter 2. But the same concept can be found in Darwin.

187   HERBERT A. SIMON, *Reason in Human Affairs* (Stanford University Press, 1983), p. 73.

187   THOMAS H. JUKES, "The fight for science textbooks," *Nature* 319:367–368 (30 January 1986).

188   Some of the cultural-evolution analogies first appeared in my article "The evolutionary sidestep," *Whole Earth Review* 60:4–9 (Autumn 1988).

189   Calvinist combination: JACOB BRONOWSKI and BRUCE MAZLISH, *The Western Intellectual Tradition* (Harper & Row, 1960), p. 94.

190   ERNST MAYR, *Toward a New Philosophy of Biology* (Harvard University Press, 1988), pp. 2–3.

191   Behavior innovates, anatomy follows: This observation is often credited to Konrad Lorenz, but it goes back several centuries to Lamarck. See also ALISTER C. HARDY, *The Living Stream* (London: Collins, 1965).

191   JANE GOODALL, *The Chimpanzees of Gombe* (Harvard University Press, 1986).

192   Biology facilitating cultural practices: JAMES L. GOULD and PETER MARLER, "Learning by instinct." *Scientific American* 256(1):74–85 (January 1987).

193   LOREN EISELEY, *The Immense Journey* (Knopf, 1957), p. 47.

193   Accommodation in middle age and other vision topics: R. A. WEALE, *Focus on Vision* (Harvard University Press, 1982).

193   Absurd evolutionary "designs" also include the female reproductive system of mammals, especially the connection (or lack of it!) between the ovary and the uterine tube. It isn't so bad if the ovum misses its narrow channel into the uterus, and thus a possible opportunity to meet a sperm; what's so absurd is that a fertilized ovum can escape back out the tube into the abdominal cavity to cause a life-threatening ectopic pregnancy. Or that the endometrium which is shed at the end of each menstrual cycle can also escape backwards and take up residence in the abdomen (the "reflux" theory for endometriosis). Or that vaginal infections can cause widespread pelvic infections.

196   ERNST MAYR, *Toward a New Philosophy of Biology* (Harvard University Press, 1988), p. 95.

196   Conversions of function obscured by subsequent streamlining: CHARLES DARWIN, *The Origin of Species* (London: John Murray, 1859), p. 182. "Metamorphosis of function" term coined on p. 204; "So important to bear in mind the probability of conversion from one function to another. . . ." (p. 191).

197   Biological underpinning of morality, or lack thereof: RICHARD ALEXANDER, *The Biology of Moral Systems* (Aldine, 1987).

198   Other genetic disorders such as the glucose-6-phosphate dehydrogenase deficiency common in Mediterranean populations are also associated with resistance to malaria ("G6PD" is an enzyme in one of the metabolic pathways that converts glycerol to glucose).

200   Tension between scientific reductionists and holists: See, for example, the exchange between ERNST MAYR and STEVEN WEINBERG in *Nature* 331:475–476 (11 February 1988). A more complete treatment is in MAYR's *Toward a New Philosophy of Biology* (Harvard University Press, 1988), chapter 1.

201   RICHARD DAWKINS, *The Extended Phenotype* (Freeman, 1982), p. 113.

203   KARL R. POPPER, "Critical remarks on the knowledge of lower and higher organisms, the so-called sensory motor systems." In *Sensory-Motor Integration in the Nervous System*, edited by OTTO CREUTZFELD, RICHARD F. SCHMIDT, and WILLIAM D. WILLIS (Springer-Verlag, 1984), pp. 19–31, at p. 28

10. Darwin on the Brain:
Self-organizing Committees

206   FRANÇOIS JACOB, *The Statue Within: An Autobiography* (Basic Books, 1988).

207   GLYNN LL. ISAAC, talk at University of Washington (31 January 1984).

208   EUGÈNE MARAIS, *The Soul of the Ape* (about 1927; Penguin, 1969), p. 56, has an account of chacma baboon nut-cracking: "On reaching the hills, the [coconut-sized hard] fruit was

placed on a flat rock and smashed with stones. . . . Great efforts were first made to break the fruit by hammering it on the rock by hand before a stone was used as a tool."

The classic accounts in chimpanzees are C. BOESCH and H. BOESCH, "Sex differences in the use of natural hammers by wild chimpanzees: A preliminary report," *Journal of Human Evolution* 10:585–593 (1981); "Optimization of nut-cracking with natural hammers by wild chimpanzees," *Behaviour* 83:265–286 (1983); "Mental map in wild chimpanzees: An analysis of hammer transactions for nut-cracking," *Primates* 26:160–170 (1984).

210   This brief explanation omits, of course, the serious problem of self-recognition: how we tell friend from foe. There is a tuning-up period during development when the immune system learns about its host's own characteristic molecules, and so doesn't play this game with them. Autoimmune diseases are what happens when the system fails. Sometimes the immune response to an infecting antigen also develops antibodies for one's own molecules, in which case all sorts of things can happen.

210   Immune-system examples of darwinism and networks: A. COUTINHO and F. VARELA, "Immune networks: A review of current work," *Immunology Today* (in press, 1988); and N. JERNE, "Idiotypic networks and other preconceived ideas," *Immunology Reviews* 79:5–24 (1984). DEBORAH L. FRENCH, REUVEN LASKOV, and MATTHEW D. SCHARFF, "The role of somatic hypermutation in the generation of antibody diversity." *Science* 244:1152–1157 (9 June 1989)

210   MARVIN MINSKY, *The Society of Mind* (Simon & Schuster, 1986), p. 73.

211   Hand-moving quotes are from a computer-mediated discussion on the Well, the *Whole Earth Review*'s conferencing system, in 1987.

214   DANIEL K. HARTLINE, in *The Crustacean Stomatogastric System*, edited by A. I. SELVERSTON and M. MOULINS (Springer, 1987), pp.181–204.

214   GRAHAM HOYLE, quoted in SUSAN ALLPORT's *Explorers of the Black Box* (Norton, 1986), p.57.

216   STANISLAW M. ULAM, *Adventures of a Mathematician* (Scribners, 1976), p. 13–14.

217   J. Z. YOUNG, *Philosophy and the Brain* (Oxford University Press, 1987) p. 216

222   Sounds overlap as when pronouncing *675*, so that you have to detect *7* in the midst of the final sounds of *6*. There is a reading equivalent to this problem, very much what has slowed down the development of good text scanners to convert printed pages into letter strings; it is the "kerning" that printers favor to reduce the space between letters, as when the *a* may nestle under the *T* in *Tap*.

222   TERRENCE J. SEJNOWSKI and CHARLES R. ROSENBERG, "NETtalk: A parallel network that learns to read aloud," *Johns Hopkins University Electrical Engineering and Computer Science Technical Report* JHU/ EECS-86/01 (1986).

224   DAVID E. RUMELHART, GEOFFREY E. HINTON, and RONALD J. WILLIAMS, "Learning representations by back-propagating errors," *Nature* 323:533–536 (9 October 1986). This was for feed-forward networks only.

224   A most interesting new field is unfortunately named: *neural networks*. It seems absurd for neurobiologists to have to start talking about "*real* neural networks" just because the physics-math-AI folk didn't learn their lessons. And I'm not referring to ignorance of neurobiology, though that too is a sore point: Remember the hyperbole in the old days when the fledgling digital computer got called a "brain"? And how soon no self-respecting computer person would call a computer a "brain" for fear of being thought a beginner? So why are we now seeing this nonsense of calling any plastic network of pseudo-neurons a "neural network"? For some simulations, it seems appropriate to use "neural network" in referring to the computer model: Those simulations of lobster networks, the simulations of the retina using state-of-the-neurobiological-art parameters, etc. But most so-called "neural networks" in AI don't even have the ambition to simulate a real neural circuit: They are seeking shortcuts around formal programming, a plastic network that can be shaped up by training until it performs a desired task (and perhaps then cloned). They should be called "*neurallike networks*" or "connectionist models."

225   GERALD M. EDELMAN, *Neural Darwinism* (Basic Books, 1987), p. 241.

225   ULAM (1976), p. 13.

226   "Connectionism" is what neurallike networks are often called in the literature; see the special issue of *Daedalus* (Winter 1988) for some excellent introductory essays.

227   Portions of this section are adapted from W. H. CALVIN, "A global brain theory (review of *Neural Darwinism*)," *Science* 240:1802–1803 (24 June 1988).

227   Glutamate receptor at synapse: I am referring here to a particular subtype, usually called "NMDA" because N-methyl-D-aspartate is the molecule to which it is most sensitive. But glutamic acid is the neurotransmitter normally used at such synapses.

229   GERALD M. EDELMAN, in *How We Know* (Nobel Conference, 1985), p. 24.

230   W. ROSS ASHBY, *Design for a Brain* (1952), p. vi.

230   RICHARD DAWKINS, *The Blind Watchmaker* (Norton, 1986).

11. A Whole New Ball Game: Bootstrapping Thought Through Throwing

234   RODOLFO LLINÁS, quoted in SUSAN ALLPORT's *Explorers of the Black Box* (Norton, 1986), p.170.

237   Sand is always imported: See THOMAS A. TERICH, *Living with the Shore of Puget Sound and the Georgia Strait* (Duke University Press, 1987), Chapters 1–3. There is actually a sand cycle, for the sand that gets swept away from the shore each winter and deposited in offshore depressions in the ocean bottom.

237   JOHN KENNETH GALBRAITH, *A Life in Our Times* (Houghton Mifflin, 1981), p. 43.

238   Arm-back-to-arm reaction time: PAUL J. CORDO, "Mechanisms controlling accurate changes in elbow torque in humans," *Journal of Neuroscience* 7(2):432–442 (February 1987). "A corrective adjustment in torque [occurred] within roughly the first 100 msec of responses. This mechanism incorporated target torque information provided by the stimulus into the response."

239   J. L. LEAVITT, R. G. MARTENIUK, and H. CARNAHAN, "Arm movement trajectories and movement control strategies of expert and non-expert dart throwers," *Society for Neuroscience Abstracts* 13:713 (1987).

239   For an introduction to reaction times, see ERNST PÖPPEL, *Grenzen des Bewußtseins* (Deutsche Verlags-Anstalt, 1985)— English translation *Mindworks: Time and Conscious Experience* (Harcourt Brace Jovanovich, 1988).

240   DENIS DIDEROT, "Locke," *Encyclopédie*, IX, cited in R. DESNÉ, *Les matérialistes français de 1750 à 1800* (Paris: Buchet-Chastel, 1965), p. 179.

240   ARTUR SCHNABEL, quoted in *Chicago Daily News* (11 June 1958).

241   WILLIAM H. CALVIN and CHARLES F. STEVENS, "Synaptic noise and other sources of randomness in motorneuron interspike intervals," *Journal of Neurophysiology* 31:574–587 (1968).

242   WILLIAM H. CALVIN, "A stone's throw and its launch window: Timing precision and its implications for language and hominid brains," *Journal of Theoretical Biology* 104:121–135 (1983). Sequencing as the neural predecessor of language is also discussed by OVID J.L. TZENG and WILLIAM S.-Y. WANG, "Search for a common neurocognitive mechanism for language and movements," *American Journal of Physiology* 246:R904–R911 (1984).

244   JOHN R. CLAY and ROBERT DeHAAN, "Fluctuations in interbeat interval in rhythmic heart-cell clusters," *Biophysical Journal* 28:377–389 (1979). A similar existence proof for the temporal precision enhancement by averaging large numbers of jittery cells is JAMES T. ENRIGHT's "Temporal precision in circadian systems: A reliable neuronal clock from unreliable components?," *Science* 209:1542–1544 (1980).

246   Eightfold reduction in jitter for throwing twice the distance:
       Essentially, a target twice as far away subtends only one-
       quarter the solid angle. But to throw with a fairly flat trajec-
       tory, you also have to throw twice as fast, which halves the
       time scale. So the "launch window" shrinks to one-eighth of
       what sufficed at the shorter distance.

247   Cell can be assigned to different tasks at different times: See
       SHAUL HOCHSTEIN and J. H. R. MAUNSELL, "Dimensional
       attention effects in the responses of V4 neurons of the macaque
       monkey," *Society for Neuroscience Abstracts* 11:364.6 (1985).

247   Redundancy in memory: Suppose that your telephone's bat-
       tery was running down and the memories were a little flaky:
       223-9077 sometimes was recalled as 324-9077 and sometimes
       as 223-9079, etc. Solution: Put the same phone number in all
       10 memories and somehow reprogram the little computer
       inside the phone to examine all 10 memories before dialing the
       first digit: Whatever digit is most frequent, dial that one
       (*2* most of the time). Next digit, survey again. With this
       redundancy, the right number will usually be dialed even
       though none of the memories was 100 percent correct on all
       seven digits. But the Law of Large Numbers operates by
       averaging, not by majority rule; either way, redundancy buys
       much more than just backup systems in case of failure.

252   ULAM (1976), pp. 180–181.

12. Shaping Up Consciousness with a Darwinian Dance: Emergence from the Subconscious

256   OLIVER SACKS, quoted in JONATHAN COTT, *Visions and Voices*
       (Doubleday, 1987).

256   JEAN-PAUL SARTRE, *Nausea* (tr. ROBERT BALDICK), Chapter
       "Saturday noon."

256   PETER BROOKS, *Reading for the Plot: Design and Intention in
       Narrative* (Random House, 1984), pp. 1–2.

257   Child development: "Life's First Feelings," NOVA television
       program (1988); and JEROME KAGAN, J. STEVEN REZNICK, and

NANCY SNIDMAN, "Biological Bases of Childhood Shyness," *Science* 240:167–171 (8 April 1988).

258   Exploit others through understanding them: See introduction to *Machiavellian Intelligence: Social Expertise and the Evolution of Intellect in Monkeys, Apes, and Humans*, edited by RICHARD W. BYRNE and ANDREW WHITEN (Clarendon Press, 1988). See also *Behavioral and Brain Sciences* 11:233–273 (June 1988).

258   DAVID BALLIN KLEIN, *The Concept of Consciousness* (University of Nebraska Press, 1984), pp. 22–23.

259   R. B. CATTELL, "Animal intelligence," in *Encyclopaedia Britannica*, 12:345–347 (1970).

260   ALF BRODAL, "Self-observations and neuro-anatomical considerations after a stroke," *Brain* 96:675–694 (1973).

260   WILLIAM JAMES, "Great men, great thoughts, and the environment," *The Atlantic Monthly* 46(276):441–459 (1880) at p. 456. James apparently started discussing the idea in letters to friends about 1874; see ROBERT J. RICHARDS, *Darwin and the Emergence of Evolutionary Theories of Mind and Behavior* (University of Chicago Press, 1987), pp. 440 ff.

261   PAUL SOURIAU, *Théorie de l'Invention* (Paris: Hachette, 1881).

261   KENNETH J. W. CRAIK, *The Nature of Explanation* (Cambridge University Press, 1943), p.61.

261   *Darwin Machine*: Term introduced in W. H. CALVIN, "Bootstrapping Thought: Is Consciousness a Darwinian Sidestep?" *Whole Earth Review* 55:22–28 (Summer 1987).

261   Idea of randomness as basis of thought: DONALD T. CAMPBELL lists 26 previous statements of same idea: "Evolutionary epistemology" in *The Philosophy of Karl Popper*, edited by P.A. SCHILPP (Open Court, 1974) pp. 413–463. See also NICHOLAS HUMPHREY, *Consciousness Regained* (Oxford University Press, 1983), pp. 178–179; and DOUGLAS R. HOFSTADTER, "Variations on a theme as the crux of creativity," in his *Metamagical Themas* (Basic Books, 1985).

262   Shaping up by selection: See the examples in RICHARD
          DAWKINS, *The Blind Watchmaker* (Longman, 1986), Chapter 3.

266   GEORGE A. MILLER, "The magical number seven, plus or
          minus two: Some limits on our capacity for processing infor-
          mation," *Psychological Reviews* 63:81–97 (1956).

267   Chunking: HERBERT A. SIMON, *Models of Thought* (Yale Uni-
          versity Press, 1979), p. 41.

271   For an example of a neurophysiological view of consciousness
          that is also oriented to time-series such as speech, poetry, and
          planning—but without the Darwin Machine at the center of
          things—see ERNST PÖPPEL's *Mindworks: Time and Conscious
          Experience* (Harcourt Brace Jovanovich, 1988 translation from
          the 1985 German original), especially chapter 19.

271   "The artificial intelligentsia" term is credited to LOUIS FEIN
          by J. WEIZENBAUM, *Computer Power and Human Reason*
          (Freeman, 1976), p. 179.

272   Linkages such as *is-a* and *is-contained-in* are used in *LISP*,
          the AI programming language.

274   ALFRED NORTH WHITEHEAD, *Adventures of Ideas*, part III,
          15.

13. The Trilogy of *Homo seriatim*: Language, Consciousness, and Music

277   Portions of this chapter and the following one first appeared
          in *Reality Club #3*, edited by JOHN BROCKMAN (Lynx, 1989).

278   ROBERT FROST, in *Selected Prose of Robert Frost*, edited by
          H. COX and E. C. LATHEM (Collier, 1986), pp. 33–46.

278   STANISLAW M. ULAM, *Adventures of a Mathematician* (Scrib-
          ners, 1976), pp. 180–181.

279   MARTIN E. P. SELIGMAN, "A reinterpretation of dreams," *The
          Sciences* 27(5):46–53 (September 1987). Argues visual bursts
          are random elements that mind finds ways of stringing to-

gether in attempt to make coherent story. Subconscious sequences rising to the level of consciousness and action without
the usual censorship are particularly well illustrated by some
of the phenomena seen in Tourette's syndrome. See OLIVER
SACKS, "Tics," *New York Review of Books*, pp.37–41 (29 January 1987).

279 WILLIAM H. CALVIN, *The River That Flows Uphill* (Macmillan, 1986), p. 365.

281 GEORGE JOHNSON, *The Machinery of the Mind: Inside the
New Science of Artificial Intelligence* (Times Books, 1986),
pp. 3–4.

282 HERBERT A. SIMON, *Reason in Human Affairs* (Stanford
University Press, 1983), pp. 12–13. Simon goes on to note at
p. 17 that "in typical real-world situations, decision makers,
no matter how badly they want to do so, simply cannot apply
the SEU model. [Human beings] have neither the facts nor the
consistent structure of values nor the reasoning power at their
disposal that would be required . . . to apply SEU principles."
See A. TVERSKY and D. KAHNERMANN, "Judgment under
uncertainty: Heuristics and biases," *Science* 185:1124–1131
(1974).

287 I am grateful to Paul Ryan for noting that Darwin Machines
do not solve the problem of value and reminding me of Warren McCulloch's model, and to Michelle DuBois for the information on naming horses (those are indeed the names and
lineages of actual horses).

291 OSCAR SAENGER, *The Oscar Saenger Course in Vocal Training*
(The Victor Talking Machine Company, 1915). Quoted by
WILLIAM ZINSSER, *Writing to Learn*, (1988), p. 227.

291 GERALD WEISSMAN, *The Woods Hole Cantata: Essays on
Science and Society* (Houghton Mifflin, 1985), p. 2.

294 *Ear worm* is one of the gems to be found in HOWARD
RHEINGOLD, *They Have a Word for It* (J. Tarcher, 1988).

294 JACOB BRONOWSKI, *The Origins of Knowledge and Imagination*
(1967 lecture; Yale University Press, 1978), p. 9.

295   Rain dance, see JANE GOODALL, *The Chimpanzees of Gombe*
           (Harvard University Press, 1986).

299   HEINZ PAGELS, *The Dreams of Reason* (Simon & Schuster,
           1988), p. 88.

299   GREGORY BATESON, *Mind and Nature: A Necessary Unity*
           (Bantam, 1979), p. 191.

14. Thinking About Thought:
Twilight at Nobska Lighthouse

302   HEINZ PAGELS, *The Dreams of Reason* (Simon & Schuster,
           1988, p. 328.

304   Species occupying same niche competing to extinction: This is
           called the Competitive Exclusion Principle or Gause's Princi-
           ple (after G. F. GAUSE, *The Struggle for Existence*, 1934),
           though Charles Darwin also recognized it eight decades ear-
           lier in *The Origin of Species* discussion of extinction (p. 110).
           An interesting ecological discussion of it relating to the com-
           petition between monkeys and chimpanzees for fruit trees can
           be found in MICHAEL P. GHIGLIERI, *East of the Mountains of
           the Moon* (Macmillan, 1988), chapter 9; since it appears that
           the monkeys are winning, it demonstrates (to supplement the
           warning in ECCLESIASTES about the race not always being to
           the swift) that the race is not always to the clever, at least in
           a rain forest!

306   HENRY BESTON, *The Outermost House* (1928; reference to
           1962 Penguin edition), p. 211.

308   PETER BROOKS, *Reading for the Plot* (Knopf, 1984), p. 3.

310   "leak in heater hose. . . .": Like most theories, this one was
           wrong. It was really the usual water pump hose. Some leaks
           are simply intermittent. But the inspiration still illustrates
           subconscious problem-solving while you go about other business.

311   DANIEL C. DENNETT, *Brainstorms: Philosophical Essays on
           Mind and Psychology* (Bradford Books, 1978). Dennett's Chap-
           ter 15 is a particularly good reference on free will and the
           generate-and-test hypothesis for mental acts.

311   CARL SAGAN, in *Skeptical Inquirer* (Fall 1987), pp. 41–42.

312   "Nietzsche noted. . . .": See also FRANCIS BACON in *Novum Organum:* "Truth comes out of error more readily than out of confusion."

312   FRANÇOIS JACOB, *The Statue Within* (Basic Books, 1988), p. 15.

313   "lobbing discus-shaped rocks into the midst of a tightly-packed herd. . . .": At least, that's my interpretation of what the Acheulian "hand axe" was primarily used for.

313   "noise window in hominid evolution": See WILLIAM H. CALVIN, *The River That Flows Uphill: A Journey from the Big Bang to the Big Brain* (Macmillan, 1986), p. 407.

314   The first collection of papers on neural-like networks was D. E. RUMELHART, J. L. MCCLELLAND, & THE PDP RESEARCH GROUP, *Parallel Distributed Processing* (MIT Press, 1986, 2 vol.).

315   ITALO CALVINO, in *Corrierre della Sera* (August 10, 1975), quoted in Calvino's *The Uses of Literature* (tr. PATRICK CREAGH), (Harcourt Brace Jovanovich, 1986), p. 138.

15. Simulations of Reality:
Of Augmented Mammals and Conscious Robots

302   ANNE SEXTON, "The poet of ignorance," in *The Awful Rowing Towards God* (Houghton Mifflin, 1975).

323   RICHARD DAWKINS, *The Blind Watchmaker* (London: Longmans, 1986), pp. 46–49.

328   MARY MIDGLEY, *Evolution as a Religion: Strange Hopes and Stranger Fears* (Methuen, 1985), p. 38.

329   JANE GOODALL, "A plea for the chimps," *The New York Times Magazine*, pp. 108–120 (17 May 1987).

329   Big machines protecting their niche need not occur for any sinister reason: There was some danger of niche domination in

the U.S. back before the microcomputer ascendancy of the late 1970s. At large universities and in many state governments trying to cope with rising expenditures for computers, one could not buy a piece of computing equipment without going through a computer committee, usually chaired by the head of the biggest computer center around. These experts naturally wanted to expand their operations and make them more efficient; they usually discouraged small, inefficient operations. When lab instruments needed computing power, they encouraged tie-lines from labs to the central computer. But some of us had data-acquisition requirements that required wider band pass than telephone lines, and so we began to escape the dominance of the central computer setup. Eventually, we learned to phrase our purchase orders to avoid any mention of "computer" and to piece together computers from components whose purchase orders escaped the purview of such committees. And because these "data-acquisition devices" could also do word-processing and statistical manipulations, we neurophysiologists (and some chemists and physicists as well) had stand-alone single-user computers much like the present microcomputers, but a decade before Apple et al. came on the scene and swamped the computer committees into impotence (before then, there were about 50,000 computers in the whole world; now that many are produced every day). See my letter "The Missing LINC" in *Byte* 7(4):20 (April 1982). In other cases, central authorities dominated, most notably in Eastern Europe and the U.S.S.R., but that central domination too started to erode when the cheap "clones" of popular U.S. computers became available from the Far East.

331   RALPH WENDELL BURHOE, "What specifies the values of man-made man?" *Zygon* 6:224–246 (1971).

331   Downloading brains into work-alike computers, see HANS MORAVEC and DANIEL HILLIS quotes in GRANT FJERMEDAL's *The Tomorrow Makers* (Macmillan, 1986), pp. 4–5, p. 96. Chaos studies are nicely summarized in JAMES GLEICK, *Chaos: Making a New Science* (Viking, 1987).

335   "the most strongly right-handed actions. . . .": A useful news article by BRUCE BOWER on handedness and brain organization is in *Science News* (7 January 1989).

338   Darwin Machine not especially suitable for depiction: That doesn't mean that you couldn't use a massively serial device

to help out with what is basically a large parallel representation. After all, you can reduce a three-dimensional house to a stack of two-dimensional blueprints, reduce the blueprint page by scanning in a Fax machine to a one-dimensional string of bits—then reconstruct the blueprint on the other end (and indeed the house). Many parallel-like phenomena seem to happen too rapidly for such serial reconstructions to assist, but depiction is often spread out over time when dealing with a novel construct, either in creating a depiction or in deciphering it. For a discussion of depiction's role in hominid evolution, see IAIN DAVIDSON and WILLIAM NOBLE, "The archaeology of perception: Traces of depiction and language," *Current Anthropology* 30(2): 125–155 (April 1989).

338   Power requirements: The fourfold larger brain now consumes about one out of every four calories, so the hominid enlargement probably ran into some problems. One of the constraints was likely overheating, when engaging in a long chase under the hot sun. Brain cells are far more sensitive than the rest of the body to an episode of overheating, and so hominid brain enlargement may have been selected against until some improvements in the cooling arrangements were made to protect the brain against the heat arriving in the arterial blood. DEAN FALK argues (*Behavioral and Brain Sciences* 1990) that the head's venous drainage system altered in parallel with the enlargement over the 2 million-year encephalization process, with the emissary veins bringing sweating-cooled venous blood from the scalp into the cranial cavity. The robust Australopithecine lineage lacked such an arrangement, suggesting that they could either run or have a bigger brain, but not both.

339   FREEMAN DYSON, interview in *U.S. News and World Report* (18 April 1988), p. 72.

339   Mental evolution of everyone in Woods Hole: Well, at least if they're not in coma. But then there are no hospitals or nursing homes in Woods Hole, only up in Falmouth. Does everyone else, awake or asleep but at least not in coma, share this evolutionary property? Certainly there are individuals who are locked into patterns (obsessive-compulsives, and perhaps some of the senile) that probably prevent new patterns from ever winning. But then there is stasis in biological evolution too, such as the horseshoe crabs, and we often label such long-lasting species as extraordinarily successful.

342   PAGELS (1988), p. 331.

A native of Kansas City, WILLIAM HOWARD CALVIN was born in 1939 into a family that had arrived in the American Midwest in the eighteenth and nineteenth centuries from English and Scandinavian roots. After much youthful experience with journalism and photography, he studied physics at Northwestern University, doing an undergraduate thesis on a neural-network model of the retina, graduating with honors in 1961. He spent a year at the Massachusetts Institute of Technology and Harvard Medical School making the transition from physics to biophysics, then moved to Seattle, where he studied the primate visual system with Mitchell Glickstein and cellular neurophysiology with Charles F. Stevens, receiving a Ph.D. in physiology and biophysics in 1966 from the University of Washington. Following his doctorate, he remained at the University of Washington School of Medicine, joined the faculty of Neurological Surgery, and also taught in Physiology and Biophysics; in the 1980s, he moved to the Biology Program, also teaching in the Department of Zoology and the Honors Program of the College of Arts and Sciences.

His neurobiological research was, for many years, primarily concerned with how single nerve cells compute using electrical signals. He became interested in the comparative aspects, recording from cells in species as diverse as sea slugs, lobsters, frogs, rats, cats, monkeys, and humans; from single peripheral receptors to the cerebral cortex to the motor neurons that run the muscles. He investigated the pathophysiological processes in epilepsy and chronic pain disorders that distort the normal physiology of nerve cells. In addition, he was an early theoretician in computational neuroscience, his input-output modeling culminating in the 1979 "Styles of Neuronal Computation" (written together with the neurobiologist Katherine Graubard, his wife). His more recent research has been concerned with theoretical problems at the interface between neurobiology, evolutionary biology, anthropology, and developmental biology; their general theme is how we evolved such a big brain.

He renewed an interest in archaeology and human evolution during a sabbatical year as a visiting professor of neurobiology at the Hebrew University of Jerusalem during 1978–1979. Subsequently, he wrote (together with his neurosurgical colleague George A. Ojemann) his first book, *Inside the Brain.* He became interested in hominid brain evolution and discovered the neurophysiological paradox of timing an accurate throw, together with the Law of Large Numbers escape from the paradox. His book of essays, *The Throwing Madonna*, was published in 1983. He wrote more broadly on evolutionary topics (and the Grand Canyon) in *The River that Flows Uphill* and began making models for the developmental modifications and Ice Age selection cycles associated with encephalization. His Darwin Machines model for human language and consciousness was published in 1987 in *Nature*, and is elaborated in this book.

He has also written on prehistoric antecedents of science, suggesting a number of ways that Ice Age people could have learned to predict eclipses of the sun and moon without the occupational specialization and record-keeping associated with agricultural civilizations. He has studied astronomical alignments at dozens of Anasazi ruins in the canyonlands of the American Southwest, including the site in the bottom of the Grand Canyon that he discovered while writing *The River That Flows Uphill*. He is a frequent contributor to the *Whole Earth Review* and *Reality Club*.

He has been elected a member of the American Physiological Society, the Biophysical Society, International Association for the Study of Pain, International Brain Research Organization, International Society for Human Ethology, Language Origins Society, New York Academy of Sciences, Sigma Xi, and the Society for Neuroscience.

INDEX